STATE OF DISASTER

STATE OF DISASTER

A Historical Geography
of Louisiana's Land Loss Crisis

Craig E. Colten

LOUISIANA STATE UNIVERSITY PRESS ▍ BATON ROUGE

Published by Louisiana State University Press
lsupress.org

Designer: Michelle A. Neustrom
Typeface: Whitman

Cover photo by Julie Dermansky.

Library of Congress Cataloging-in-Publication Data

Names: Colten, Craig E., author.
Title: State of disaster : a historical geography of Louisiana's land loss crisis /
    Craig E. Colten.
Description: Baton Rouge : Louisiana State University Press, 2021. | Includes
    bibliographical references and index.
Identifiers: LCCN 2020057361 (print) | LCCN 2020057362 (ebook) |
    ISBN 978-0-8071-7570-5 (cloth) | ISBN 978-0-8071-7629-0 (pdf) |
    ISBN 978-0-8071-7630-6 (epub)
Subjects: LCSH: Coastal zone management—Government policy—Louisiana. |
    Louisiana. Coastal Protection and Restoration Authority. | Louisiana—
    Environmental conditions. | Louisiana—Population.
Classification: LCC HT393.L8 C65 2021 (print) | LCC HT393.L8 (ebook) |
    DDC 363.739/409763—dcundefined
LC record available at https://lccn.loc.gov/2020057361
LC ebook record available at https://lccn.loc.gov/2020057362

To my students,
who inspired me and fueled continual rejuvenation

CONTENTS

ILLUSTRATIONS

PREFACE

I left Louisiana in 1978 for what turned out to be an extended, vagabond career that took me to New York; Illinois; Washington, DC; and Texas. Before my departure, I had brief flirtations with the land loss issue as a student in the 1970s. I did some very rudimentary digitizing of land cover change in the Atchafalaya Basin for Johannes van Beek, a longtime collaborator with Woody Gagliano. I also spent a few days in the field with Shea Penland, who became a noted expert in coastal issues, while he was doing measurements of barrier island washovers for his MS thesis. My highly peripheral role in those projects made me aware of processes at work, but my understanding was entirely superficial. Coastal land loss at the time was a topic largely confined to a group of academic specialists.

When I returned to Louisiana in 2000, land loss had become a prominent concern that reached well beyond scholarly journals and graduate seminars. Once settled back into Baton Rouge, I commuted to my campus office and regularly caught the "coastal minute" public service announcements on the local radio station that reported on the unfolding crisis. Colleagues at LSU were deeply immersed in studies about the many processes contributing to coastal wetland loss, and there was ample material available to include a rich discussion of the subject in my Louisiana geography class. Indeed, a new building appeared on our campus, not long after my arrival, to house the College of the Coast and the Environment—

which was and remains the principal hub of scientific research on Louisiana's coastal region. Baton Rouge and LSU were the unquestioned crucible of scientific inquiries into this slow-motion emergency.

During my tenure on this campus, I've been fortunate to get to know some of the stalwarts of the science community who pioneered investigations into the coastal issue. In addition, I went on field trips into the coastal region, attended and participated in academic conferences on the topic, and received grants that supported my own work on the state's threatened communities. Each of these experiences expanded my knowledge of the situation, yet I was slow to dive in deeply. This changed when I took a position with the Water Institute of the Gulf in 2013, where I focused on the coastal crisis. As director of human dimensions for two years, I interacted with the state agency charged with restoring the coast and found myself much more directly connected to the institutional inner workings of the coastal issue. I witnessed decision-making that seemed tentative to address the human dimensions using humanities and social science research, conducted workshops with community groups who were frustrated with their exclusion from the planning process, participated in forums that sought to address the shortcoming in dealing with people, and encountered a simmering resentment among academic scientists about being sidelined in shaping the plan for the coast. Despite the bold proclamations of stakeholder engagement by the state, from nearly every angle I discovered exasperation and a sense of exclusion.

Granted, for a historical geographer, my position with the Water Institute afforded me a healthy research budget that led to several reports and a fine atlas by my colleague Scott Hemmerling. Ultimately, seeing little institutional interest in the work I was proposing, I opted to return to the academy full time. This book arises from my work over the last dozen years or so, and was shaped in part by my time with the Water Institute. It is, however, a reflection of my own interests and inclinations and does not purport to be a product of the institute. Nonetheless, all my interactions with colleagues, agency personnel, elected officials, NGO staff, and the public profoundly influenced my understanding of this complex situation. I am deeply grateful for the opportunity I had to peer behind the curtain, and this work owes its genesis to that period of employment and research support. I cannot identify any particular threads of thought or nuggets of empirical information that derive from my relationship with the institute, but want to acknowledge, appreciatively, the crucial role it played.

I am also grateful to several funding agencies that supported portions of this long-term project. In particular, several grants from the Community and Regional Resilience Institute (CARRI) enabled me to begin working on the topic of resilience in the wake of Hurricane Katrina. Robert Kates and Tom Wilbanks were instrumental in enabling my participation in CARRI's work. At the invitation of a group of scientists with the University of Texas Medical Branch in Galveston, I continued investigating community resilience on Louisiana's coast in the wake of the Macondo oil gusher. My participation with the Department of the Interior's Strategic Working Group during and after the Deepwater Horizon blowout provided additional intellectual inspiration. Louisiana Sea Grant funded a remarkable "rolling seminar" that brought together a lively group of scholars to spend three days touring the coastal region and discussing this topic with a range of experts.

I need to also acknowledge the special place that the "Coastal Cleritics" played in the gestation of this project. Weekly gatherings at Len Bahr's house allowed me to converse with a group of science experts which helped me build this work on a solid foundation. Len, Paul, Michael, and Doug, you all made an impression on my thinking.

One of the immeasurable benefits of external funding was having resources to support graduate students to work alongside. I want to dedicate this book to the students who collaborated with me on these projects and to all my graduate students—here at LSU and elsewhere. There are moments when a graduate advisor grumbles and mutters to himself, "When are they gonna get it? When are they gonna see the big picture?" For every such moment, there are also occasions when the students, through their own initiative, their particular genius, their singular set of talents, and their personal motivation enlighten the mentor and make what had been obscure, clear and comprehensible. I commend and thank the students who have worked with me for providing such moments. It is on these occasions that I am less a teacher and more a student. It is a glorious experience. Students have more than compensated me for the time I spent instructing, counseling, and editing when they ultimately transformed a sketchy idea into a meaningful contribution to our academic enterprise. They make me proud when they venture forth and do good work. There is no greater satisfaction in this business of the mind.

Students who have been directly involved in work on the coast include Scott Hemmerling, Amy Sumpter, jenny hay, Alexandra Giancarlo, Zack Delaune, Lauren Morris, Audrey Grismore, and Jessica Simms. In addition to helping with the basic research that undergirds much of this work, they are contributing coauthors in a chapter. Students assisting with recent riparian flooding in the Amite River Basin include Yi-Ling Chan, Kelly Haggerty, and Ria Mukerji.

Other PhD students have pursued their own research agendas and enlightened me on a host of fascinating topics. They include Jacqueline Mills, Meg Streiff, Yi-Chia Chen, Ryan Orgera, Louise Bordelon, Aubry Kyle, and Ashley Allen. Here at LSU I've had the privilege to work with Samantha Chaisson, David Farritor, and Sandra Soto as they earned their master's degrees. Current students include Melanie Tagiamamao, Juliana Delgado, and Roycean Philson. I must also acknowledge Diane Mulville-Friel, the first graduate student who invited me to serve on her committee, who later proved to be a splendid colleague at the Illinois State Museum. There have been numerous other students at Southwest Texas State University who also shared their wisdom with me—most notably Rebecca Sheehan, who went on to earn her PhD. I've been honored to serve on a number of dissertation committees with students at other universities, and I thank all for permitting me to watch their work take shape.

There have also been several students who, for personal reasons, never completed their degrees or opted to shift to another advisor. I also appreciate the time they spent with me and applaud their accomplishments.

Working with graduate students is an exceptional part of our work, but I also want to express my appreciation for the undergraduate students—not only geography majors but those who just happened to sign up for one of my classes. Every class has a student of two who slip off into brief naps, and others who rhythmically nod their heads acknowledging that the message is getting through. This latter group impel me to return, year after year, and are contributors to the exchange of knowledge that goes on in the classroom. Sharing with them the story of Louisiana's coastal crisis has been a consistent mission over the past two decades.

There are countless other contributors to works of this sort. LSU Press and its capable staff have been steadfast and reliable collaborators. In a time when the monograph has declined in value for academic advancement and in the midst of a revolution in publication, they have continued to produce a splendid catalog of books. Jenny Keegan and Catherine Kadair have been supportive editors on this project, and freelancer Stan Ivester provided valuable copyediting to refine my clumsy prose and clean up other details. I also want to thank the anonymous reviewer who provided insightful and constructive comments on the draft manuscripts. I found this review of exceptional caliber, and the book certainly benefited from the reviewer's suggestions. I remain responsible for any shortcomings.

Librarians, archivists, and public records officials, whom I pestered over the years, have with remarkable aplomb helped me uncover the sources behind this work. Mary Lee Eggart has been an amazingly efficient graphic artist/cartographer for this and other projects. I am deeply grateful to them all.

Colleagues, on campus and around the globe, have spurred me to continue with this endeavor. They have endured countless presentations at professional gatherings as well as having conversations over drinks, and they have offered critiques that sharpened my thinking. The faculty and students who participated in the Human Coast Initiative and my recent classes on that topic also bolstered my desire to complete this manuscript.

A list of acknowledgments would be incomplete without mentioning my wife, Marge Campane. A constant and supportive companion, she has been at my side through our emotional ups and downs, numerous interstate relocations, and during disappointments and celebrations. She even endures my daily pauses when I ignore her standing over my shoulder as I try to preserve a fragile idea before finally acknowledging her morning greeting.

ACKNOWLEDGMENTS

A portion of the introduction appeared previously as "Adaptive Transitions: The Long Term Perspective on Humans in Changing Coastal Settings," *Geographical Review* 109, no. 3 (2019): 416–35, and is used here with permission.

The resilience research mentioned in chapter 1 was funded in part by Award Number U19ES020676 from the National Institute of Environmental Health Sciences (NIEHS). The content is solely the responsibility of the author and does not necessarily represent the view of the National Institute of Environmental Health Sciences or the National Institutes of Health. Additional funding came from the Substance Abuse and Mental Health Services Administration, through the NIEHS. The author also drew on research that was carried out as part of the Water Institute of the Gulf's Science and Engineering Plan and received several grants from the Community and Regional Resilience Institute based at Oak Ridge National Laboratory.

Chapter 1 contains excerpts from the following publications:

Colten, Craig E. 2015. "Historic City with a Poor Memory." In *The Katrina Effect: On the Nature of Catastrophe*, edited by William M. Taylor, Michael P. Livine, Oenone Rooksby, and Joely-Kym Sobott, 305–30. London: Bloomsbury Academic, an imprint of Bloomsbury Publishing Plc.

Colten, Craig E. 2019. "Adaptive Transitions: The Long-Term Perspective on Humans in Changing Coastal Settings." *Geographical Review* 109, no. 3: 416–35, reprinted by permission of American Geographical Society (AGS), https://americangeo.org.

Colten, Craig E., Audrey A. Grismore, and Jessica R. Z. Simms. 2015. "Oil Spills and Community Resilience: Uneven Impacts and Protection in Historical Perspective." *Geographical Review* 105, no. 4: 391–407, reprinted by permission of American Geographical Society (AGS), https://americangeo.org.

Colten, Craig E., jenny hay, and Alexandra Giancarlo. 2012. "Community Resilience and Oil Spills in Coastal Louisiana." *Ecology and Society* 17, no. 3. dx.doi.org/10.5751/ES-05047–170305.

A previous version of chapter 2 appeared as "Environmental Management in Coastal Louisiana," *Journal of Coastal Research* 33, no. 3 (2017): 699–711. It is reprinted here with permission. Chapter 3, in a different form, was published as "Cartographic Depictions of Louisiana Land Loss: A Tool for Sustainable Policies," *Sustainability* 10, no. 3 (2018), doi:10.3390/su10030763 and is reprinted here with permission. An earlier version of chapter 5 appeared as "The Public in Louisiana's Coastal Restoration Public Works Project," *Louisiana Voices* 1, no. 1 (2019), img1.wsimg.com/blobby/go/05e43d27–5e27–4ec0-b1ee-5319e8259ad2/downloads/Louisiana%20Speaks%20_2018.pdf?ver=1583166372623.

Peter Kamu, Audrey Maass, and Bethany Garfield provided essential research assistance on chapter 4, and Charles Camillo, with the Mississippi River Commission, provided historical documents for my use in that chapter. Their contributions are greatly appreciated.

STATE OF DISASTER

Introduction

Louisiana, my longtime home, is a remarkable place, remarkable in many respects. It has a distinctive cultural heritage. A Francophone colonial settlement history, overlaid on a persistent if diminished indigenous population, with subsequent arrivals of multiple ethnic and national groups, created a rare assemblage of inhabitants in a Deep South state. French, German, African, Spanish, Irish, and Italian immigrants contributed to a remarkably diverse population by the end of the nineteenth century. Hispanics and Asians, mainly from Vietnam, infused the state with additional complexity in the twentieth century. These people, many residing on the state's coastal margins, constitute not just demographic statistics, but a vital and dynamic collection of families and communities with diverse interests, customs, livelihoods, and ambitions, creating a rich cultural gumbo. This work addresses the state's humanity.

Louisiana's citizens face remarkable environmental challenges. The state's broad southern coast consists mainly of an expansive marshland. Large bays, fed by freshwater rivers and bayous, the marshes, and inland swamps constitute a remarkable ecology that provides a habitat for many commercial species of fish, migratory waterfowl, and other wildlife. With a combination of subsiding wetlands and rising oceans, the state has the highest relative sea-level rise in the country. Aware of the coastal land loss issue for decades, scientists and engineers have assembled a remarkable knowledge base about the biophysical processes contributing to this dire situation, and they have constructed a remarkable plan to mitigate the effects of a disappearing littoral landscape. This plan has a remarkable budget that far exceeds the state's capacity to pay for it. Backing away from fiscal challenges has not been a common trait among Louisiana political leaders, who have demonstrated a remarkable ability to find others to pay for their efforts to cope with environmental crises. From levees for flood protection to deadly epidemics to rebuilding in the wake of hurricanes and restoring the wetlands after major oil spills, outside funds have consistently provided a remarkable lifeline.

Louisiana has endured an overabundance of environmental crises. For a state so inclined to adopt a mascot for every occasion—the pelican, the crawfish, the strawberry, the Catahoula Leopard Dog, the green tree frog—it is surprising the legislature has not selected a particular tragedy to best represent the state. Another option might be to revise the state motto to be "Louisiana: The State of Disaster." In fact, the agency heading the restoration effort has observed that Louisiana is experiencing a "coastal crisis" (Coastal Protection and Restoration Authority [hereafter CPRA] 2012, 36). Responding to crises such as hurricanes is almost habitual among coastal residents who treat the frequent, but irregular, exercise like a trip to the fitness center. A common, if erroneous, attitude is that repetition builds strength. Add river floods, oil spills, epidemics, and economic crises to the suite of historical disasters, and you have a location with ample experience dealing with tragedy and recovery.

The earliest prehistoric settlers followed the aggrading delta as it extended into the Gulf of Mexico. They had no maps or satellite imagery to allow them to recognize the land-building process, but they stayed within reach of the shore for sustenance. They also began the process of landscape manipulation. Dumping empty rangia shells, they created mounds in the marshes that provided dry footing for villages. These indigenous people had disappeared by the time Europeans arrived, but their mounds provided important resources for French settlers. Subsequent societies undertook considerable effort to adjust to an unfamiliar environment and, through a set of disconnected adaptations, over the course of several centuries, society persists, in a very different form than in the 1700s.

Throughout its three-hundred-year history since Europeans, Africans, and Asians arrived within the state's borders, residents and outside experts have concocted ever-expanding plans to manage the riparian and coastal landscapes to minimize risk and enhance economic opportunity. Each plan, when implemented over the course of decades, produced both environmental and social impacts that have persisted for centuries, and in some cases, complicate the demands on successive plans. Until fairly recently, those entitled to guide the decisions for considerable social investment in environmental manipulations represented only a small segment of society—largely those with economic, political, or technological authority. Consequently, these plans have been selective in who benefits, and they have not always served the full diversity of the state's residents.

The current planning for protecting and restoring portions of the coast is a prime example. It builds on deeply embedded environmental management systems guided by and built by a select few. Robust public involvement has been minimal over the centuries. The long-term cascading consequences of these prior projects are a major reason the current plan is needed, but the plan does not include removing the structures that created the problem in the first place. It contains ambitious projects for marsh restoration and creation, ridge and barrier island rebuilding, structural protections, sediment diversions, hydrologic restoration, and nonstructural projects. A response to centuries of human adaptations and interventions, it has a fifty-year objective to reduce the rate of land loss and build some critical areas of coastal land to protect inland population centers and economic activity. Although the plan's authors tout its attention to the state's cultures, the plan offers little to restore the families, communities, and cultures that will be impacted by both land loss and deliberate restoration efforts. It is not entirely surprising that people have been neglected. From the earliest maps of Louisiana's coast to the current illustrations of projected land loss, people have not appeared prominently (fig. I.1). With modest opportunities to contribute to past plans, the state's marginal residents are not major beneficiaries in this enterprise. Their exclusion has become standard practice. I seek to insert people more directly into the planning process, to illustrate how the plan can include the people and cultures that it professes to value in a way that parallels the attention given to the biophysical environment. I hope to bring the state's people into a more obvious view among planners and policy makers and

Fig. I.1. Coastal population, 1752 to 2012. The presence of humans is virtually invisible in this pair of maps. Upper map is a detail from *Carte de la Louisiane par le Sr. d'Anville,* 1752, Library of Congress. Lower map is after CPRA 2012. Map by Mary Lee Eggart.

to illustrate how this might be done in other settings facing sea-level rise and the dislocation of threatened communities.

HUMANITIES AND THE COASTAL CRISIS

The state's master plan proclaims to be science driven. Science is absolutely essential, where science applies, but it does not negate other approaches. The 2017 version asserts that the planning process has put Louisiana "at the forefront of using science and innovation to plan a sustainable future" (CPRA 2017b, ES-11). Science and modeling future conditions are at the core of the state's approach. While science expands our understanding of many biophysical processes, deploying "objective" science distances the planners from the appearance of political bias and obscures the notion that science itself is a social process that is replete with its own biases. It provides a justification for hard and sometimes unpopular decisions without full public participation, free of culpability, that have profound impacts on already marginalized citizens. Through each iteration of the planning process over more than thirty years, government officials have expanded stakeholder participation and proclaimed that cultural heritage is a primary objective. Such actions provide a mantle of fairness and community mindedness. Indeed, the plan notes the need to demonstrate "sensitivity and fairness . . . to those whose homes, lands, livelihoods and ways of life might be affected" (CPRA 2017b, 48). Yet, by utilizing a science-based "systems approach," the planning process rejects how society functions, that people, families, and communities do not operate as systems. It sidesteps the complexities found in the human past and the future contingencies that cannot be predicted or accurately modeled.

As projects in Louisiana move forward, there is an increasingly desperate need to fold humanities perspectives fully into our planning for a future with a changing climate that will alter the countless environmental modifications already in place along the coast. The same holds true for coastal areas around the globe. Planning seeks to project conditions into the future and in doing so relies on knowledge of past rates of change. A longitudinal perspective is fundamental to the task of dealing with changes that will bring disastrous results, especially those with a protracted timescale (Knowles 2014). The earliest maps of land loss relied on historical maps. Also, the study of climate, an important factor in Louisiana's land loss crisis, is based on historical records, along with multiple proxy measures for long periods before systematic record keeping (Lamb 1982; Brázdil et al. 2005). The challenge remains to bolster the planning process with reliance on a wider range of historical documents and to use them in ways other than as basic scientific data. These sources can reveal an understanding of the erratic and discontinuous human past in the face of changing environments.

With its chronic history of disasters, there has been a tendency in Louisiana to frame extreme events as "natural" when the underlying force behind them has been meteorological or geological—such as a hurricane or an earthquake. This course of action disconnects human agency from tragic consequences. Wise scholars, for more than half a century, have tried to dissuade policy makers from this impulse. Gilbert White's profound statement, "floods are acts of God, flood losses are acts of man" (1945) prefaced multiple academic declarations that there are no natural disasters (O'Keefe, Westgate, and Wisner 1976; Steinberg 2000; Bankoff 2010; Knowles 2014; Chmutina and von Meding 2019). Using the term "natural disasters" expunges or at least diminishes the role of multiple human decisions and actions that contribute to risk and loss in the wake of a natural hazard. Natural forces do produce extreme conditions, but human agency underlies the exposure of people and property to risk. Making deliberate adjustments and adaptations to risk are traits of human society. These adaptations, or implementation of lessons learned, are also deeply infused with social and cultural influences (Knowles 2014). An adaptation in one location might not be transferable to another where it would not be suited to either the local culture or the geographic setting. The Louisiana master plan is a product of scientists operating within a host of social and cultural frameworks and is not entirely value free. Members of society guide the planning process, and the crisis driving the master planning process is fully rooted in its host society and the decisions that contributed to its creation.

With sustainability as a governing principle for the master plan, has there been adequate inclusion of humanities perspectives that shed light on issues of justice and equity? Is there a model for Louisiana planners to draw on from this global approach? In the early 2010s, sustainability scientists were grappling with how to change personal attitudes and institutional structures to employ a broadly based methodology that would influence a wider audience (Wiek et al. 2012). In terms of climate change, a key issue within the realm of sustainability science, scholars have pointed out that there is a place for human dimensions in research and findings. They note that social sciences and humanities are commonly absent from strategies for coping with climate change, and the research behind the plans fails to consider the values and the ends and means that guide human decisions (Castree et al. 2014). Adger and associates underscore the importance of cultural dimensions. They point out that the analysis of culture is "central to understanding the causes and meaning of, and human responses to climate change" (2013, 112). Holm and Winiwarter tabulated the contributions of social scientists and humanities scholars in the Intergovernmental Panel for Climate Change reports and discovered a stunning dearth of noneconomic contributions to this important work (2017). This deficit exists despite notable observations that breaking down barriers to the adoption of sustainable policies requires penetrating the social and cultural realms of human activity. The underlying resistance to this approach stems from a failure by the scientists to take into account human "motivations and goals" or to address deep-set "habits" of behavior that are difficult to overcome (Holm and Winiwarter 2017, 5). Likewise, Adamson and colleagues conclude that adaptation to climate change "is constrained by social and cultural factors and requires an understanding of values and knowledge" (Adamson, Hannaford, and Rohland 2018, 195). The acceptance or rejection of the very concept of climate change is rooted in cultural values, which is acknowledged by scientists. But resolving this vexing problem remains beyond their customary tool kits. Hence, when the biophysical sciences do not address such important topics or employ methods from the humanities, they only partially address the basis for the crisis.

One core component to an intellectual methodology that embraces the humanities and social sciences is the use of robust public participatory methods at the outset of planning. This approach ensures the assembly of information not typically used in scientific analysis. According to Innes and Booher, public participation goes beyond the traditional public hearing process and even the more recent stakeholder engagement approach. They assert that it brings the full spectrum of potentially impacted citizens into the process at the earliest stages of environmental management decision-making (before the first decisions are made), uses direct dialogue between specialists and citizen groups to educate the public on the technical nuances of the projects, builds institutional capacity for the direct involvement of citizen groups, and regards citizen input as crucial to defining the goals and outcomes of public investments in environmental management (2004). Granted that participatory methods can be time-consuming and messy, still they are best suited to uncover often overlooked cultural concerns. By revealing the underlying cultural values and social memories, these methods get at what actually counts to local community members, and not just the proxy indicators that scientists can count and analyze.

The neglect of humanities and the social sciences is a characteristic of Louisiana's master planning process. It quite simply has not invested in noneconomic or non-demographic social science or humanities research. So what can be gleaned from such research? Scholars in England have investigated the role of social memory in adapting to flood risk, and they have identified processes that undermine the perpetuation of risk-reduction policies over time (Holmes and McEwen 2020). Comparable studies have not been launched by restoration authorities. Numerous scholars have begun inquiring about attachment to place, adaptation to new environmental conditions, willingness to migrate, the relationships among diverse ethnic and social groups, and other culturally based values (Burley 2010; Simms 2017b, Hemmerling 2017). Such inquiries can illuminate the foundations for resistance to change or pathways to promote effective adaptations. State planners have yet to fold the findings of such investigations into their plans. This type of activity has fallen to other organizations without the ability to secure their inclusion in the planning process (Manning-Broome, Dubinin, and Jenkins 2015; Oxfam 2014; Louisiana Office of Community Development, hereafter Louisiana OCD 2019). Numerous scholars have made noteworthy contributions to the state's coastal society as well (see Laska 2020, Mandelman 2020, Randolph 2018, Burley 2010), and there has been pioneering work on the history of restoration efforts that could yield insights for Louisiana officials (Hall 2010, Martin 2015).

Additionally, the historical perspective can enrich public and professional understanding of the current crisis. Multiple centuries have passed since human adaptations and environmental manipulations of the coast began. Modern planning often begins with the assumption that adaptations will proceed at the same pace as restoration projects, without actually considering the disparate temporal scales of those two separate actions. Historical analogs offer one method to gauge the pace of past adaptations in relationship to changing environmental conditions (Glantz 1988, Colten 2018). A longitudinal perspective can also expose the convergence of multiple adaptations into long-term adaptive transitions.

Singular, uncoordinated adaptions do not always result in a robust and enduring society. The concept of sustainability rests on the belief that multiple local adaptations can add up to a global sustainability transition (National Research Council, hereafter NRC 1999; Colten 2019). Examining the numerous past adaptations can help select and coordinate viable options for a more resilient and sustainable future.

ADAPTIVE TRANSITIONS

Resilience studies have emphasized the importance of adaptations in coping with changing environments. W. N. Adger's widely cited 2000 work examines the relationship between ecological and social resilience. Adger notes that social resilience is a key component in how societies adapt to environmental change and recognizes the central connection of ecological and social resilience through human dependence on ecosystems (347). Ultimately, he defines social resilience as "the ability of communities to withstand external shocks to their social infrastructure" (361). Adger and his collaborators subsequently examined coastal resilience to disasters, which is of particular relevance to Louisiana (2005). This work underscores the vulnerability of coastal societies by virtue of their tighter linkages to global economic and political processes than in the past and their geographic susceptibility to rising sea levels. Yet it also points out that social memory serves as a reservoir of practices, knowledge, values, and worldviews as a foundation for resilience in the wake of disturbances. Social memory is rooted in local experience with ecological conditions and enables the establishment of community resilience in particular places. Thus, social memory reinforces the vital role of human agency in adaptation and complicates the notion of human activities as wholly systematic, or mechanistic and predictable. The master plan, while attentive to historical structures, has overlooked the powerful influence of social memory.

Adaptation and adaptive capacity are core components of a resilient society (Smit and Wandel 2006). The ability to make decisions and undertake actions in response to changing environmental conditions which enable a society to continue represents a form of human agency. Adaptation may be very deliberate and swift, or it may represent a collection of minor adjustments over the course of generations. Those societies with the capacity to adjust quickly have greater adaptive capacity than more rigidly tradition-bound people. Sustainability as a global goal, unfortunately, rests on an assumption that all societies will be adapting towards a common goal or sharing comparable adaptive capacities. Locally based social values, attachment to place, and an openness to external values complicate adaptation (Adger et al. 2009). Pelling discusses transition theory and notes that transitional adaptation fails to fundamentally alter political or cultural regimes, but it can open pathways for more complete, although incremental, transformation (Pelling 2011, 82). Despite the unlikelihood that all adaptations will be coordinated toward sustainability, there exist opportunities for widespread social adaptation. In Louisiana, the adaptation strategies embedded in the master plan deal primarily with reshaping the biophysical environment and not the political or cultural regimes noted by Pelling.

Kates, Travis, and Wilbanks offer the notion of transformational adaptation in contrast to incremental adaptations. They define incremental adaptations as the many small, discrete actions or behaviors that society takes to reduce loses or enhance benefits arising from natural climate variations. They identify three types of transformational adaptations: collective adaptations that are larger in scale or intensity than incremental efforts, truly new adaptations to a region or location, and adaptations that either transform a location or result in populations migrating to new places. These specific types of adaptation may operate in tandem, further accelerating or enhancing the transformation. In their discussion, transformation begins with adaptations that are more than just reengineering biophysical systems, and they may include technological, institutional, and normative change (2012). Pelling, O'Brien, and Matyas take this idea a step further and point toward transformative adaptations as a possible outcome for multiple, interrelated, and deliberate adaptations with thorough penetration through society (2015). Although they do not specifically state it, they suggest that the timescale is decadal or generational—or observable in a human lifetime. Others have proposed the term "adaptation pathways" for broad and deliberate sets of changes and responses that demand addressing the underlying causes of vulnerability. They also underscore the uncertainties that confound decision-making for the long term (Adamson, Hannaford, and Rohland 2018).

"Transitions," as used here, include both deliberate and unplanned adaptations, those that are not directed at either modifying the environment or human activities that impact the environment. The fundamental concept of transitions rests on the notion that both deliberate and unintended adaptations can add up to consequential and transformative changes at multiple social, environmental, and geographic scales across considerable time spans. Such transformations are rooted in deep-set social and cultural matrices that more ephemeral public policies can influence.

Karl Butzer and colleagues have presented a critical model of social collapse/resilience that emphasizes both the long-term nature and complexity of the process (2012). The model is not deterministic, nor does it presuppose a singular progression—so it is not a predictive model. It allows for a range of outcomes, with multiple points of inflection along the way where adaptations may change the prevailing trajectory, and it offers a realistic framework for complex social responses to change. In each stage it incorporates social, political, economic, environmental, and other human factors. It acknowledges that societies can make adjustments in the course of a crisis that may lead toward stability or instability and possibly collapse. One of the core ideas presented is that climate or environmental conditions alone do not enable the reconstitution and perpetuation of a society, nor do they predetermine collapse. Such notions are far too simplistic. Louisiana's coastal restoration plans rely heavily on changing environmental conditions, presupposing environmental change is the principal driver, and do not blend in the many key social issues reflected in Butzer's model. In effect, it assumes that, by solving an environmental problem, society will successfully adapt. This is a serious weakness because the history of multiple adaptations in the past do *not* offer a precedent for long-term success.

In 1999 the National Research Council (NRC) published an overview of what it termed the "sustainability transition" and asked the question: "can the people living on earth over the next half-century meet their needs while nurturing and restoring the planet's life support systems?" The report claimed that the transition was a process that would foreground sustainability in public and political discussions and was fundamentally a "reconciliation of society's developmental goals with the planet's environmental limits over the long term" (1999, 1–2). It posited that human decisions could guide this sustainability transition, which it described as an ongoing, adaptive process and not a static goal. In doing so it recognized human agency and the fundamental role that society would play in the process, including many social, cultural, technological, economic, and political activities.

For quite some time there have been deliberate attempts to merge scholarly inquiries concerning the relationships between humans and the environment they inhabit. Authors use terms such as the "human environment," "human ecosystem," "socio-ecological systems," "socio-nature," and "nature-society" to characterize the object of study (Kates et al. 2001; Machlis, Force, and Burch 1997; Berkes, Colding, and Folke 2003; Swyngedouw 1996; and Russell et al. 2011). Scientists using the first three terms seek to integrate the analysis of biophysical and human systems, to acknowledge the interconnectedness of ecological and social processes. This approach seeks to redress the traditional conceptual separation of humans and the environment that prevailed in ecological studies for many years.

A spate of recent reports on the need to infuse climate change research with humanities and social sciences offers a complementary perspective (Castree et al. 2014, Adger et al. 2013). Historians in particular have pointed out why it is critical to look at cultures and environments as agents of change within the realm of nature-society relations (Russell et al. 2011, Holm et al. 2015, Adamson, Hannaford, and Rohland 2018). Humanities scholars acknowledge systems in the biophysical realm, but they see the imposition of a systems approach on humans as being deterministic, and instead strive to foreground the unpredictable and interrelated social, cultural, political, technological, and economic processes as well as the particularities of place and time. They also emphasize that science itself is a human endeavor and therefore is infused with political and other social influences. Likewise, it is influenced by the historical and geographical settings in which it functions (Livingston 2010). Historical contingency, not systemic consistency, is the prevailing concept in the study of human pasts.

Much of the research on long-term climate change relies on modeling both biophysical systems and the related socio-ecological systems, and this is the case with Louisiana's projects for its changing coastline. If we accept that humans are not systematic creatures and contingency looms beyond the horizon, are models up to the task of forecasting long-term nature-society relationships and conditions? Models tend to neglect erratic and often unpredictable contingencies in human history and often build in assumptions of steady states (albeit running multiple models or inserting hypothetical disruptions in a model address this deficiency to an extent). When will there be a massive hurricane that disrupts the steady state, or a war, a major economic recession, a spiral in fuel prices, a global pandemic, a fundamental shift in political policies? Contingencies are impossible to accurately predict and extremely difficult to factor into models, and this is where long-term historical analyses can complement models of biophysical systems and provide a way to incorporate long-term adaptive transitions (Adamson, Hannaford, and Rohland 2018; Colten 2018; Holm et al. 2015).

AUGMENTING SCIENCE

If Louisiana hopes that multiple, culturally and locally based adaptations will occur in alignment with its restorations in ways that will enable a sustainable transition, it has an obligation to move beyond a strictly science-based approach. Scientists tell us that simply knocking down the levees and allowing the river to rebuild its delta will not restore the coast. The detailed analysis behind this knowledge and for planning diversions and other projects is essential. Deep inquiry into the social and cultural processes at work are just as fundamental to fathom how restoration and land loss are impacting the people who live and work in the littoral region. Human futures are filled with unpredictable contingencies. With a dwindling supply of petroleum reserves and a declining population, the state will face incalculable challenges financing its ambitious restoration goal, let alone maintaining flood-mitigation structures in an increasingly precarious setting. Armed with a greater understanding of human motivations and culture, it might avoid some costly investments that could unleash adverse social impacts, undermine public confidence, and that may not provide a long-term solution based on the imperfect, albeit best, current science.

My intent is not to undermine or challenge the immense volume of science on Louisiana's existential coastal crisis. Sound science is required in the master planning process. Rather, I hope to reveal the neglected voices of marginalized coastal citizens as crucial to the planning process, to incorporate the underlying cultural values and attitudes relevant to life on the coast, to expose the agency of humans who are directly engaged in a form of social behavior as they labor on the plans, to restore the recognition that human decisions and actions are part of the scientific process. Toward that end, I seek to answer several broad questions.

The first chapter foregrounds the underlying process of human interaction with a changing environment. It considers adaptations that make coastal communities more resilient to change and disaster. It points out the subtle and vital role of inherent resilient practices, rooted in social memory, that have enabled community survival in a perilous place for centuries and how they have not been incorporated into formal resiliency plans introduced by external entities. Ultimately, the disconnection between local, informal practices and external, formal procedures have become normalized in the coastal master planning process. This has provided an underappreciated social impediment to robust public participation and locally responsive planning process. I ask the questions: How do the practices of families and communities factor into resilience? Are the multiple adaptations enabling the state to move toward a more sustainable future? Does the master plan adequately address the unpredictable nature of humans in charting its future investments? Is there a place for locally based, human-centered adaptation in the planning process? What are the timescales of these many human adaptations?

The second chapter sets the current restoration planning in the wider context of human management of the environment. In particular it traces how several different management regimes have contributed to the current crisis and the enduring environmental legacies they passed on to subsequent generations. It asks how the uncoordinated intellectual roots and guiding theories of past management policies remain influential in the decisions of current planners, and how well-intentioned science has produced unintended consequences that have erupted into the current crisis, and how current planners are interacting with both the intellectual and environmental legacies of their predecessors. What are the enduring impacts from previous management policies that are difficult to overcome in coping with the future, and how has each subsequent management strategy dealt with its predecessors? Do the timescales of environmental management align with those of human adaptations?

The third chapter examines the cartographic visualization of the land loss crisis. Early mapmakers largely ignored the coastal wetlands, but by the mid-twentieth century concern with the potential loss of oil revenue prompted detailed mapping of the retreating shoreline. Maps have obscured the presence and significance of certain segments of society, while also mobilizing society to accept science-based plans. How has land loss been displayed in cartographic form? What biophysical processes did the maps portray? Have the images adequately mapped people in the effort to mobilize the massive restoration-planning enterprise?

The next two chapters follow the evolving process of public input to major environmental management decisions that influenced the current coastal crisis. Government fiat largely guided the earliest decisions, but by the nineteenth century, local leaders appealed to the federal government for flood protection; public hearings with limited participation became a part of the process, followed by a more inclusive effort to allow stakeholder engagement. And yet, how geographically inclusive have these opportunities for input been? Has there been congruence between the people and communities providing input and the places most directly impacted by the decision-making process?

The state is investing huge sums of money in its restoration and protection projects that will have profound impacts on people of the coast, as it is currently configured and as it will be in the future. The people who will be affected by this plan and its projects deserve to be just as much a part of the process as the ecological, hydrological, and geomorphological settings that are the primary focus now.

1

Louisiana's Coastal Societies

Adaptation and Resilience

With contributions from Alexandra Giancarlo,
Audrey Grismore, jenny hay, and Jessica Simms

Louisiana is an ever-changing and distinctive physical place. At the same time, it is populated by a diverse set of people with varied settlement histories that have created a complex social and cultural geography. One does not determine the other. That is, although there are deeply intertwined and inextricable relationships between the environment and society, there is not a rigid set of causal relationships between the two. A flood or hurricane does not determine a particular response or outcome. Many factors based on human decisions shape the scale of damage or deliverance. The geography of human settlement is one prominent factor. In coastal Louisiana, linear villages with nodes of urbanization line the numerous bayous and their natural levees (figs. 1.1 and 1.2). Elevation above sea level and the presence or absence of levees further influence a community's ability to withstand a powerful storm. Much of the coastal territory is bordered by expansive but low-lying marshes. The wider the marsh buffer between people and the coast, the greater the potential for a diminished impact.

The state master plan calls for multiple changes to the biophysical setting, with little regard for how society will change—either voluntarily or unwillingly. A fundamental assumption, however, seems to be that either

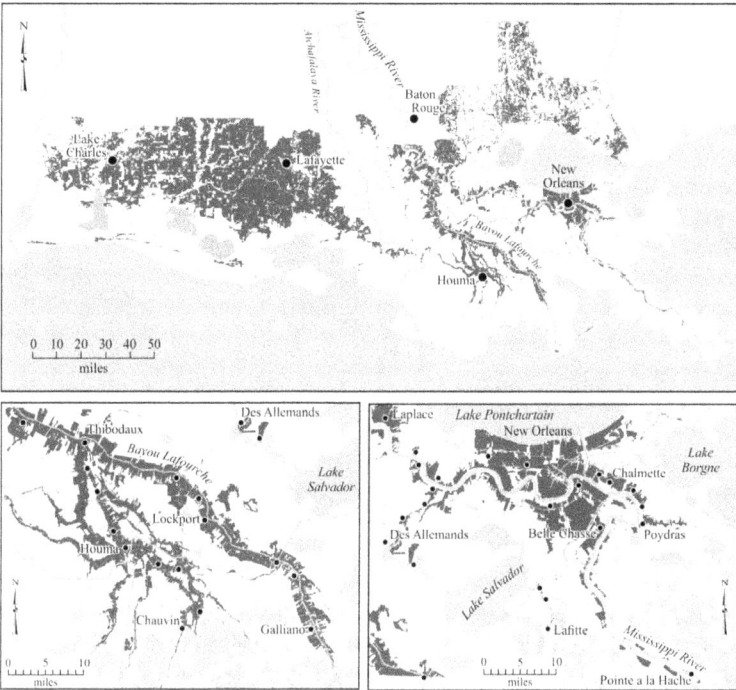

Fig. 1.1. Coastal population distribution, 2010. Map by Mary Lee Eggart, after Hemmerling 2017.

current conditions will prevail or positive social change will flow from changes engineered to the biophysical setting. The human considerations associated with this ambitious enterprise to salvage the coast have long been neglected. Resilience is a process that has enabled some members of society to adapt to this dynamic setting over the past several centuries. A host of ad hoc, unplanned adaptations should be seen in their multigenerational historical context—which extends most notably over the centuries since European and African arrivals to the Louisiana coast. Adaptations, both to an unfamiliar setting and to environmental changes in the new location, have been unevenly employed by different segments of society with unequal access to the means to invest in the resources that enable effective change with minimal disruption. Deliberate efforts to manage the environment have prompted or forced adaptations. Attitudes, beliefs,

Fig. 1.2. Fishing boat at a dock in Delacroix, Louisiana, 1925, with linear settlement along bayou in the background. Percy Viosca Jr. Photograph Collection, Mss. 4948, Louisiana and Lower Mississippi Valley Collections, LSU Libraries, Baton Rouge, La.

and values that arise from cultural backgrounds have influenced adaptive capacity. While certain types of hazard events have motivated particular adaptations, the practices used by society to cope with threats are not all transferable among the range of menaces. Furthermore, social and political commitments to adaptations are not all perpetuated over time. Thus, preparedness for disaster can wane, and social susceptibility can increase. Despite the professed political support for the state's master plan, there remain deep-set differences in the ability of segments of Louisiana's coastal population to accommodate the environmental changes built into the restoration program. Grave questions remain about the long-term political commitment to the project and how effectively it will protect and support society into the future. The state's planners have intensively studied many aspects of the biophysical environment in anticipation of implementing each component of its ambitious efforts, but there has been no comparable consideration of the social and cultural dimensions.

ADAPTATION AND RESILIENCE

The state asserts that its master plan offers a path towards sustainability, and resilience is generally considered a trait of a sustainable society. Resilience, at least in the realm of social sciences, means the ability of a society to absorb the impacts of both expected and unexpected disturbances, to recover and rebuild itself to a functional state (NRC 2012). In order to absorb a blow, society needs to be able to plan for extreme events and organize to a sufficient level to mitigate their impacts. Tom Wilbanks identifies the four elements of resilience as the ability to anticipate disruptive events, to reduce their impacts, to respond effectively fairly and equitably, and to recover from them (2008). This definition identifies these elements as active and deliberate steps taken by society, covers the fundamental capacities required to take these steps, and provides a useful framework for this discussion about resilient practices. Most importantly, it recognizes resilience as a process and not an outcome, which guides our efforts to document actions and not static demographic or economic measures. It also allows for deliberate adaptation, which is the key distinction between human societies and biological communities and can occur within each element. I contend that there is also a fifth element that needs to be added to Wilbanks's set. It is to *remember.* Storing the knowledge of resilient practices in social memory and passing them down to future generations is a necessary step in perpetuating all capacities to adapt and rebound.

Community-level research in coastal Louisiana has shown that resilience works at multiple levels, and I consider two: inherent and formal (Colten, Hay, and Giancarlo 2012). Inherent resilience is locally adapted, community-based practices that provide families and communities with essential tools to cope with and respond to disruptions (fig. 1.3; Colten, Hay, and Giancarlo 2012).* These capacities are not always deliberate or codified in emergency plans and manuals, and they do not have government or corporate finances or infrastructure supporting and perpetuating

---

*Cutter and associates refer to "inherent" resilience as those qualities that function effectively in between crisis periods and "adaptive" as those that can be applied in response to extreme events (2008, 601).

Fig. 1.3. Blessing of the shrimp fleet, Morgan City, Louisiana, 1946. Livelihoods, culture, family, and community were tightly intertwined in coastal Louisiana and provided the essential lineaments for inherent resilience. Photo by Arnold Eagle, courtesy State Library of Louisiana.

them between events. Rather, these sets of *practices* are place based, they reside in social memory, and communities draw on them when needed (Adger et al. 2011; Adger et al. 2005; Colten and Sumpter 2009; and Colten, Hay, and Giancarlo 2012). Their somewhat ephemeral qualities mean they hold less value in terms of anticipating disruptions, but at the same time, they emerge, even if in a fragmented way, in the wake of an event and operate at the local level even before government or corporate responders have arrived. They also persevere well after an event during the long-term recovery and exist in a somewhat dormant state between infrequent events. A long-term perspective is necessary to see the reappearance of these vestigial practices following extended intervals between extreme events. Yet some can also be fragile and erode over time, especially as external formal programs arrive. By identifying and focusing on the actual practices used at the community level, it is possible to more closely follow the processes and avoid the pitfalls of the commonly used proxy measures that were not assembled to measure resilience (Abramson et al. 2015).

Formal resilience, in contrast, is top-down. Well before the term permeated the hazards literature, organizations such as the Civil Defense and Red Cross devised anticipatory plans for responding to extreme events. Corporations produced emergency response plans as well. Developed by specialists, set down in hefty manuals, practiced in drills, and funded with public and private dollars, these programs focused on three of Wilbanks's elements: anticipate, reduce, and respond. For many years, anticipation and emergency response were the primary focuses, with the exception of the flood-protection levees, although mitigation has gained prominence in recent years. Long-term recovery often was set aside until it was needed in the aftermath of a disaster.

In its study of resilience, the NRC (2012) has recognized the top-down and bottom-up forms of resilience and stressed the need to foster both and to find ways to integrate the two approaches. Research on inherent resilience in coastal Louisiana points toward areas of opportunity and challenges to accomplish this goal (Colten, Hay, and Giancarlo 2012, Colten et al. 2018).

Social scientists have, some would argue, overused resilience as an approach to hazard management in this century. Beyond becoming almost trite, it is subject to some serious critiques. Government programs tend to push capacity building to the local level, which, in contrast to vulnerability studies, can absolve higher-level bodies of some responsibility. Political spokespeople commonly reinforce a mythic tradition of self-reliance and individual ability to pull oneself up out of desperate conditions as a foundation of resilience. According to MacKinnon and Derickson (2013), the concept of resilience is fundamentally conservative and privileges established social orders, thus doing little to address social inequities. In their critique, government programs that promote resilience are fundamentally inequitable. Also, resilience is based on a scientific concept of ecological resilience and thus treats complex human societies as mechanistic systems. By considering the practices deployed at the community level, we move away from a systems approach by recognizing historical contingency. MacKinnon and Derickson argue that the prevailing approach to resilience is "top down." They do not, however, consider resilient practices that existed at the local level well before formal programs came into existence. Recognizing locally based inherent resilience, as done here, addresses that shortcoming. While far from perfect, reorienting our approach to social resilience around the actions taken at the family and community level can reveal the processes at work in resilient communities that are neglected in the proxy-based methods.

Coastal Louisiana has dealt with its share of natural and technological hazards, from river floods to hurricanes, deadly epidemics, military invasion, and economic boom and bust cycles. The frequency of tragic events has provided residents and institutions of the Gulf Coast with ample experience in coping with environmental trauma and an opportunity to store the memories of these events and how they responded.

Neil Adger points to the importance of social institutions in harboring the capacity to rebound after disruptions, to be resilient (2000). By serving as "reservoirs of practices, knowledge, values, and world views," individuals and institutions serve as the basis for "building resilience and coping with surprises" (Adger et al. 2005). Social memory is the repository for the "accumulated wisdom, knowledge, skills and experience" that are "passed on within a community" and serve as the history for decision-making that enables resilience (Wilson 2013, 208). Decisions about how to cope with floods, hurricanes, epidemics, and other potentially disastrous environmental conditions tap a community's social memory.

Yet social memory is far from perfect. Susan Cutter and her collaborators (2008) observe that "lessons learned" after a hazard event are often merely "lessons identified." If we accept adaptation as a key component of resilience, and adaptation as a process of continual learning and making adjustments to contend with hazards, then merely identifying lessons and not perpetuating them in plans, institutional processes, and physical structures renders them valueless in the long term. Residents along Louisiana's Gulf Coast have amply demonstrated the ability to "learn lessons" and then to fossilize at least portions of them in impressive structures, while promptly discarding others in the face of economic aspirations. This type of selective retention represents what English memory scholars refer to as the active forgetting of past tragedies (Garde-Hansen et al. 2017): the deliberate setting aside of lessons learned. This fragility of social memory contributes to the erosion of resilience.

ADAPTATIONS AS PART OF LONG-TERM TRANSITIONS

River Flood Adaptations

Humans began modifying the coastal environment in what is now Louisiana as physical processes created this marshy landscape several millennia ago. Prehistoric mounds are abundant in Louisiana's coastal zone. Early geomorphological research on the progression of delta building relied in part on archaeological dating of the contents of Native American mounds (Kidder 2000 and Kniffen 1936b). Prehistoric people followed the shoreward extension of the deltas to stay within reach of the resources they relied on. Land building prompted a slow-motion migratory adaptation with mound building in what are now Orleans, Plaquemines, and St. Bernard parishes in the period from roughly 100 to 1200 CE (Kniffen 1936b). As best we can tell, land building and climate change did not prompt a wholesale transition of this coastal society although coastal inhabitants did migrate incrementally.

Native Americans relied on rangia, a shellfish found in the brackish coastal waters, and oysters as key elements of their diet and built settlements on the ad hoc refuse heaps of the discarded shells (Kidder 2000). Early coastal dwellers also deliberately built mounds, but these marsh residents had largely disappeared by the time Europeans arrived. When the French began settling coastal Louisiana, they took advantage of the shell middens for camp sites and also mined them for road-building materials and other purposes. Europeans displaced indigenous populations through disease and warfare, although survivors retreated to remote wetland locations, adapting to new conditions in the process (Swanton 1946; Kniffen, Gregory, and Stokes 1994; Kidder 2000; Unser 2003).

European societies that settled along the lower Mississippi River in the 1700s were unfamiliar with the subtropical climate and deltaic environment. Numerous unplanned, uncoordinated adaptations over centuries represent a long-term adaptive transition to sustain the settlements along the Mississippi River. As for the efforts to cope with the environmental hazards and the resources they came to rely on, we can trace a series of adaptations that include social, political, economic, and technological components. I will discuss two broad categories: protection from river and tropical cyclone flooding, which advanced initially as incremen-

tal efforts, and wetland modification, which includes several more deliberate efforts (Colten 2017). When viewed as part of a multidimensional
long-term transition, they highlight both the temporal scale and interrelated human endeavors that were involved. Each set of adaptations was
intended to facilitate survival in the low-lying delta and created opportunities for some members of society while imposing conditions that forced
further adaptations on others. The historical social ripple effects and the
environmental and technological path dependencies were not foreseen in
the distant past, but they are evident today.

First among the notable adaptations was the construction of levees to
protect against annual spring floods. The explorer Pierre LeMoyne d'Iberville reported on evidence of high water on his spring 1699 voyage up
the river (Iberville 1661–1706). Subsequent French settlers were aware
of the risks posed by the riparian location of their initial settlements.
European colonists brought knowledge of riverine hydrology and levee
building from their homelands and constructed structural protections
on the lower Mississippi River landscape (Rohland 2018). The French,
along with subsequent African, German, Spanish, and eventually English
settlers occupied the relatively narrow natural levees that hug the river.
Unlike most locations in Europe and in French Canada, the highest land
was immediately adjacent to the river and gradually sloped downward
as one moved away from the crest of the natural levee near the water-
course. These earthen shoulders that paralleled the river were the last to
flood and the first to drain and consequently attracted human habitation.
Nonetheless, annual inundations were common, and the company that
established New Orleans built low levees to protect the initial urban settlement, and it required landowners to erect comparable barriers fronting
their properties as well. The overall intent was to create a continuous
wall along the waterway. By the end of the colonial period, levees extended well upstream and a modest distance downriver from the colonial capital. They were inconsistent in quality, and frequent crevasses, or
breaches, allowed the river to invade the floodplain (Elliott 1932; Colten
2005). Elevated housing, another adaptation, introduced from the French
Caribbean, offered protection to domiciles against the regular threat of
high water. It became common for residents of the flood plain to abandon
the more traditional French *poteaux en terre* construction, which placed

houses directly on the ground, and to build houses with the living spaces elevated five to six feet above the ground (fig. 1.4). This allowed flood-waters to pass beneath the house and offered the additional benefits of allowing breezes to moderate the oppressive temperatures and raising living areas above the most intense mosquito zone (Edwards 2011).

Over the two centuries following New Orleans's founding, responsi-bility for building and maintaining levees shifted from private landowners to the parishes, to the state, and finally to the federal government. Design and construction passed from individuals to government authorities, and resilience became more formal. Administrative responsibility changed over time, as did the size, length, and strength of the levees. These changes took place amid social turmoil and debate about the role of the federal government in public works (Paskoff 2007 and Wood 1996). During the nineteenth century, crevasses in the inconsistently built levees tormented floodplain dwellers with all-to-frequent inundation. Considerable debate

Fig. 1.4. Raised house in New Orleans. Madame John's Legacy, built in the 1780s, is one of the few remaining examples of French architecture in the French Quar-ter. The living quarters stood over six feet above ground level and offered pro-tection from inundations. Photo by author.

and persistent lobbying by Louisiana's delegation preceded Congress's authorization of federal involvement in levee construction in 1879, and by the early twentieth century the legislative branch extended the role of federal bodies in building and maintaining a more consistent barrier along the river. Federal levees, particularly since a major change in the engineering approach following the epic 1927 flood, have effectively contained the lower river. After that devastating flood, the Army Corps of Engineers shifted from a "levees only" approach to a "levees and outlets" strategy. This adaptation introduced human-made outlets to replicate the function of the severed distributaries and to provide safety valves during extreme floods. The Corps created a more secure system that has more consistently rerouted the massive load of waterborne sediments from the floodplain into the deep waters of the Gulf of Mexico (Reuss 1998, Colten 2005). The adaptative use of levees has contributed to the so-called sediment starvation of the lands along the river's course, and this contributes to the general subsidence of the lower delta (Colten 2018) and the severing of the river from the wetlands. Just over two centuries elapsed as floodplain residents experimented with flood-mitigation structures and adapted to the conditions that existed on the lower Mississippi River. Ad hoc efforts gradually morphed into highly engineered works which the state does not want to abandon along much of the lower river. It took decades after 1927 to design and build the current configuration of levees and outlets, which remains in place in the 2020s. This multi-century timescale of flood protection is beyond the temporal horizons of the current master planning process which suggests human adaptations can occur over twenty years (CPRA 2017a, 4) and allowed for gradual social adaptations.

Coping with the recurrent river floods provided a proving ground for adaptive responses. Charitable organizations arose in New Orleans to provide aid to flood victims when levees failed (Rohland 2018, Colten 2005, Kmen 1957). Disaster relief became more formalized as it shifted to federal organizations, particularly during the devastating 1927 flood. The Red Cross, the Coast Guard, and other organizations mobilized to provide shelter and food to the hundreds of thousands of displaced people that spring, albeit not equitably (Barry 1998, American National Red Cross 1929). Eventually the federally organized Civil Defense took on the lead role for flood response planning in the 1940s, which eventually transitioned to the Federal Emergency Management Agency in 1979. Overall, the regularity of river floods prompted efforts to protect lives and properties and not to retreat from risky locations.

The levees have also provided an opportunity for reworking the floodplain's economic and social geography. Rice, which was the first successful staple commodity grown adjacent to the river, relied on annual flooding. Africans provided vital knowledge about manipulating floodplains to implement this type of cultivation (Morris 2012, Mandelman 2020). Flues allowed the introduction of water to specific fields even as the levees fended off most high water. Sugar cultivation, which requires low-moisture soils, expanded after its late-eighteenth-century introduction and, unlike rice, demanded an impervious levee system. Adam Mandelman (2020) provides a compelling narrative of the technological, economic, and political adjustments to improve the levees for sugar while reducing the privileges of rice growers to maintain flues for seasonal flooding of their fields. Additionally, the sugar-plantation economy encouraged investment capital from other regions of the country during the first half of the nineteenth century (Vaughan 2003). The lure of wealth brought entrepreneurs to the floodplain who, in many cases, acquired land from the *petit habitant* Acadians who had secured riverfront property during the Spanish colonial period. Not inclined to scale up their agricultural activities, the Acadians sold out and migrated into the Atchafalaya Basin, down the bayous, and into the prairie parishes to the west where they adapted to new conditions (Estaville 1986, Comeaux 1972). By the late nineteenth century, small farmers and rice cultivation had largely departed from Louisiana's delta floodplain. Sugar came to dominate the riparian landscape and the local economy (Mandelman 2020; Colten 2012; Rehder 1999). Over the ensuing decades, Congress enacted complex federal programs that supported the industry which operates at the climatic margins of viable cane cultivation and in ways that are too costly to compete in the global market (Vaughan 2003).

With emancipation of the former enslaved sugar-plantation workers during the Civil War, there was a reconfiguration of the region's social landscape. Some African Americans migrated to nearby cities, and others sought new opportunities outside the South. Many former agricultural workers remained in the region, where they commonly clustered in narrow villages on slivers of property carved out of former plantations (Rosner and Markowitz 2002; Rodrigue 2001). During the twentieth century, petrochemical industries acquired property and erected refineries and processing facilities protected by the federal levee system. A massive expansion of the industry took place, especially after the Second World War (McMichael 1961, Colten 2012). Encouraged by state tax incentives, industries took advantage of locally abundant oil and natural gas resources as well as the river's transport and waste-removal capabilities. The oil and gas industries now support thousands of jobs and occupy a favored status in the state's politics. Yet exposure of Africans in the "fence-row" settlements adjacent to the emission of the newly arrived industries has created environmental justice conflicts and few jobs for the marginalized residents (Lerner 2005, Rosner and Markowitz 2002).

The flood-protection system has had direct impacts on marginalized communities (Barry 1998). In the face of the 1927 flood, local officials convinced the Army Corps of Engineers to deliberately breach the levee downstream from New Orleans with the intent to reduce pressure on the levees along the city's waterfront by creating a temporary second mouth to the river. The crevasse flooded much of the wetlands of St. Bernard Parish, which had been the leading fur-producing region in the country. The high water devastated the trapping economy of the parish for years and seriously impacted the Isleño residents of the area (Gomez 2000). Following that flood and with the construction of the two artificial outlets, the engineering changes altered the hydrology of the Atchafalaya River Basin. Sedimentation in the lakes of the lower river transformed a viable commercial fishery into a backwater swamp and displaced many fishing families (Delahoussaye 2014). Periodic opening of the Bonnet Carré Spillway has harmed oyster fisheries in Mississippi Sound as well (see chapter 2; Colten 2018). The cascading consequences were felt well beyond the immediate floodplain and prompted enduring, multigenerational social changes (see chapter 4).

Hurricanes and Adaptation

The extreme winds and storm surge associated with tropical cyclones were less frequent than river floods and did not retrace the same path with each occurrence, but adaptations, while drawing on some of the riparian experiences, were essential for survival in the coastal region. They included multiple practices, but the variable paths of levees limited the viability of levees. Instead, geographic relocation was common. After the devastating Last Island hurricane in 1856, the property owners never restored resort functions on the barrier island, even though they flourished elsewhere temporarily. When the 1893 hurricane destroyed the lavish hotel on Grand Isle, investors never rebuilt. That storm also devastated the fishing community of Chenier Caminada, and most survivors turned to relatives and friends up the bayou as they resettled further inland. Pre-existing networks or social capital, cultivated over the years through day-to-day interactions, provided the linkages that led to temporary shelter, and employment for those who lost boats and businesses. Following storms, friends and family lent skills and time to help repair houses and fishing boats. Modest investments in housing and furnishings functioned as a type of self-insurance and reduced losses caused by surge. Local charitable drives, often conducted through churches or local government, collected cash and essentials to enable individuals to survive and then get back on their feet. Even before the advent of the Red Cross and Civil Defense, response and recovery efforts flowed through these networks (Fogelman 1958, Laska et al. 2005, and Burley et al. 2007). Additionally, during the first half of the twentieth century, fishermen were commonly aware of the meteorological signs of an impending storm and thus heeded visible indications of foul weather along with Weather Service warnings ("Delacroix Island" 1947, GC-Harms interviews, Simms 2017a).

Locally based adaptive response and recovery efforts followed storms such as Audrey in 1957, Betsy in 1965, and Camille in 1969 (Fogelman 1958, Colten et al. 2008). In addition, parish governments took action to assemble funds to help residents rebuild houses and to foster wildlife-conservation efforts to restore economically valuable species that residents harvested (St. Bernard Police Jury 1970, Plaquemines Parish Council 1970). Such actions, initiated at the local level and sustained through local networks, were oriented toward long-term recovery.

Geographic and economic mobility provided other means for communities to persist in place. When storms disrupted oyster beds, fisherfolk redirected their efforts to unaffected locations. Shrimpers delivered their catches to different ports where facilities were not destroyed. If those choices were not available, they might deviate from their normal pursuits and work for a friend or relative engaged in different resource-based livelihood. It has been commonplace for coastal residents to follow seasonally available resources, so adjusting from one activity to another is a small adaptation to a disruptive event. Work in the oil industry offered another employment option (Comeaux 1972, Gramling and Hagelman 2005, Maass 2014). Despite reserves of social capital, massive storms such as Katrina were highly disruptive to coastal communities, particularly to those dependent on the shrimping industry (Petterson et al. 2006, GC-Harms interviews). Mobility offered a critical means for survival.

The same type of ingenuity and adaptation moved from the floodplain to the marshes in the use of raised houses by oystermen, trappers, and residents in low-lying coastal areas prone to storm surge (Kniffen 1936a, Kniffen and Wright 1963, and Kniffen 1965). Local charitable fundraising drives functioned through local networks to alleviate suffering ("City's Hurricane" 1947). Inland migration is an adaptation that reflected the mobility component of inherent resilience (Laska et al. 2005). In addition to the flight from Chenier Caminada after the 1893 storm, residents have departed from numerous other coastal towns following devastating storms (Hemmerling 2017). Deep attachments to place, cultivated through intimate knowledge of the local environment and natural resource cycles, have enabled adaptation and survival in the wake of disruptions, while proving elastic enough for short-distance migration toward safer ground (Burley et al. 2007).

Familiarity with hurricanes has fostered a confidence among coastal residents. Most adults have endured more than one storm, and they feel that their experiences have prepared them to cope with future events (GC-Harms interviews). The relatively short duration and limited area of impact, even when severe, enable relatively swift initiation of recovery efforts and tapping resources from unaffected communities. The support structure of family or ethnic and church groups provides a security net even when individuals have to flee their homes for several days. Thus, when weather forecasts alert residents to the approach of a massive storm, they can deploy well-known resilient practices. Through familial and social networks, this informal knowledge persists and assists communities in enduring the storms and mobilizing recovery efforts (Fogelman 1958; Airriess et al. 2007, GC-Harms interviews).

For New Orleans and its suburbs, hurricane adaptations included numerous locally devised practices along with several more formal approaches. Buffered by extensive marshes on its south and east, the low-elevation city could endure flooding across its unprotected and thinly populated lakefront before 1900. In advance of the massive 1915 storm, the weather service sent warnings to rural coastal communities. Families with the means evacuated to the city, where public shelters were available. Shipping companies advised captains to remain in the river and delay setting out into the Gulf of Mexico, while railroads pre-positioned materials to rebuild bridges ("Tropical Storm" 1915; Colten 2009, 21). After the storm wreaked havoc to the stilt houses on the city's lakefront, residents began the process of rebuilding without external aid ("Old Bucktown" 1915). The city initiated a nearly twenty-year campaign to armor the highly susceptible lakefront district with a concrete seawall (Orleans Levee Board 1954). This project reflected local confidence in the viability of levees. Filling the wetlands with dredged lake-bed sediments behind the structure created marketable real estate and thus underwrote its costly construction. The barrier provided a sense of security and contributed to the subsequent "levee effect" that motivated residential development in a high-risk setting (Colten 2015). It also began a greater dependence on structural protection and not the traditional inherent practices.

Before the next major hurricane, civic leaders in adjacent Jefferson Parish appealed to the Army Corps of Engineers to build a levee for their rapidly growing suburbs (US Congress, House 1946a). They were not completed as the 1947 storm approached, and weather forecasters issued a warning that compelled some area dwellers to evacuate. Nonetheless, the storm surge poured over the lakefront seawall. With the levees and building codes that promoted slab-on-grade construction, new development had largely abandoned traditional raised-house construction (Orleans Levee District 1950). Consequently, the newest postwar homes suffered the greatest damage in New Orleans. In addition, lake water inundated the emerging suburbs in Jefferson Parish and provided the impetus for extending levees across its lakefront. The potential for economic development provided an adequate "benefit" to justify the Corps's work on this project. Postwar suburbanization followed and enlarged the population in the risky, albeit structurally protected, lakefront districts (Colten 2009). Inherent resilience practices had been designed out of both land use and building practices.

Formal resilience before the 1950s was not limited to hurricane-protection levees in the New Orleans area. There existed capacities available to the entire coastal region such as weather forecasting, loosely organized Civil Defense and Red Cross efforts, and regionally organized evacuation/shelter efforts. Weather forecasting was rudimentary by today's standards, but the Weather Service issued notifications, and local officials hoisted hurricane-warning flags with some modest advance notice (Colten et al. 2008). Charitable organizations in New Orleans provided shelter for evacuees from coastal communities. Yet this option required individuals to travel on their own, and fatalities among the poor and minorities who were unable to flee often were disproportionate (Colten 2011, "City's Hurricane" 1947). In addition to preparations taken by railroads and shipping companies, utility companies also developed plans to restore telephone and electrical service in the wake of storms (Colten et al. 2008). As utilities and transportation businesses consolidated during the second half of the twentieth century, formal resilience enlarged in scale.

After the enactment of the Disaster Relief Act (1950), additional federal programs offered assistance (Platt 1999, Dauber 2013). Louisiana's Civil Defense developed an extensive plan complete with pre-storm designated shelters, plotted evacuation routes, and allocated duties among local organizations for the post-event emergency response (Louisiana Military Department 1949, Louisiana Civil Defense Agency 1957). The Coast Guard and National Guard had key roles to play in the emergency response phase as well. To help spur recovery, Congress made available low-interest loans to impacted businesses and enabled disaster declarations to initiate restoration of key infrastructure. In the mid-1950s, a series of hurricanes that struck the heavily populated eastern US seaboard gave rise to additional federal investigations and the development of a model hurricane plan for coastal communities (Dorst 2007, US Dept. of Commerce 1959).

As Hurricane Betsy approached the Louisiana coast in 1965, residents deployed the customary, inherent resilience practices. Rural residents assembled essential supplies, evacuated to higher ground with family members, and secured fishing vessels and houses. The plans for formal resilience saw the evacuation of military aircraft, stockpiling of emergency provisions and equipment, and opening of multistory schools in the city as neighborhood shelters. The city's levees were not wholly effective, and storm surge inundated some 40 percent of the city. Nonetheless, the combination of inherent and formal resilience minimized loss of life. Damage was costly nonetheless, and efforts to fortify the structural protections for the city and nearby areas began almost immediately (Colten 2009, US Army Corps of Engineers, New Orleans District 1965).

Congress approved a previously drafted plan for a more extensive hurricane-protection levee system, and work began within weeks of its approval (fig. 1.5). Although intended for a 1978 completion, the project dragged on for decades. There were multiple causes for the delays. Challenges of constructing a heavy levee system on spongy marsh soils

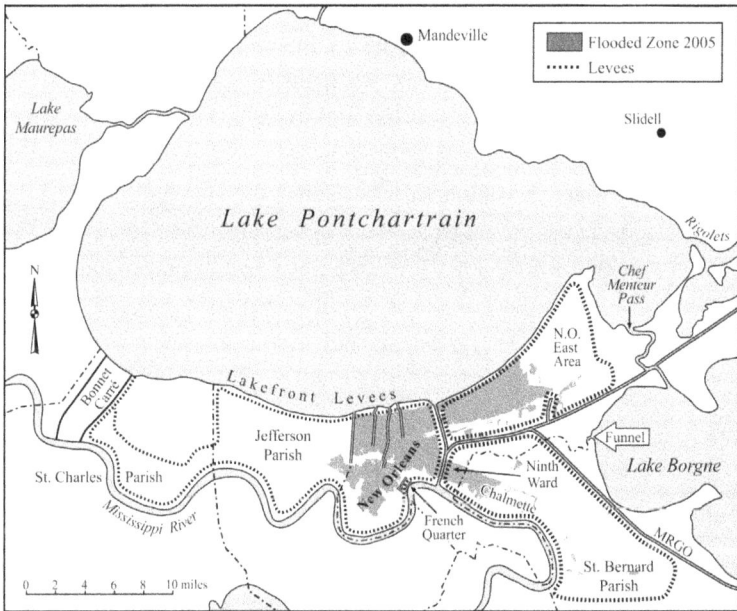

Fig. 1.5. New Orleans's protective levee system, built mostly after Hurricane Betsy in 1965. It failed in 2005, and a large portion of the city flooded. Map by Mary Lee Eggart.

prompted experimentation. Legal challenges by residents on the north shore of Lake Pontchartrain who feared the levees would divert surge to their communities interrupted work and prompted a major redesign that set back completion. Jefferson Parish temporarily wrested the project from the Corps with the intent to protect a larger territory to expand its taxable real estate (Colten 2009). The conflicts with parish governments and citizens in the early phases of the environmental review process reflect the shortcomings of existing public participation (chapter 5) and caused delays. As the years passed without a major tropical cyclone, residents assumed a false sense of security, and urgent demands for levee completion declined. When Hurricane Katrina arrived in 2005, the system was still incomplete.

Beyond New Orleans proper, the Corps's cost-benefit accounting system excluded some small coastal communities while offering lesser protection to residents of the lower bird's foot delta—the narrow land areas adjacent to the diverging channels of river where it empties into the Gulf of Mexico. The uneven treatment established by the 1965 hurricane-levee plans became a template for dealing with more remote, nonurban residents in subsequent coastal restoration plans.

By the eve of Hurricane Katrina in 2005, Congress had established FEMA to lead federal efforts in combination with the Red Cross, the Coast Guard, and the National Guard. There was much greater reliance on formal resilience by this time, and inherent practices had waned. The sense of urgency fostered by Hurricane Betsy had declined, and with it formal resilience had deteriorated. Social memories of hurricane preparation and response were no longer vivid.

Erosion of Resilience

Weather forecasting improved dramatically between 1965 and 2005 and enabled a longer advance notice before Hurricane Katrina arrived on the Louisiana coast. Nearly three days before landfall, the National Hurricane Center posted its advisory, which showed potential landfall just east of New Orleans, and this allowed extensive preparation, including staging of relief supplies and enabling an unprecedented evacuation of some 800,000 people. But the levee system failed, and the inundation of 80 percent of the city far exceeded preparations and thoroughly strained all elements of resilience. This storm was more destructive to New Orleans than Betsy, even if wind speeds were less within the city. Winds at the airport registered only eighty-nine miles per hour (Kates et al. 2006). Katrina exposed, in a deadly fashion, the funnel effect of the converging levees near the Industrial Canal that facilitated overtopping of the floodwall in the Ninth Ward and caused it to collapse. The most heavily relied-upon formal resilience system failed (fig. 1.5). Horrendous destruction in the lower Ninth Ward resulted. Shortcomings in the levees along two of the city's drainage canals permitted additional dramatic failures and extensive flooding in lakefront neighborhoods. The storm's havoc left more than one thousand people dead and seriously damaged over 140,000 houses. Structural protections were not up to the task. Much like the 1927 river flood exposed the shortcomings of the river levees, Katrina revealed similar inadequacies with the hurricane barriers. One of the principal reasons given for the tragic failure was the loss of the coastal marshes as a buffer from storm surge. This observation linked the multi-century diversion of sediment, along with natural subsidence and other processes, to the threat of storms. In addition, rising concern with sea-level rise in the environmental science community further heightened concern with future storms. Hurricane levees demand a fundamentally different level of government involvement than river levees, but in many respects they were used as if the two different risks were comparable.

Memories of Betsy arose in the midst of tragedy and prompted assignment of blame to those responsible for formal resilience systems. When floodwaters entered the city, some residents retreated to neighborhood schools to escape the rising flood in the multistory structures. Such action reflected the 1960s-era evacuation plans, but not those in place in 2005. Schools formerly used as shelters were locked when terrified residents sought entry. Frantic individuals nonetheless gained entry and huddled in the buildings, which had no electricity, for days after the storm passed. As in the wake of Betsy, residents of the Ninth Ward reported that the levees were blown to sacrifice their neighborhood and reduce the risk in affluent neighborhoods (Giancarlo 2011, Kelman 2009, Landphair 2007). This was one of many expressions of public doubt about the authorities' sincerity to safeguard disadvantaged neighborhoods.

As the global media focused on the emergency response, they reported on shortcomings in planning and emergency response—the bold promises made after Betsy had not been remembered nor fulfilled by a later generation of leaders (Freudenburg et al. 2007, Colten 2015). Since Katrina, politicians have pledged to rebuild the city, to make it more resilient. Lessons-learned reports tabulated the many failures leading up to the hurricane's landfall (Office of the President 2006; US Congress, Select Bipartisan Committee 2006; Colten, Kates, and Laska 2008). Post-Katrina critiques have found fault in nearly every facet of preparation and response, but also elements of resilience that surprised observers (Parker et al. 2009, Green and Olshansky 2012, and Airriess et al. 2007).

With an emphasis on formal resilience, community-support networks within the city were less agile and, with the extensive flooding and evacuation, social capital was extremely low. There was a surge of voluntary organizations that arose to provide medical care and food to stranded residents. They became even more critical when federal services were slow to arrive on the scene (Kates et al. 2006; Colten, Kates, and Laska 2008). The Vietnamese community, with strong leadership from church officials, defied the general trend and rebounded with remarkable rapidity (Airriess et al. 2007). Yet recovery required massive state and federal expenditures and coordination which lasted for years.

One of the great inadequacies linked to lost memory was the absence of a recovery plan before the storm. The initial post-storm plans showed little regard for reconfiguring the obliterated city's layout to enhance long-term safety. After Katrina, city leaders sought outside assistance that stimulated a vigorous pushback from a shaken and dispersed population. A plan prepared by the Urban Land Institute called for limiting development in the footprint of disaster and conversion of this territory to green space for future flood overflow. However, many displaced residents understood it to mean a government land grab and a taking of their damaged properties. Fear of this possibility sparked a "right to return" movement which rejected the creation of parks in some low-lying areas with the greatest future flood risk. Citizens called for a more inclusive planning process, which ultimately became the guiding principle for recovery. Using this reworked approach required almost two years for the city, neighborhood committees, and outside consultants to chart a course that won municipal approval—the Unified New Orleans Plan. A refined Target Areas Plan, rolled out under recovery "czar" Edward Blakely, sought to promote redevelopment in key economic nodes as growth points for long-term restoration. All but two were in areas that had endured the worst flooding (Nelson, Ehrenfeuct, and Laska 2007; New Orleans 2007; Olshansky and Johnson 2010; Blakely 2012). Opening expansive green spaces in high-risk areas disappeared from the plans entirely. As was done after previous hurricanes, safe land use was designed out of the plan.

Granted there have been adaptations that proved effective. In 2008, officials expressed great pride in the city's response to Hurricane Gustav. It came ashore while the memory of Katrina was still vivid, and the city, the state, and residents of the region took satisfaction in their reaction to this threat. Formal preparations were thorough, and all phases of the response prevented loss of life. The worst of the storm bypassed the city and did not really test the region's ability to respond to a major storm. After-action reports nonetheless pointed out the need for better integration of plans among the multiple entities (Louisiana Governors Office 2008, 19). And by 2012, following Hurricane Isaac, one of the criticisms voiced by parish officials was the failure of emergency personnel to consult the very emergency response plans assembled in the wake of Katrina (Louisiana Governor's Office 2012, 28). It is important to underscore that, by pointing out this deficiency, authorities are in a position to remedy the situation. But is the failure to use on-the-shelf plans an indication that the region has already lost the impetus to sustain its preparations?

Early assessments of the city's post-Katrina recovery progress were far from optimistic. At the one-year mark, the *Katrina Index* reported that "New Orleans is showing signs of rebirth" (Liu, Fellowes, and Mabanta 2006, 1). It noted that tourism was on the rebound and the housing market was recovering, but the population, city services, and urban infrastructure were far from satisfactory in the eyes of the authors. Slightly more than a year later, a follow-up report observed that promising signs were emerging: New Orleans reached 70 percent of its pre-storm population levels, but useable housing remained in short supply and high real estate prices limited access and return to many with limited financial means. There remained considerable economic and racial disparities in the returning populations with the poor and African Americans lagging behind their wealthy white counterparts. Progress on infrastructure plodded along. Huge sums of federal funds assisted with recovery and rebuilding (Brooking Institution 2007), and this infusion of dollars helped the urban area escape the worst of the national recession between 2008 and 2010.

A central issue that gained considerable public attention after Katrina was the need for repairs to the levee system, the outfall canals, and closure of the MR-GO (Mississippi River–Gulf Outlet)—a canal completed in the 1960s that enabled oceangoing ships to reach the city without navigating upstream against the river's current. Work quickly progressed on restoring the levees. The Army Corps of Engineers has completed impressive gates to seal off the outfall canals that allowed levee failures in 2005. These devices can be closed when a storm approaches, and massive pumps will lift water around the gates into Lake Pontchartrain. This arrangement will prevent surge from entering the canals and breaching the combined earthen levee-floodwalls. In addition, the Corps closed the Mississippi River–Gulf Outlet and erected a giant surge barrier at the mouth of the "funnel" where two levees converge east of the city. This new structure will greatly reduce the risk of flooding in the Ninth Ward (Reid 2013).

Yet critics point out that the Corps has merely patched the existing system and recalibrated risk. The levees were designed in the 1960s to repel the "project storm"—or the most severe storm characteristic of the location. Since Katrina, a critical issue has been restoring the levees to a level that will enable property owners to purchase flood insurance, not to ensure safety. Consequently, the design standards have been adjusted to meet the hundred-year standard for insurance, and not a more rigorous standard to protect lives and property. With sea-level rise, the loss of a wetland buffer, and a subsiding land surface, long-term safety is not assured by levees with a design that is not readily adjusted to changing environmental conditions (Marshall 2014, 1, 3).

In addition, the city has now become more geographically dispersed and reflects an atomistic process of migration and resettlement. New Orleans proper had only about 80 percent of its pre-storm population at the ten-year anniversary, and restoration of some of the worst flooded areas in New Orleans East has languished especially in the lower Ninth Ward and New Orleans East. Also, St. Bernard Parish's population return was less robust than Orleans's and was only at about two-thirds of its pre-storm count in 2019. There has been obvious population movement away from heavily damaged neighborhoods, and population growth in areas that did not flood in 2005—reflecting a memory of recent events (Horowitz 2014, Zaninetti and Colten 2012). Suburban population has increased north of Lake Pontchartrain, on the west bank, and in up-river parishes. This demographic rearrangement, in effect, has diminished the value of the investments in the levees protecting New Orleans. With fewer people to protect, the expenditures now might seem ill placed given recent incidents. Flooding caused by Hurricane Isaac in 2012, in areas previously immune from storm-driven inundations, prompted residents in St. John Parish to request additional levee protection that was funded in 2018 (Thibodeaux 2012, Thompson 2013, Thompson 2014, Bacon-Blood 2013). Expanded levee protection will stretch the budget for construction and maintenance of the existing system during federal and state political regimes stressing fiscal restraint—which translates into limited funding. The memory of Katrina may have prompted some people to move to what they considered safer locations, but as the risks of those places have become evident, the familiar sequence of expanding the levees to encircle new neighborhoods is occurring. Additionally, sea-level rise increases risk further inland. Structural protections all have design limits which have been exceeded in the past.

An unsettling development that has weakened the post-Katrina adaptation has also unfolded. One recommendation to ensure more professionalism within the local levee boards was to consolidate them and require appointment of appropriately trained professionals to the boards. The Southeast Louisiana Flood Protection Authority–East, one of the consolidated organizations, came under political attack after filing a lawsuit against major oil and gas companies. The suit sought compensation from the companies that dug thousands of miles of canals through Louisiana's coastal wetlands in their quest to extract petroleum and natural gas. These canals have contributed to the loss of coastal wetlands that once protected New Orleans and its levee system and represent the complex overlap among interests in the coastal region. Louisiana's governor during the litigation was sharply critical of this lawsuit and worked to replace the levee board members who backed the legal action—re-politicizing the organization (Adelson 2013, Frierson 2014). A court threw out the suit, although parishes have filed similar lawsuits. In 2020, the legislature considered bills to eliminate these suits but did not pass them. The state's coastal restoration program seeks to rebuild one of the lines of defense—but lacks the funds to implement it in full and has not taken action to join the parishes in seeking funds from oil and gas corporations (CPRA 2012 and 2017b).

Meanwhile the city is basking in its inclusion in the Rockefeller Foundation's list of the hundred most resilient cities ("New Orleans Is Exemplar" 2013, Rockefeller Foundation 2013). Achieving this distinction is an honor but does not guarantee perpetuation of resiliency. Among the measures of resilience touted by the New Orleans Data Center is the number of start-up businesses. In 2013, there were 501 startups per 100,000 residents—a number well above the national average of 320 (Greater New Orleans Community Data Center 2013, 2). And yet, is the proliferation of new enterprises a reflection of resilience in a city which still faces serious threats from hurricanes and sea-level rise—particularly as the region continues to subside and coastal land loss continues? Small businesses, like these start-ups, were hardest hit in the wake of Katrina. National big-box stores could redistribute staff and restore supply chains during urban infrastructure repairs. They could even wait until a sufficient number of customers returned to reopen. Small family-operated businesses, many of which did not have disaster plans, had to cope with a loss of customers while also dealing with rebuilding in a chaotic situation—all in the absence of external corporate support. There will be hurricanes in the future that will disrupt local businesses. Economic diversity, as reflected by new businesses, is often equated with resilience. However with more businesses, some owned by people without hurricane experience, rapid rebound following subsequent events might not be as swift as hoped for.

Local experts have attributed the impulse to push economic development over safety to the local "growth machine" (Freudenburg et al. 2009, chap. 4). Powerful citizens and organizations have for decades sought various public works projects to spur economic growth. Beginning in the nineteenth century with the river levees and the massive drainage works, their efforts continued in the latter half of the twentieth century with the MR-GO and hurricane protection levees (Colten 2009, chap. 5).

Funded largely with public dollars, these impressive fixtures have become landscape features reflecting the success of these influential individuals and organizations. Over the years, the most potent impetus has been growth, not safety. Memories of devastation and death do not mesh with the growth narrative, and already the boasting of entrepreneurial enthusiasm is eclipsing the pleas for a secure setting.

At the start of the 2014 hurricane season, a local public safety official observed, "Our concern is that complacency has now set in, and people will find a reason not to listen to us" (Schleifstein 2014). Such a comment may be motivational as much as a well-founded fear, but it exposes recognition that memories are fading and urgency diminishing. Public apathy diminishes interest in deliberate planning for a safe future.

Severe, but not extreme, rainfall in August 2017 caused extensive flooding in New Orleans. On the eve of the most severe portion of the annual hurricane season, local downpours exceeded the city's pumping capacity, compromised by several compounding power and pump outages ("New Orleans Scrambles" 2017). The failure of an aging and inadequately maintained drainage system during a brief but intense storm exposed a shortcoming to sustain preparedness for even larger hurricane-produced precipitation. Intense rainfall and flooding again in April and July 2019 reminded residents that the city remained ill equipped to cope with copious precipitation. A combination of ancient equipment, staffing shortages, budget shortfalls, and failure of related electrical infrastructure contributed to the problems that persist (ABS Group 2018). The technological fixes continue to show signs of faltering resilience.

Over the past three centuries, Louisiana's coast has been repopulated by a diverse assemblage of Europeans, Africans, and Asians who live alongside a diminished number of indigenous peoples. A host of adaptations that evolved over centuries has enabled societies to persist in this perilous place. Adaptations, rooted in social memory, include practices that make it possible for society to rebound following the all-too-numerous disasters that have beset this place. These adaptations add up to community resiliency. Inherent or locally based informal resilience resides in social memory. Over the decades, formal resilience—that is, practices implemented by government bodies and corporations—has supplemented inherent resilience. Most notably, the practice of moving away from risk has been neglected in such efforts and in the state's master plan.

A pair of shortcomings have become apparent in terms of the disjunction between inherent and formal resilience. Formal plans seldom build or even consider the preexisting inherent social networks and capacities. Thus, they do not effectively draw on local expertise and experience and attempt to impose external solutions on localities. This is one way that local communities come to feel excluded from important external planning endeavors. It breeds a democratic deficit according to some. Additionally, the formal resilience efforts have failed over the long haul even as they allow inherent resilience to erode. It took about half a century for the federal government to create what was considered a viable river-levee system only to have the flood of 1927 expose its shortcomings. Revamping the system took another quarter-century. Likewise, an enlarged hurricane-protection levee system begun in 1965 was incomplete in 2005. Both these formal resilience systems fostered a decay of inherent resilience and encouraged settlement in risky areas.

Certainly, when disasters have occurred, enthusiasm for recovery is intense and has supported massive engineering revamps. Nonetheless, several disasters revealed shortcomings in engineering and construction, and also the impermanence of resilience. Just like the state's master plan, the river and hurricane protection levees relied on science and engineering without factoring in local expertise and inherent resilience practices such as mobility. Levees have specific design limits and have tended to encourage development in risky locations. When there has been faltering support for project completion, maintenance, or improvements, tragedy ensued when environmental conditions exceeded the design limits of the structures. Devastation was due not just to nature or structural failure, but to the false sense of security offered by these very defensive systems and expanding urban development in the shadow of the levees. Social, cultural, political, and economic decisions, not just natural conditions, produced the unfortunate outcomes. The calls for an ever-expanding scale of structural protections—from river to hurricane to land loss and sea-level rise—place greater demands on government institutions to deal with growing costs and engineering complexities. With a history of periodic failure, levees have not been wholly reliable, but they remain the method at the core of flood-protection plans.

Adaptations for coping with an unfamiliar and changing environmental setting have been multigenerational or multi-century in their timescale, not decadal as projected by Louisiana planners (CPRA 2017a, 4). The responses and recoveries have not taken the protracted process of human adaptation into account, focusing instead on their importance to reinvigorating the economy and the time needed for construction projects. This incomplete approach persists in Louisiana's coastal restoration planning. Numerous environmental management strategies, of which the master plan is one example, have been used to manage risks and modify the region's wetlands. The timescales do not mesh with the processes that produce resilience-boosting adaptations, and this is an obvious shortcoming to those who approach the topic from the humanities or social sciences.

2

Changing Environmental
Management Strategies

Coastal Louisiana was undergoing extensive biophysical change as indigenous people migrated toward the Gulf of Mexico atop the newly river-laid delta. These tribal societies sought marine and estuarine resources and moved seaward with the land-building processes. They also undertook modifications of the coastal wetland. Mound building, both ceremonial and as midden heaps, elevated small parcels of land above the marsh and above riparian flooding (Kidder 2000, Kniffen 1936b). These deliberate and ad hoc constructions reflect the earliest forms of prehistoric environmental management and underscore the long history of human interaction with this dynamic environment. The mounds persisted as part of the coastal landscape long after the societies disappeared, and they provided resources for European settlers in the 1700s (Kidder 2000).

A critically important aspect of human occupation of the Gulf Coast has been the inhabitants' deliberate role in modifying the physical environment, transforming it into a humanized landscape that better serves their goals, and then adapting to each new set of ecological, geomorphic, and hydrologic conditions. When unsatisfied with existing conditions, society has sought ways to change them. This was true in prehistoric times, in the colonial era, and most dramatically in the last two centuries. Human decisions and actions along with the underlying government policies and investments are just as important, if not more so, in the ongoing set of nature-society relationships in this region. The consequences of each management phase produced lingering consequences that contributed to current conditions and then compelled subsequent management efforts. The vast body of research on Louisiana's coastal crisis has focused on the biophysical processes (Peyronnin et al. 2013). This line of inquiry has been absolutely essential, yet it operated on the assumption that science could uncover the processes at work, and science and engineering could chart methods to remedy the crisis without comparable investigation into the complex social, cultural, economic, and technological processes that ultimately shape the restoration agenda and determine how people adapt to environmental change. Deliberate environmental management has guided human transformation of the Louisiana littoral region through various phases, or regimes, within broader social and cultural contexts that framed decision-making.

PEOPLE AND COASTAL MANAGEMENT

Each environmental management regime in coastal Louisiana has had influences on and has been influenced by natural changes (fig. 2.1). Prehistoric efforts combined waste management with flood protection, and to a degree cultural ritual. The first non-indigenous impact, and the one with the most dramatic and lasting effects, has been flood protection. From early colonial settlement to the present, levee construction to fend off high water has transformed the local environment to protect riparian residents and businesses from inundation. Wetland reclamation, the next tactic, sought to remove moisture from the extensive marshes and swamps that were considered wastelands and convert them to productive farmland. This approach arose as a form of public and private environmental management in the late nineteenth century and continued well into the twentieth century. Conservation practices emerged full-blown in the early twentieth century and drove government involvement in the protection of certain wildlife species and other natural resources. It contributed to the prioritization of certain desirable forms of wildlife and protection of habitats that were important to their perpetuation. Conservation remains a cornerstone in some management programs. Since the 1980s, ecological restoration has emerged as the dominant management regime. It seeks to reestablish wetlands to a condition

Fig. 2.1. The Louisiana coastal region contains two major wetland plains–the deltaic and chenier plains. Several major rivers pass through these coastal wetlands, and human settlements cluster on the slightly higher ground of natural levees. Map by Mary Lee Eggart.

that will protect the region's ecology and the state's major resource-based economies.

To some extent restoration has been merged with practices framed by the concept of sustainability, which seeks to ensure that future generations will be able to enjoy nature-society relations comparable to those of current populations. Each of these regimes is prominent in current programs, has a strong science/engineering foundation, and seeks to produce predetermined ecological outcomes. They are not directed toward human communities—although sustainability is much more attuned to both health and well-being in the future, along with just outcomes. Yet, as Ludwig and others noted in the 1990s, environmental management is a human undertaking—that is, humans make the decisions and guide efforts to manage nature, and humans live with the consequences (Ludwig, Hilborn, and Walters 1993). Policy makers followed the lead of influential citizens and businesses in rolling out these management regimes. With a focus on the biophysical environment and with little input from the populations most affected by changing conditions, they often neglected the citizens who had to adapt to changes. There remains ample opportunity to bolster this critical relationship in planning Louisiana's coastal future.

The early management policies had relatively narrow objectives which restricted the vision of engineers and scientists to the primary purposes, whether it was flood protection, converting wasteland to productive real estate, species perpetuation, or rebuilding wetlands. These diffuse management agendas could have results that were at odds with other programs. Since the implementation of the environmental impact assessment procedures in the 1970s, recognition of the interrelationships among the many ecological systems and society has become more pronounced. Additionally, ecological science has acknowledged the prominent role of humans in environmental change (Balee 1998, McNeill 2001). Critics of current practices note that social impacts remain a secondary consideration, particularly in relationship to coastal management (Vanclay 2012). In addition, there are those who argue that ecological restoration should seek to restore not only the biotic, geologic, and hydrologic environments but the social-economic ecology as well (O'Brien and McIvor 2007, Morris 2016). And proponents of sustainability emphasize the need for management decisions to strive for socially just and equitable outcomes.

These objectives would require a more exhaustive analysis of both the human past and social trends within the local environmental setting. Proponents of social and cultural analysis point out that exposing underlying values and beliefs can better attune management decisions to a local situation and diminish conflicts (Castree et al. 2014, Adger et al. 2013). Yet there is seldom parallel documentation and analysis of the social and cultural circumstances before or after the environmental change. This shortcoming undermines the premise that "restoration cannot proceed without recognition of human impacts and cultural significance . . . [that] historical fidelity is as important as ecological integrity" (Guerrini and Dugan 2010, 133; Higgs 2010). Desbiens argues that sustainable resource management, a goal of current plans, demands collaborative development of project goals. Collaboration relies on equity and reciprocity in understanding both the linked human-environmental factors and the viewpoints of all who interact with a managed landscape (Desbiens 2013). To achieve the ambitious goal of mutual restoration of the ecology and society, a solid foundation of the past nature-society relationships and incorporation of that fundamental history into shaping plans for the future are essential. How were decisions made and plans carried out in the past? Who were the beneficiaries in the past, and how do past policies and programs continue to impact the society making current decisions?

THE COMMONS, ENVIRONMENTAL MANAGEMENT, AND SOCIETY

Before European colonization of the Louisiana coast, Native Americans followed the gradual growth of the deltas as they extended into the Gulf. They adapted to continually changing environmental conditions and treated the landscape as a common resource. When French settlers arrived in Louisiana in the early eighteenth century, the French explorer Robert de La Salle had already staked an imperial claim to the entire Mississippi River Valley, thus superimposing royal authority on indigenous lands. Colonial officials, both French and later Spanish, granted lands to settlers and considered the unsettled territory and waters as commons. Over time the commons has been narrowed by public policy. Europeans arrived with concepts of two types of commons: the more intensively used agricultural commons and the so-called wastes, or less-used peripheral territory (Greer 2012). Much of the land beyond the crown's grants atop the natural levees in colonial Louisiana fell into that latter category. These "wastes" were the swamps and marshes that constituted the landscape of much of the territory's coastal fringe. These lands remained central to the survival of a greatly reduced indigenous population. European landowners could harvest cypress in these lands, enslaved laborers often hunted and fished the unbounded territory, and some escaped African Americans used this space for clandestine settlements. Additionally, landowners, both large and small, grazed cattle in the unclaimed marshes. Thus the commons provided a valuable resource used by all segments of society.

Increasingly, land moved from public to private ownership and thereby reduced the terrestrial commons. Private landowners acquired the vast majority of Louisiana's coastal wetlands. Also, after the Louisiana Purchase in 1803, US policy began shifting the orientation of public lands policy from one of a commons to that of commodities (Wilson 2014). A series of legislative and regulatory actions aimed at flood protection and maintaining selected species of wildlife and other resources restricted legal access to public lands. These adjustments had clear impacts on the natural-resource-based societies in south Louisiana although the plans did little to assist with social adjustments demanded by the policies. With each change, people in Louisiana's coastal margins adapted to new conditions (Colten, Grismore, and Simms 2015).

A related series of federal environmental protection policies enacted in the 1960s and 1970s sought to address fears engendered by the so-called "tragedy of the commons." Garrett Hardin's landmark article on this subject in 1968 prompted the public and policy makers to think of the environment as something more than personal property and economic resources. Rather, the environment had value in its own right. And since all members of society shared water and air, they also bore a joint responsibility to protect it. While this idea was a powerful influence in the post-1960s environmental movement and in the development of policies, this chapter follows historians' usage of the term in reference to access to public lands (Greer 2012, Wall 2014).

FLOOD PROTECTION

Flood avoidance was an adaptation among indigenous people and early settlers that became the first major European-inspired, large-scale, and deliberate environmental management policy. Flood protection initially centered on protecting the tenuous settlement of New Orleans from regular high-river stages. Colonial policies as early as 1723 provided for the erection of levees around the incipient city and required landowners beyond the city to build levees along their river frontage. Essentially a form of courveé labor, this policy required private landowners to use their own resources, enslaved labor at the time, and to dedicate a portion of their private land to purposes other than crop production. This system directed private investment in structures to protect the larger public (Colten 2005). The batture, or the narrow swath of land between the levees and the river itself, remained a commons, and urban dwellers were allowed to scavenge sediment from the riverfront to fill their low-lying lots in the city (Kelman 2003). Likewise, French law treated the waterway as navigable and open to public passage.

After France sold the Louisiana Territory to the United States in 1803, a series of policies impinged on common use of the river and riparian lands. New Orleans imposed a tax on boats tying up along the waterfront. The tax policy recognized the batture as public land, but the city used the revenue, collected from those using the waterfront, for levee maintenance (Colten 2005). Also under US authority, the state created levee districts which assumed the responsibility formerly imposed on individual landowners. These bodies did not own land, but were semi-autonomous government authorities that could impose taxes on landowners within their jurisdiction and apply those revenues to building and maintaining levees (Owens 1999). By the mid-nineteenth century, the US government transferred millions of acres of swamplands to states like Louisiana and Florida. The intent of this action was to permit the states to sell the "wastelands" and use the proceeds to build and maintain effective levees without tapping the federal coffers. In order for this system to work, it necessitated the sale of public lands to individuals or companies. With transactions of this sort, the vast wetlands of the interior swamps and coastal marshes would become less accessible to hunters, trappers, and fishermen (Colten 2014b). Despite poachers continuing to harvest cypress, sale of land to large timber companies after 1870 limited legal access to the wetland forests. Nearly complete removal of the extensive cypress stands by the 1930s disrupted traditional resource-collection practices in the Atchafalaya Basin.

Following the Civil War, the US government gradually assumed responsibility for levee building in the lower river. With the creation of the Mississippi River Commission (MRC) in 1879 and eventual funding in 1882, federal authorities launched a more systematic phase of design and construction that involved enlarging the footprint and height of levees, although irregular funding hampered its progress. Federal levee administration effectively transferred the land beneath the levees from private to public control but removed the responsibility for levee maintenance from agriculturalists. While some property owners were not pleased with more of the prime lands going under the enlarged levees, the trade-off for safety was acceptable. Also, the science providing justification relied on the concept that a levee-confined waterway would continually scour a deeper channel, thereby ensuring more reliable navigation with commercial benefits. Although contested by alternate theories at the time, this hydrologic argument fit with the political compromise to use federal dollars for interstate commerce and not flood protection (Pabis 1998). Local interests had lobbied for federal levee oversight to prevent inundation although, in the wake of the Civil War, congressional delegates from defeated southern states welcomed support from northern states that sought improved river shipping. Ultimately, Congress justified expenditures that offered safety to formerly rebellious planters as a means to promote interstate commerce—not floodplain safety. Thus, the science behind flood protection thoroughly interwove flood-protection and navigation concerns (O'Neill 2006). The chief beneficiaries were large planters and urban entrepreneurs. By the early twentieth century, public policy reinserted flood protection, and not navigation, as the primary purpose for levees.

After the great flood of 1927, federal policy shifted to include "outlets" or engineered floodways to carry large volumes of floodwater to the Gulf of Mexico via human-designed and -built channels (Camillo and Pearcy 2004, Reuss 1998). Central to this discussion were contrasting viewpoints: create a diversion to send a portion of the river down the natural distributary, the Atchafalaya River, or raise the levees below that waterway's headwaters. There were contentious public hearings on the changing policy and the option of using the Atchafalaya River basin as a floodway to ensure the safety of the entrepôt of the lower river (MRC 1927). Ultimately, the outlets argument prevailed in the interest of protecting the shipping infrastructure and dense urban population at New Orleans. By the 1950s, it also became apparent that control structures as part of this diversion were necessary to prevent the Atchafalaya from capturing the Mississippi. Consequently, the outlet option became even more essential (Reuss 1998, Barnett 2017).

The Corps completed the Bonnet Carré Spillway by 1931 to divert excess flow through Lake Pontchartrain toward Mississippi Sound and launched planning and design work for the larger Atchafalaya Floodway (fig. 2.2). As flood-control projects moved forward, the increasing volume of Mississippi River water and sediment flowing through the Atchafalaya River Basin contributed to the silting of large inland lakes (Reuss 1998). These lakes were major commercial fishing areas, and fishermen treated their waters as a commons (Comeaux 1972). By the time the Atchafalaya

Fig. 2.2. Historical diversions and spillways on the Mississippi River. Since the 1920s there have been several efforts to reconnect portions of the coastal wetlands adjacent to the Mississippi River with fresh-water diversions. The construction of two major flood-control outlets followed the 1927 flood, and they provide occasional relief from high water for the lower river. Map by Mary Lee Eggart.

Spillway was operational in the 1950s, the commercial fishing activities on Grand Lake had largely disappeared due to sedimentation in the water-body (Delahoussaye 2014).

The outlet option encountered challenges from neighboring Mississippi as early as 1923. Oystermen voiced concern about a potential diversion that would reroute river water through Lake Pontchartrain into their prime oyster grounds. Meanwhile, fishing-industry trade organizations indicated their approval of the spillway with the stipulation that it would not injure oyster beds in Mississippi waters (Krebs 1923). When the Bonnet Carré Spillway was opened to its full flow for the first time, in 1945, there was extensive damage to the oyster beds in Mississippi Sound, followed by resounding criticism from the fisherfolk. The increased flow through the Atchafalaya in 1945 also damaged coastal fishing and again when the Corps opened Morganza Spillway for the first time in 1973 (Delacruz and O'Neal in US Congress, House 1946b, Gulf South Research Institute, hereafter GSRI 1973). Damage to the Mississippi Sound fisheries followed the spillway opening once again in 2011 (US Army Corps of Engineers 2012). Thus, the use of outlets has had repeated, episodic, and relatively short-lived economic impacts on resource-based societies. Despite damages to oysters and objections against this environmental management approach by fisherfolk, planners prioritized protecting New Orleans and shipping infrastructure, and the outlets remain in place for occasional use in the interest of flood control without standing authorization for compensation for occasional damages to fisheries livelihoods. Economic priorities and not just environmental sciences have been highly influential in flood-protection decisions.

The construction of levees and outlets—along with numerous other influences such as navigation canals, agricultural chemicals, and intensive resource use—has also contributed to an entirely reconfigured coastal ecology. Annual floods no longer spread across the lower delta and add sediment to the wetlands. Rather, levees confine the sediment and direct it into the deep waters of the Gulf. This arrangement has created a new ecology for shrimp, oysters, and other wildlife in the coastal estuaries and an ecology without the annual pulses of fresh water. The range of consequences were becoming apparent by the 1920s and 1930s and were intensively studied by the 1950s (Viosca 1928; Russell 1936, chap. 2).

WETLAND RECLAMATION

Early wetland policy in the United States favored the draining of wetlands, principally for agriculture (Tzoumis 1998, Vilesis 1997). Fear of miasmas in the Midwest and the urge to convert wetlands to farmland propelled a massive land-drainage effort in the late nineteenth and early twentieth centuries (Miller 1989 and Prince 2008). As a consequence, the lower forty-eight states lost approximately 53 percent of their wetlands—or about 117 million acres—due to hydrologic alterations between the 1780s and 1980s (Miller 1989). Both wetland drainage and forest removal across the Midwest, driven by commercial agricultural interests, contributed to increased runoff. By accelerating the rate of upstream discharges, flood risks in the lower Mississippi River rose and contributed to distant unintended consequences and thereby reinforced the commitment to structural flood protection. Meanwhile, despite Acadian cultural affiliation with swamp livelihoods and a rising aesthetic fascination with swamps in the later nineteenth century, marshes remained a setting viewed as ripe for reengineering and commercial exploitation (Wilson 2006, Vilesis 1997, Miller 1989).

Reclamation in the South addressed some of the most expansive wetlands in the country. Congress passed the Swamp Lands Acts of 1849 and 1850, and this legislation represented a major step in this direction by transferring extensive wetlands territory to states as an indirect subsidy for flood protection. One idea behind the acts was that states could sell the property for agricultural development and use the proceeds for flood protection. The reclamation spirit was shared by the American Society of Civil Engineers, which touted reclamation of Louisiana's delta and coastal marshes for rice cultivation (Corthel et al. 1852). Yet neither Louisiana nor Florida, the principal recipients of swamplands, was able to convert sizable wetland tracts to agriculture by the mid-nineteenth century. Much of the ten million acres transferred to Louisiana remained as part of the commons through the Civil War and persisted as undeveloped wetlands, although an important setting for traditional natural resource collection pursuits (Blake 1980, Norgress 1947).

Undeterred by a lack of actual land drainage in southern states, the US Department of Agriculture (hereafter USDA) resumed the campaign in the later years of the century. It noted the extensive coastal wetlands in the country and promoted their development as pasture and cropland. A USDA report challenged some of the prevailing objections raised about wetland reclamation by pointing out that it was both technologically practical and economically feasible. The rich soils of these undeveloped wetlands, the author argued, offered great potential for expansion of agriculture and resource development as the western frontier receded (Nesbit 1885). Wetlands offered an entirely new, although previously bypassed, frontier. Public spokespeople advocated for wetland drainage, specifically in Louisiana. A 1914 USDA bulletin noted that about a third of Louisiana was wetland and that levee protection precluded annual inundation, thus making reclamation feasible. A thorough review of several existing reclamation projects, along with climatic and hydrologic conditions in the state, led the author to conclude pump drainage of wetlands was a viable option and that existing projects had proven successful.

With levees in place that enabled reclamation, along with concerns about the exhaustion of most other public lands in the state, the author advocated for further reworking of Louisiana's marshes (Okey 1914). Local entrepreneur Edward Wisner acquired approximately 1 million acres of Louisiana wetlands for drainage and developed some 250,000 acres (US Army Corps of Engineers 1993, 37–40). Statewide by the late 1920s, most reclamation projects proved to be failures, and some of the larger areas reverted to open water (Viosca 1928, 227). Overall, reclamation projects focused the effort of reengineering specific parcels of the environment, and the USDA did not mention that the reclamation projects would displace traditional wetland livelihoods and subsistence pursuits (Comeaux 1972). Nor did government bodies hold hearings on the private projects. Entrepreneurs built levees, drained the wetlands, and displaced traditional pursuits without soliciting the opinion of traditional fishermen, hunters, or trappers.

By the late 1940s, however, reclamation had not produced economic windfalls and lost most public support. Land speculators had been the primary operators of land-reclamation districts, which required state approval, during the early 1900s, and they drained over a quarter of a million acres in Louisiana. By mid-century, scientists recognized that subsidence of coastal lands was occurring, rendering levees built to keep out storm surge less effective over time (Harrison and Kollmorgen 1947). Storm surge flooded some of the projects and prompted the withdrawal of financial backing. Additional maintenance costs, such as increased pumping to keep pace with subsidence after drainage, the need to frequently dredge the internal drainage canals, along with poor management of drainage districts, led to their eventual failure. Project investors had targeted farm families in the Midwest as customers and seldom sought to sell to local farmers. Despite limited cultivable land on the natural levees, speculative projects did not include residents whose local knowledge and family networks might have provided a cushion against failure. Furthermore, these projects excluded traditional hunters, trappers, and fishermen from the wetland commons, and they transformed wetland habitat, at least temporarily, into dry lands, further interfering with resource-based pursuits. In the long run, none proved successful as agricultural projects, and several became hunting clubs for urban sportsmen, not local hunters (Harrison and Kollmorgen 1947). Despite optimism in the early twentieth century and some temporary financial success, drainage efforts largely fell by the wayside as a form of wetland management by mid-century.

CONSERVATION

Fear of resource exhaustion across the country provided a compelling argument for the emerging ideas of conservation in the late nineteenth century. Disappearing supplies for hardwoods for railroad ties and trestles inspired early private-sector efforts to replant forests and use wood preservation techniques (Olson 1971). Louisiana timber and paper companies began replanting pine forests to extend the life of their mills. Over the course of about fifty years before 1930, timber companies had cleared 1.6 million acres of cypress forests in the Atchafalaya, Calcasieu, and Maurepas swamps without any attempts at reforestation (Williams 1989, Norgress 1947). Conservation practices have maintained the rapid-growth pine forests outside the major swamps over the past century, but similar efforts to sustain cypress yields have not been as successful.

As Samuel Hays argues, conservation or managed wise use of resources was at its core a "scientific movement." Advocates proclaimed that the application of sound science could offset the depredations of ravenous and unchecked wildlife hunting, fishing, timber removal, and mineral extraction and sustain the yields of natural resources that society desired. Proponents presented conservation in terms of opportunity, not limitations (Hays 1959). Management of forest resources would ensure a dependable timber supply, and likewise limits on fishing and hunting would halt destructive practices and assure future harvests. Restrictions impinged directly on the commons and traditional livelihoods—some of which seriously threatened wildlife populations. Conservation policies sought to reverse unregulated depletion of resources, examples of the tragedy of the commons, but regulations made no accommodation for social transitions necessitated by regulatory changes.

Louisiana, like other states at the time, moved gradually to implement conservation policies. As early as 1877, the legislature granted parishes (counties) the authority to set aside wildlife preserves, although none took action to do so (Louisiana Commission of Birds, Game and Fish 1910). In 1908 through 1910, the state took more assertive action. It created a Commission for the Protection of Birds, Game and Fish in 1908 (Act 278); declared waters of bayous, lagoons, lakes, bays, and rivers property of the state (Act 258); took steps to regulate shrimping in the coastal bays; and established fish and game preserves (Louisiana Commission of Birds, Game and Fish 1910). Over the next several years, the state imposed numerous conservation-oriented limits on hunting and fishing seasons and equipment, all with the intent to manage wildlife populations. Couched in terms of wise use and scientific management, these policies gained political support outside the wetlands region when state authorities characterized market hunters and commercial fishermen as a menace to wildlife and fish populations (Louisiana Commission of Birds, Game and Fish 1910). In addition, private citizens and national charitable organizations set aside sizable tracts of wetlands as wildlife preserves, which eventually became the core of the state and federal wildlife refuge program (Gomez 1998, McIlhenny 1928). Under a mix of private, state, and federal ownership, there are more than 920,000 acres of protected wetlands in Louisiana's coastal parishes today, all with some degree of conservation-oriented limited access. They have contributed to the successful perpetuation of waterfowl for sport hunters and also alligators.

Depletion of oysters presented another serious problem, and the state followed the lead of other states, creating a leasing system that made oyster production mariculture (fig. 2.3). As with its initial efforts to conserve other natural resources, the state initially delegated authority to the parishes, but an 1898 federal oyster study exposed ineffective management by the local authorities (Moore 1899). To counter this situation, the state created an oyster commission in 1902 to oversee the conservation of this valued commodity. It established a system that allowed oyster gatherers to secure leases of waterbottoms from the state and work these beds as if they were private property. They had exclusive rights to the harvest and in theory would be good stewards if they managed their leases for continued income. McGuire and Leard argue that the oystermen's support for the leasing system in Louisiana has been effective (Maass 2014, Dyer and Leard 1994, Wicker 1979). In 2005, over 400,000 acres of state waterbottoms were under lease and reflect a collaborative approach.

The transition to conservation practices was not without difficulty for oystermen. Fishermen and the state recognized by 1914 that levees pre-

Fig. 2.3. Unloading oysters, around 1940. Oystermen were involved in the shaping of early conservation policies that granted rights to lease waterbottoms and cultivate oysters. Courtesy State Library of Louisiana.

vented annual freshwater flushing to the coastal marshes, which raised salinity levels and damaged oysters. The state, at the request of oystermen, constructed several freshwater siphons—structures built into river levees that allowed controlled release of fresh water into coastal bays—and other structures between the 1920s and the 1960s that offset the combined effect of salinity and fixed leases (fig. 2.2) (McGuire 2008). By the 1950s, however, further analyses had identified land loss and salinity changes due to levees as significant processes forcing geographic shifts in oyster production in the state's coastal bays (Schlesselman 1955). Oystermen have had a prominent voice in environmental management practices that has produced mixed results.

In the long term and with considerable federal assistance, the state's conservation measures restored populations of waterfowl and alligators in the coastal margins. Yet, as the state implemented its policies, other than oystermen, those who either benefited or endured impacts from these policies had limited opportunity to voice their opinions on how the procedures were put into place. As in other parts of the country, conservation efforts were inspired by national organizations and guided by elite citizens, often recreational hunters and fishers, and state officials. Edward McIlhenny, a prominent landowner and businessman, was a powerful advocate and influential voice for conservation in Louisiana (1928). McIlhenny, along with public officials, wrote disparagingly about the traditional resource gatherers and identified them as a problem. Sport hunters and recreational fishermen pushed for new conservation-management policies. McIlhenny, in collaboration with wealthy sportsmen from outside the region and the state, actively participated in creating wildlife preserves in the coastal region which precluded market hunting, trapping, and oyster harvesting. Furthermore, state policies limited fishing/hunting seasons, thereby removing the temporal flexibility that resource gatherers had previously relied on (Louisiana Commission of Birds, Game and Fish 1910). Granted these efforts served the public good by reducing pressure on wildlife, but they presented challenges to resource-dependent residents. Inclement weather or other vagaries were irrelevant to the conservation calendar. Even following a tropical cyclone that kept fishers or hunters at home during a key period of the season, they were not allowed to "catch up" after the disruption. With little voice in the process, commercial fishermen, hunters, and trappers found these policies disruptive to their traditional livelihoods. Their initial recourse was to continue hunting and fishing in open resistance to the regulations and in some cases to unleash violence against game wardens. In at least one case hunters, in defiance of state policy, shot and wounded a game warden who was attempting to enforce state regulations in 1918 (McIlhenny 1918).

State officials applied science-based conservation policies to shrimping as well. They had the authority to close certain areas to shrimping during specified seasons, again limiting access to the commons (Tulian 1921). In addition, regulations prescribed minimum size for shrimp to be sold and set specifications for nets. These restrictions implemented widely used wildlife-conservation practices. Additionally by the 1920s, in order to reduce pressure on the shrimp population and the number of boats on state waters, the state prohibited out-of-state fishermen from working Louisiana waters (Marks 2012). These restrictions impinged on the mobility or adaptive capacity of those pursuing natural-resource-based livelihoods and prompted legal challenges (Louisiana Commission for the Protection of Birds, Game and Fish 1912; McIlhenny 1918; Tulian

1921). In addition, fishermen formed unions to improve their bargaining power. Changing technologies, high fuel prices, and global competition have accounted for some of the greatest pressures on shrimp fishermen in the twenty-first century, but conservation policies continue to frame how and when they can pursue their livelihoods (Marks 2012). Conservation restrictions continue to foster tensions between fishermen and government authorities.

Commercial fishing on the inland waters has declined precipitously under conservation policies, with the exception of crawfishing. State programs emphasized the stocking of waterways with sport fish, not commercial species, and private aquaculture was able to supply consumer with consistently sized catfish filets. These trends contributed to the decline. Market hunting and trapping have also nearly ceased. Conservation programs helped restore alligators and enable the resumption of trapping these large reptiles, with a recent spike in interest as a sporting activity. Successful development of alligator farming now supplies much of the marketable hides. Trapping of fur-bearing animals has declined mainly due to changing fashion demands and the market for furs. Introduction of the exotic fur-bearing nutria to Louisiana marshes by trapping interests has produced serious impacts to marshland and prompted the state to offer a bounty for these rodents.

Conservation policies, which geographically fixed the operations of oystermen and eliminated their mobility, endowed them with effective property rights that enabled legal action against oil companies that had damaged their leases with canals, pipelines, or pollution. In some cases, courts awarded them for damages that resulted from extractive activities. Some oystermen gained additional income either by conducting assessments of leases before oil-related activity or collecting payments from oil companies when their operations traversed unproductive leases (Maass 2014, Theriot 2014). The overall importance of Louisiana's natural resources and their fundamental social and cultural significance were not factored into contemporary appraisals (Viosca 1928).

Conservation policy also accommodated the emerging oil and gas industry—another commodity that fell under wise-use principles (Banta 1981, Gorman 2001). Massive waste of oil and natural gas prompted conservation measures designed to reduce losses and direct more product to consumers. Short-term utility rather than long-term conservation was the motivation for these policies. Conservation principles shaped the state's severance tax on oil and gas as well as its early policies calling for restoration of wetlands disturbed by canals (Banta 1981). Royalties yielded substantial income for the state although they did little to impede the near depletion of onshore oil reserves by the 1970s. Permitting thousands of miles of canals dredged in the wetlands to enable mineral exploration and extraction was a way the state could promote use. Viewing this as an efficient means to transport oil and gas from remote marshland wells and as an additional source of employment, the state was not inclined to erect policy obstructions (Theriot 2014). These canals remain a lasting impact of policies that facilitated oil and gas extraction. These waterways, along with other transportation canals, have contributed to the loss of coastal wetlands. Despite recognition of wetland damages by the early 1950s, canal excavation and use faced little regulation until the 1980s (Houck 2015; Scaife, Turner and Costanza 1983; Turner and McClenachan 2018).

ECOLOGICAL RESTORATION

Ecological restoration, according to historian Laura Martin (2015), emerged from conservation practices dating back to the 1930s. Yet most ecologists would point to the formation of the Society for Ecological Restoration in 1987 as the effective formalization of this approach to environmental management. Despite the rich history of restoration, scientists tend to treat it as ahistorical, and few environmental historians have delved into its origins and evolution (see Hall 2010). Regardless of the moment of its inception, ecological restoration became the most prominent intellectual framework used since the 1980s to stabilize and reverse the state's "coastal crisis" that was propelled by prior management regimes (CPRA 2012). At its core, restoration assumes that human intervention can reverse the degradation of prior regimes and reinvigorate a prior ecosystem or create a new ecosystem with desired conditions. With intellectual roots in conservation concepts, it takes an ecological, rather than species-specific approach, and fosters active efforts to rehabilitate larger habitats and not just territories that serve single species.

Defined as the practice of reestablishing a particular ecological community of species and landscapes that had been damaged, through human agency, restoration relies on extensive ecological, hydrological, and geologic analysis of past and current conditions and modeling of future conditions to design a path toward rehabilitation. It has found considerable traction in addressing wetlands. During the second half of the twentieth century, the emergence of wetland science uncovered important functions of wetlands to store floodwaters, recharge groundwater, purify pollution, support recreation, sustain biodiversity and critical habitats, and more (Tzoumis 1998, Stine 2008, Martin 2015). This knowledge, aligned with emerging public support for environmental protection in the 1960s, propelled wetlands into a more favorable position in public policy (Beck 1994, Stine 2008).

The passage of the Federal Clean Water Act of 1972, and subsequent court rulings on the extent of the controversial Section 404 which dealt with wetlands, recast federal policy in lasting ways. In 1975, a federal district court concluded that the "waters of the United States" were not limited to navigable waters, but included waters distant from major waterways and also isolated waters (Tzoumis 1998, Stine 2008). This decision expanded the provisions of the Clean Water Act to include wetlands. Ultimately, with the development of regulations and amendments to the Clean Water Act, the Corps of Engineers gained authority to permit or deny wetland development (Tzoumis 1998, Stine 2008). Wetland filling and drainage slowed dramatically as a result, and wetland mitigation arose as a tool for creating offsets for developers intent on draining commercially desirable wetlands. Following the initial federal legislation, there was a surge in the study of creation and restoration of wetlands, and research continued at a pace well above previous levels through the 1980s (Steller-McDonald, Sischinger, and Auble 1990). Historian Laura Martin, in fact, declares the 1972 act was the first to be used to require mitigation (Martin 2015, Roberston 2000). Compensatory mitigation, as Martin refers to it, enables the sacrifice of one place along with the restoration of another. An outcome of this approach was widespread research about and experiments in restoration and in creation of wetlands *de novo*.

Restoration arrived in Louisiana as part of this larger concern with wetlands and in many respects represents an attempt to reverse or repair unintended damages from prior management efforts. Although sub-sidence in coastal Louisiana had been acknowledged for over a century (Corthell et al. 1852, Russell 1936, Morgan and Larimore 1957), discussions about taking action to halt this situation and restore the coast was a late-twentieth-century development. Studies in the 1970s and 1980s provided detailed assessments of the rate of land loss that went far beyond the early observations of subsidence (Gagliano and van Beek 1970; Gagliano, Meyer-Arendt, and Wicker 1981; Penland and Boyd 1981) and redefined this region as a damaged territory. The disappearing Louisiana coast and a desire to restore the littoral landscape became the rallying cry both for scientists and for citizen activists in the late 1980s. The first restoration plan emerged from an organization known as the Coalition to Restore Coastal Louisiana (CRCL), an agglomeration of scientists, citizen activists, fishermen, and public officials.

The plan called for three principal related actions: enhancement of fresh water and sediment flow into the coastal marshes, repair or restoration of disturbed wetland and barrier islands, and the phasing out of canal construction in the coastal zone (CRCL 1987). The initial report recognized the interconnected environmental and social systems and emphasized the need to restore the region's ecology, which would in turn sustain fisheries and other wetland livelihoods. It also pointed out that historical policies prioritized flood control and navigation and tolerated largely unchecked scarring of the wetlands with canals dredged by mineral companies. This assignment of responsibility is an important indicator in subsequent plans and highlights the social role in mobilizing science in environmental management. Past policies had greatly accelerated damage to the naturally subsiding coastal territory. This situation was, in the eyes of the coalition, a human-damaged environment that demanded human-guided ecological restoration relying on science. Its great success was galvanizing support for the ultimate passage of federal legislation. Signed into law in 1990, the Coastal Wetlands Planning, Protection and Restoration Act (CWPPRA) (Public Law 101-646, Title III), known locally as the Breaux Act, dedicated funds to support restoration.

In hearings before the US House of Representatives while deliberating this landmark legislation, a Louisiana congressman and a representative for the CRCL identified the principal causes of the land loss as

Fig. 2.4. Canal carved through the Louisiana wetlands, 1925. Notice the sizable spoil bank adjacent to the waterway. Percy Viosca Jr. Photograph Collection, Mss. 4948, Louisiana and Lower Mississippi Valley Collections, LSU Libraries, Baton Rouge, La.

levee building for flood protection and navigation and the extensive canal networks excavated for mineral extraction (figs. 2.4 and 2.5; Boggs, Kemp, and Tauzin in US House of Representatives, 1990). As part of their 1990 testimony, Louisiana's elected officials positioned the state's littoral marshes within the larger context of national attention to wetlands. They also presented compelling commentary about the scale of Louisiana's wetlands at the national level. Breaux reminded his colleagues that Louisiana contained about 80 percent of the country's wetlands and that they were a national resource (U.S. House 1990, 3–5). He also underscored that wetland loss resulted from levee building to protect vast portions of the nation's interior from river floods (3). Congressman Billy Tauzin emphasized the significance of Louisiana oil and gas to the nation's energy supply as he pointed out the impact of canals that contributed to land loss. In an era before the birth of activists' campaigns opposing widely accepted views of climate scientists, he squarely situated the situation in

Fig. 2.5. A series of canals cut through the marsh for oil exploration and extraction in lower Lafourche Parish just west of Golden Meadow. Some 10,000 miles of canals have pierced the coastal marshes. The post-1965 hurricane protection levee is visible to the left of the settled area along Bayou Lafourche. US Department of Agriculture 1980. Courtesy of the LSU Cartographic Information Center.

the arena of human-induced climate change. He asserted that Louisiana was taking a hit from "global warming" and sea-level rise—or as he put it, consequences of "global industrialization" (13). While Tauzin's comments seem striking coming from a Louisiana elected official in the 2020s, he relied on the prevailing scientific consensus.

Their efforts led to the passage of the so-called Breaux Act or the Coastal Wetlands Protection, Planning, and Restoration Act (CWPPRA, Public Law 101–646, Title III). It provided a dedicated, albeit modest, funding stream of about $40 million annually. It formalized restoration as part of the environmental management strategy and has paid for more than a hundred restoration projects. It defined coastal restoration projects as: "any technically feasible activity to create, protect, restore, or enhance coastal wetlands through sediment or freshwater diversions, water management, or other measures" (Act in US House of Representatives 1990, 96). In addition to specifying the ecological value of wetlands, the act specifically noted their value "forming barriers to waves and erosion and helping to reduce flood damage" (96). By adding flood protection as a benefit, the legislation broadened support to urban areas and neighboring states.

A series of restoration plans since the early 1990s have prioritized science-based ecological restoration as the centerpiece of wetlands management (CPRA 2007; CPRA 2012; Louisiana Coastal Wetlands Conservation and Restoration Task Force, hereafter LCWCRTF 1993; LCWCRTF 1998; US Army Corps of Engineers, hereafter USACE, New Orleans District 2004). Each successive plan, using updated information, has emphasized the perilous situation facing the coast and how, without restoration, the coastal ecology and economy will fail. The CRCL report and the 1990 CWPPRA act had identified levees and loss of regular sediment delivery to the marshes, along with the extensive canal system carved through the marshes, as the primary causes of damage. The *Coast 2050* report, published in 1998, provided more detailed planning for restoration that included swamp and marsh restoration, sediment diversions, and barrier island restoration (LCWCRTF 1998). There was a strong emphasis on habitat repair and creation. When Congress considered reauthorizing CWPPRA in 1999, the Senate committee noted the cause of land loss as "the great decrease in sediment deposition while subsidence has remained constant " (US Senate 1999). Canals and navigation-oriented alteration of the Mississippi River and wetlands faded from the public narrative. Louisiana's primary coastal official, Len Bahr, emphasized the value of wetlands for protection from tropical weather: "The loss of Louisiana coastal wetlands threatens coastal infrastructure, harms wildlife populations and increases the vulnerability of Louisiana cities to devastating hurricane damage" (Bahr in US Senate 1999). Sediment starvation and flood/storm protection rose to prominence as the causes of damage and justification for funding. The subtle shifts in assignment of blame contributed to parallel shifts in the scientific enterprise behind the coastal crisis and greater emphasis on protecting the prominent economic activities in the coastal region, namely cities, mineral extraction, and navigation.

By the end of 2001, with a combination of state and CWPPRA funds, some 125 discrete projects had planted marsh grass, diverted fresh water to deliver nutrients and sediment, used dredge material to build up marshlands, and installed "Christmas tree fences" to act as baffles against erosion (Louisiana Dept. of Natural Resources, hereafter LDNR, 2001). A 2004 report prepared by the Corps of Engineers declared its goal to "reverse the current trend of degradation of the coastal ecosystem" (USACE, New Orleans District 2004, ii). It sought to identify and prioritize specific projects that would maximize "restoration strategies" (ii). A status report on CWPPRA projects in 2005 reinforced the emphasis on restoration, noting that fifteen projects that would restore fresh water, repair barrier islands, and implement environmental restoration along the MR-GO canal had received prioritization (LDNR 2005, 4).

The ultimate question is: Did these projects accomplish ecological restoration? Extensive tabulations accompanied the reports for projects that were still in process. The Louisiana Department of Natural Resources reported in 2005 that federal and state partners had initiated some 635 projects "to ameliorate the state's wetland loss" (LDNR 2005, 95). Subsequent evaluations pointed out continuing land loss even as agency personnel reported success stories. As small projects restored some coastal wetlands, the larger processes creating the crisis continued to operate. The science of ecological restoration, given the constraints of social processes such as politics and economics, was unable to match the pace of land loss. Ecological expertise alone was insufficient to save the coast, and little attention was given to either the underlying social factors contributing to land loss or the residents on the state's littoral margins.

SUSTAINABILITY

Similar to the sequence of conservation policies merging into restoration ecology, restoration ecology blended into the next major coastal environmental management paradigm: sustainability. In 1999, the NRC's Board on Sustainable Development, drawing on more than a decade of discussions on the topic, defined sustainable development as "the reconciliation of society's developmental goals with its environmental limits over the long term" (NRC 1999, 22) The group described the need to undergo a sustainability transition to achieve this lofty goal, which they defined as society's movement toward meeting "the needs of a much larger but stabilizing human population, to sustain the life support systems of the planet, and to substantially reduce hunger and poverty" (4). This report stressed the importance of deploying science and technology to address the critical issue of overtaxing the earth's resource base and helping society meet its aspirations. Both conservation principles and ecological restoration could contribute toward this goal. But sustainability encompassed more than the sciences that could identify the biophysical challenges to the earth's life-support systems; it explicitly sought to address justice and equity in society as well. These objectives are woven into the United Nations' sustainability goals (United Nations 2015).

Louisiana adopted the term "sustainability" for its coastal management polices in its 2007 coastal master plan (CPRA 2007). Entitled *Louisiana's . . . Comprehensive Master Plan for a Sustainable Coast,* the document spells out its principal goal as emphasizing the "sustainability of ecosystems, flood protection, and communities" (2007, 7). Successive reports use the same title. These plans make clear that ecosystems are fundamental to long-term goals, but equally important are the main economic activities that operate in the coastal region and the communities that live there. The term "sustainability," as used by the state, is the same as used in scientific literature and by the United Nations, but there are subtle differences in what it means to Louisiana's planners. The plan's projects seek to sustain the most important economic activities, centering on the non-sustainable oil and gas industry. Indeed, the plans make no effort to address the state's dependence on an industry contributing to greenhouse warming (Randolph 2018). While the designs of engineered works intend to use the energy of the river to place wetland-rebuilding sediments, the designs are not sustainable in terms of energy use, funding, nor in keeping pace with projected sea-level rise. They are temporary at best and not regenerative. The successive plans prioritize numerous science-driven projects to restore the coastal wetlands, while protecting jobs and residents from flooding (CPRA 2007, 2012, 2017b). Plans acknowledge the importance of the state's cultures, yet the plans contain no concrete projects dedicated to their preservation or restoration. The principal attention given to humans is the flood protection offered to urban centers and coastal businesses, and not equity or justice.

The most recent budget reflects the emphases of the state's plan. Of the $50 billion budget, nearly $20 billion targets ecological projects defined as barrier island, ridge, and hydrological restoration, along with marsh creation. The $5 billion devoted to sediment diversion (to restore marshes) has parallel goals. Another $19.9 billion is earmarked for structures—such as levees and armoring shorelines (CPRA 2017b, 96). This is obviously an ambitious plan which seeks to offset the multiple ongoing processes contributing to coastal land loss and flood risk. Using a moderate projection, the planners forecast that the plan will create or maintain some eight hundred square miles of land (CPRA 2017b, 99). Nonetheless, projected losses will exceed gains/maintenance over the next half-century. The reduction of flood damage could be considerable—a scenario with a medium rate of land loss projects the prevention of $150 billion in damages (CPRA 2017b, 100). By this accounting, reducing risk to economic activities, not ecological restoration, appears to provide a powerful political justification for the huge investment. The plan estimates a massive annual value of ecosystem services that would be protected, but includes flood-damage reduction in that tabulation, thereby obscuring the benefits to coastal fisheries (CPRA 2017b, ES-10). There is no attempt to tabulate the value of restoring culture or community.

The primary emphasis in past expenditures has been on structural and ecological restoration, which to some extent aligns with a portion of the sustainability goal. Yet the sharpest criticism of the plan has been the anticipated impacts of new levees and sediment diversions on coastal wetlands and marginalized populations (Colten 2015, Randolph 2018). Thus, the plan has omitted the issue of equity in terms of its dedicated expenditures.

The 2012 plan includes a discussion of cultural heritage, but the depth and thoroughness of the analysis of the potential social and cultural losses are scant when compared to the analysis of land loss. This document casts restoration as a science-and-engineering enterprise that will provide a mixture of structural (levees, sediment diversions, and hydrologic infrastructure) and nonstructural (flood-proofing structures, building codes, and land-use planning) projects. The 2012 plan concedes that the nonstructural component of the plan is largely voluntary, whereas other components are not. Of the 116 potential nonstructural projects analyzed by the state, not a single one directly addresses social or cultural restoration or preservation (CPRA 2012). The orientation of restoration efforts is directed toward ecological and hydrological projects. Although "support of cultural heritage" is one of the decision criteria identified in the plan, no project directly addresses this specific area. At the core of this criterion is the intent to reduce risk for coastal communities and provide "high levels of traditional natural resources" to residents of the region (2012). The plan includes no discussion of the linkages between society and natural resources. Thus, projects prioritized for funding target ecological and not social/cultural conditions. The 2017 plan emphasizes a bolstered public outreach effort to overcome the neglect of marginalized coastal citizens. Overall, the most recent $50 billion proposed budget allocates $6 billion for nonstructural work which touches on social/cultural issues (CPRA 2017b, ES-19). Structures and ecological restoration are the assumed tools for cultural protection and restoration. Both structures and ecological restoration will impinge upon or disrupt traditional resource-based livelihoods, and thus threaten the viability of communities on the state's coastal margins. What the cities and commercial interests gain in flood protection might not translate into sustainable economies for others in rural locations.

The plan asserts that it seeks to provide "a sustainable long-term solution" (CPRA 2017b, 48). As for "long-term," they state the use of a fifty-year planning horizon. This is comparable to the temporal scope commonly used by other engineered projects and is in line with the "two generations" time horizon used by the NRC in 1999 (NRC 1999, 3). Yet, in the scope of human occupation and modification of the lower Mississippi River, it is a relatively brief time span. Flood management and the numerous alterations in structural approaches have been going on for nearly three centuries. Conservation programs have been underway for more than a century. Both demand continuing expenditures and maintenance or operational support. They also, in some respects, work in opposition, thus perpetuating the need for environmental management and offsetting the aspirations of a sustainable ecosystem. Also, the state's plan provides funding for structures and other components that will require maintenance and modification over time—even without sea-level rise. Core components, such as the sediment diversions to rebuild marshes that will rely in part on the power of the Mississippi River to deliver sediment-laden water and the action of gravity to spread the material across the coastal margins, will require maintenance. Dedicated funding for maintenance is of concern to residents of the coast, but does not adequately factor into the current budgets. Sea-level rise will ultimately offset the protection of fixed infrastructure and will require renewed investments if lessons from river levees are applicable to coastal levees (Törnqvist et al. 2020).

The series of wetland-management policies, consistently and sometimes in tandem, have contributed to long-term environmental change, which has prompted policy decisions that have at times compounded negative effects of prior environmental change. The more dramatic changes to restrict flooding began in the early 1700s and expanded in scope and impacts over the following centuries. Levees and the ensuing diversion of sediment into the deep Gulf of Mexico are major contributors to Louisiana's coastal crisis today. Despite negative impacts, flood-protection structures have provided a high degree of safety for farms, cities, and industries along the river during the last century. Consequently, there is no active discussion about removing the levee system, so it will remain a component of the future planning process. Conservation polices have helped perpetuate valuable marine commercial species and sport fishes and thus some livelihoods that depend on them. Yet they have also impinged on the commons and prompted some coastal residents to adapt to changing conditions. Abandoning market hunting and commercial inland fishing were among the adaptations, as was the shift to fixed leases for oystering. Ecological restoration has produced modest successes but, given social constraints and the inherited flood-mitigation infrastructure, these projects are not able to keep up with the ongoing land loss processes. Even the more socially conscious sustainability paradigm has selectively prioritized biophysical environmental solutions that aid prominent commercial activities and not social solutions. The plan's timescale is relatively short-term when compared to the evolution of the situation confronting the coast and its residents, and there is no parallel effort to address the underlying causes of climate change at the state level or programs to restore coastal cultures and communities.

3

Cartographic Revelations
Mapping Land Loss

Mobilizing scientists, NGOs, and government bodies to confront Louisiana's land loss crisis required the transformation of a slow-moving, largely invisible, process into a threatening and high-profile situation that non-coastal residents could readily imagine. The power of cartography proved to be a key catalyst. Presenting a compelling visualization required detailed mapping of the changing coastline, but persuading the wider public of a crisis required a social context sympathetic to ecological losses, political opportunities to deliver funding to local projects, and an effective public relations campaign to spread the word. Cartography transformed the Louisiana coast from a *terra incognita* to a *cause célèbre*.

Early cartographic renditions of the Louisiana coast are vague in their delineation of the shore. There were no bold headlands, no stark cliffs, no tall forests, no obvious indigenous settlements to plot onto maps. Rather than recognizable topography, the coast is mostly a vast low-lying marsh where it is difficult to distinguish where water ends and land begins. The blurry boundary has been an element in the long-standing debate about René-Robert Cavelier, Sieur de La Salle's failure to return to the Mississippi River in 1685 (Wood 1984, De Vorsey 1988). The shoreline, while not invisible, was largely unpopulated and conspicuously disregarded by early European explorers and colonists. It offered poor footing and thus inhibited direct inspection by Europeans. In Mississippi and Alabama, the French established settlements on solid ground near the beach while, in Louisiana, the principal settlement was some one hundred miles upstream on the firm banks of the Mississippi River, admittedly taking advantage of a portage that provided ready access to Lake Pontchartrain—in reality a large bay with a wetland fringe. What was dismissed by early European explorers and cartographers as insignificant is now the centerpiece of the state's most ambitious public works spending program.

How have cartographic depictions of the coast and the protracted process of land loss drawn the attention of scientists, mobilized public interest, activated political actions, and galvanized the state's commitment to a costly campaign that is well beyond its own fiscal resources? Depictions of land loss have changed, particularly since the 1950s, and corresponding developments in ecological science and public policy along with dramatic hazard events shaped the understanding of possibilities for coastal renewal, and the combination of all these elements contributed to the emerging discussion about coastal restoration. Visualizations of this process illustrate how effective cartographic presentations can expose critical issues facing coastal societies in other regions of the world and perhaps contribute toward more sustainable policies. Maps have been an important tool behind the decisions about environmental management.

AN INVISIBLE COAST

European explorers traversed the Gulf Coast and selected sites for early outposts on headlands in protected bays such as Pensacola and Mobile. Terra firma mattered, as did the advantages of safe harborage and military defense. The murky bayous and shallow bays surrounded by marsh in what became Louisiana offered no such site advantages. Nonetheless, control of the Mississippi River Basin thoroughly offset any disadvantages of the French colony's unappealing coast. By the time the United States acquired Louisiana in 1803, settlers had expanded across the inland natural levees of south Louisiana while largely avoiding the neighboring marshes and swamps. Only the displaced Houma Indians, escaped slaves, and a few other marginalized groups found refuge in the coastal wetlands. Geographic depictions of the region expose the neglect of this avoided expanse.

Colonial cartography reveals only vague knowledge of the shoreline. It shows an uncertain border between land and sea with much of the coastal territory labeled as wetlands. In 1747 French cartographers used the term *terre basse inondée*, or "low flooded land." Terms such as "marshy islands," "lagoons," and "broken land" appear in a 1770s map, while *terres tremblantes et marécageuses*, or "shaking land and marsh," describes the Biloxi Marsh in the 1750s (fig. 3.1). This territory was not an appealing landscape to European colonizers. Contemporary notions of marsh were at odds with European settlement and economic pursuits. Europeans viewed

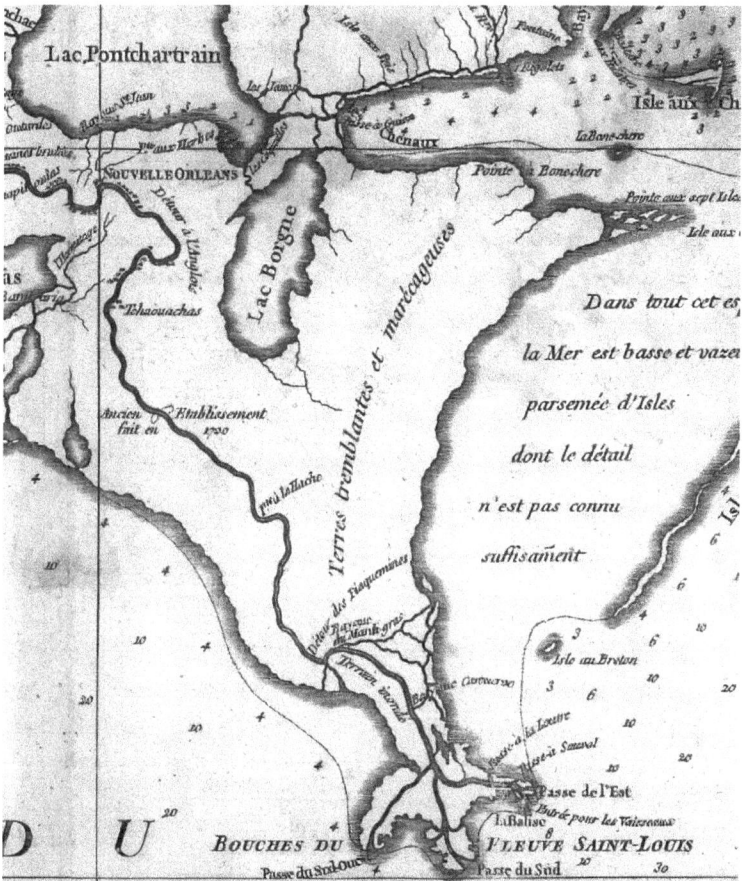

Fig. 3.1. Marshes are shown as *terres tremblantes et marécageuses*. Detail from *Carte de la Louisiane par le Sr. d'Anville*, 1752. Library of Congress.

them as worthless, unless drained and reclaimed for productive purposes (Vilesis 1997, Giblett 2016).

In 1817, William Darby observes that most early European accounts of the lower delta yielded little accurate information. He is critical of their lack of detail and notes that "little knowledge of Louisiana can be gained from the perusal of works published in Europe" (Darby 1817, iv). His own description of the coastal region is exceptionally thin on detail. Darby reports that to the southwest of the Mississippi River there exists "another intermixture of bayous, lakes, woods, and morasses" that terminates in the Gulf of Mexico (41–42). He describes the numerous bayous and distributaries that course through the coastal region, but dismisses the areas away from the waterways as "too monotonous to demand much detailed description; mostly morass, devoid of trees, and sunk to nearly the level of the high tide" (51). He points out much of the area of St. Bernard Parish as "one vast grassy marsh interspersed with lakes" (52).

After the American Civil War (1861–65), Samuel Lockett embarked on a statewide tour to update Louisiana's geography. His account of the coastal parishes in the 1870s highlights the cultivated lands along the bayous and rivers. He notes that extensive but unoccupied marshes made Terrebonne Parish one of the state's largest political units (Lockett 1874, 116). For St. Bernard Parish, he observes that much of it is "low, flat sea marsh subject to tidal overflow" (119–20). Likewise for Plaquemines Parish he dismisses the marshes: "An enumeration of these multitudinous islands and sheets of water would add nothing to the foregoing description of the parish" (120). Although he acknowledges that sportsmen frequented the marshes for hunting and fishing, this territory nonetheless was of little significance in his account. The absence of people and the difficulties of traversing it made the marshland unappealing to explore and unthinkable to inhabit or develop.

In the early twentieth century, a burst of conservation efforts raised the value and visibility of the coastal wetlands. National organizations such as the Audubon Society were active in campaigns to protect birds of plume and migratory waterfowl which were declining in number due to intensive commercial hunting. Local sportsmen, most notably the wealthy businessman Edward McIlhenny, lobbied for the state to acquire marshes to serve as refuges for migratory waterfowl. McIlhenny also was effective in leading the charge for conservation laws at the state level and in recruiting national foundations to purchase and set aside vast tracks of marsh. These state changes paralleled national conservation policies that sought to preserve some wetlands as habitat for migratory waterfowl. These efforts led to the mapping and dedication of some 300,000 acres of wetland in southwest Louisiana as refuges by the late 1930s (Lockett 1874, Beck 1994, Gomez 1998, Colten 2014b). While their new status as protected areas limited access by traditional resource gatherers, it allowed urban sportsmen greater access and introduced this unknown territory to the politically powerful. This would factor into subsequent management strategies.

The principal nineteenth-century geographical compilations underscore the lack of attention given to the coastal marshes (Darby 1817, Lockett 1874). Protection as refuges raised their visibility among sportsmen, as did limited, and largely unsuccessful, attempts to drain wetlands to expand agriculture, but they remained invisible to the majority of the state's residents. Wetlands remained in the imaginary pale to the wider public in the 1920s.

CARTOGRAPHIC DISPLAY OF LAND LOSS
AND WETLAND POLICIES

Well before systematic mapping began, there were cursory comments about the loss of land on the delta. Publications contained brief statements based on direct observation (Cortell 1897, Russell 1936), but they offered no measurements or depictions of the pace of land loss.

Louisiana's concern with its coastal wetlands soared in importance during the Tidelands controversy of the 1950s. This episode was a protracted legal battle between the state and the federal government over the outer boundary of the state's territorial limits—which defined the area subject to the state's severance taxes on oil and natural gas. Early measurements of a retreating shoreline revealed a threat to future taxable offshore mineral reserves. One of the first systematic attempts to map shoreline change appeared in 1957—authored by the coastal scientist James Morgan and cartographer Philip Larimore. Based on a comparison of the shore shown in navigational charts and topographic maps at intervals from 1812 to 1954, it indicates that portions of the southeast coast experienced retreat of sixteen to sixty-two feet per year (Morgan and Larimore 1957). The landward movement of the shoreline revealed in their map forecast a retreat in the territory where oil taxes would flow to the state. These early maps triggered no ecological alarms, even though the message was a clear warning, and few beyond the coastal science community or the litigators took note, particularly after the Tidelands issues was finally settled in 1975 (Miller 1997, Priest 2008). Nonetheless, a vigorous research effort focused on changing coastal conditions had commenced and would continue.

Several related issues converged over the next ten to fifteen years that gave the land loss issue greater prominence. At the national scale, policies and judicial decisions that protected wetlands transformed what had long been considered wastelands into highly valued ecosystems (Tzoumis 1998, Miller 1989, Dahl 1990, Prince 2008, Stine 2008). Alongside the recasting of wetlands as desirable ecosystems, restoration ecology came into play as scientists sought ways to rehabilitate degraded wetlands or to create new ones (see chapter 2; Steller-McDonald, Sischinger, and Auble 1990; Martin 2015). In Louisiana, geographers and ecologists assembled more detailed maps which recast the problem of land loss as one of declining acres of critical habitat and not just the retreat of taxable seabed. Within the context of national policy concern for preserving wetlands, restoration offered hope for reversing the disappearance of Louisiana's coastal marshes.

Through a combination of protection policies, wetland mitigation, and restoration the pace of wetland loss nationally fell from 458,000 acres per year between the 1950s and the 1970s to only 58,500 acres per year between 1980 and 1997 (Stine 2008, 46–47). There were even modest gains in certain types of wetlands (Steller-McDonald, Sischinger, and Auble 1990, 1). Federal policies, with public support, drove this turnaround. Since the 1990s, farmers have set aside over two million acres in wetland reserves (USDA n.d.), to say nothing of the extensive coastal restoration efforts in Louisiana (CPRA 2012 and 2017b). Jointly, wetlands preservation and restoration ecology provided a framework to advance the analysis of land loss in Louisiana as the state's coastal marshes assumed greater public significance.

Beginning in the early 1970s, geographer Sherwood "Woody" Gagliano spearheaded several projects that more accurately measured the rate of land loss than preceding efforts. Along with collaborators, he produced a steady stream of reports based on careful historical analysis of sequential coastal maps and aerial photographs. Among his earliest works, funded by the Corps of Engineers to gauge the potential impacts of diverting a portion of the Mississippi River to Texas, was an article that mapped the areas losing land most rapidly, and which recommended restoration as a "cure" to the problem. He traced shoreline loss by comparing areas depicted in sequential topographic maps produced by the US Geological Survey (USGS) since the 1890s (fig. 3.2). Based on his measurements, he reported that Louisiana had been losing an average of 16.5 square miles per year for the preceding twenty-five to thirty years (Gagliano and van Beek 1970). He shifted the unit of measure from a linear measure or miles of retreat to an areal measure of square miles per year, which became the standard in subsequent discussions. This adjustment set aside the concerns prompted by the Tidelands controversy about offshore oil revenues and replaced it with attention to the wetlands themselves. The new emphasis was on a complex ecological territory or habitat for multiple plants and animals. The map also shows areas of land gain, notably areas in the Atchafalaya Basin where sedimentation was filling inland lakes. The presentation of areas of both gain and loss, in black and white, did little to spark widespread concern since one appears to offset the other. By showing both, the map indicates the creation of new wetlands was possible, even in the face of massive losses. Gagliano was unambiguous in his overall assessment. He states that there was a "progressive landward march" of the coast and that "major estuaries were undergoing rapid and drastic changes" (Gagliano, Light, and Becker, 1973).

Gagliano's detailed observations also revealed that some of the small subdeltas of the active Mississippi River Delta had experienced some cyclic land building. Based on this observation, he recommends the installation of structures, known as diversions, that would allow river water to flow through the levees into adjacent wetlands and deliver sediment to targeted areas, thereby mimicking the natural land-building processes

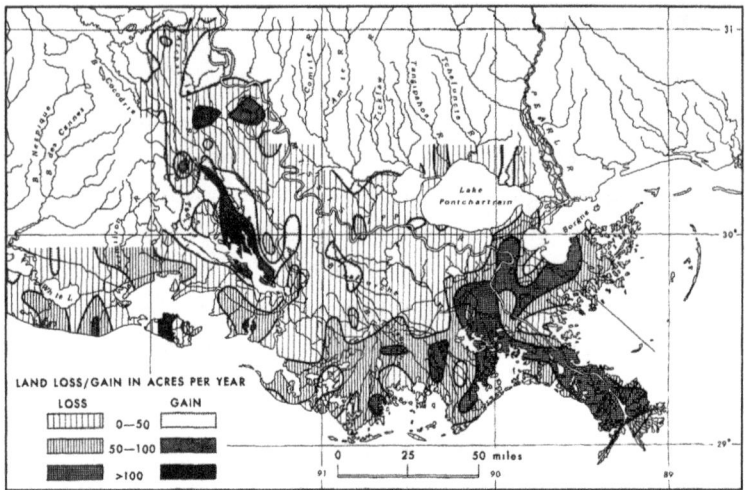

Fig. 3.2. Rates of land loss and land gain in Louisiana, 1970. Gagliano and van Beek 1970.

and restoring portions of the deteriorating wetlands. Although he uses the term "restoration," he does not appear to draw on the ecological restoration scholarship of the time (Martin 2015). Nonetheless, restoration using diversions assumes an ability to set hydrological and ecological systems in motion that would continue over time. Hence, this early recommendation reflected larger conversations with restoration ecology and most notably a strategy to use nature to rebuild the wetlands of coastal Louisiana that persists, in a modified form (Steller-McDonald, Sischinger, and Auble 1990; Martin 2015).

In a subsequent assessment of land loss, Gagliano and his associates plot only areas of loss (fig. 3.3). Their 1981 map of loss between 1955 and 1978, based on sequential aerial photography, clearly depicts serious rates of land loss in the lower delta (Gagliano, Meyer-Arendt, and Wicker 1981). It also reveals substantial losses inland. The research team went a step further and projected land loss into the future, using medical terminology to report the "life expectancy" of four coastal parishes. The anticipated life span ranged from a mere 52 years to 205 years. The projections of loss relied on basic notions of ecological progression—change that could be forecast based on current conditions and processes. The discussion by the early 1980s focused largely on local processes—subsidence and canal

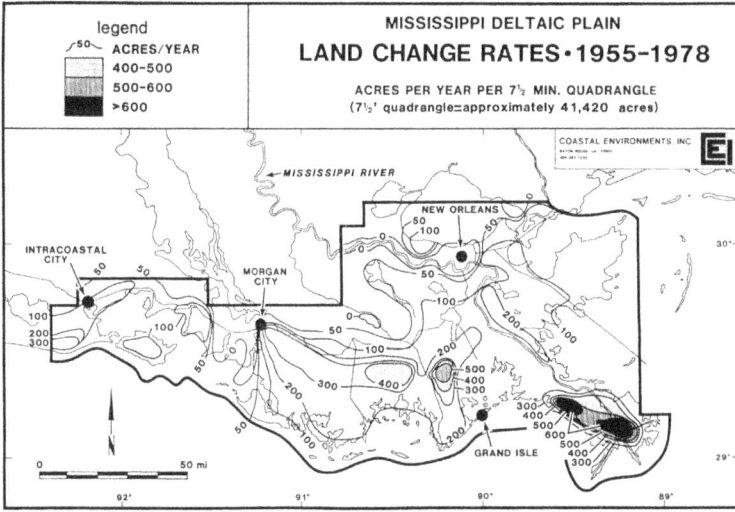

Fig. 3.3. Louisiana coastal land loss, 1955–78. Gagliano et al. 1981.

dredging and the associated deterioration of wetlands—as opposed to climate change or sea-level rise. After more than a decade researching and reporting on this problem, with little public policy response, Gagliano, Meyer-Arendt, and Wicker issued an urgent conclusion: "A great natural catastrophe is occurring in the deltaic plain of coastal Louisiana" (1981, 298). It also reflected Gagliano's frustration in compelling public officials to take effective action up to that point in time. Federal and state agencies had shown no interest in mobilizing a massive program to restore the coast. Nonetheless, this presentation marks something of a turning point. The efforts of Gagliano and others had raised the wetlands into a more visible position, and the maps provided a compelling summation of a process that was too slow to observe without the aid of maps. The political inaction that frustrated Gagliano and others began to change in the ensuing years.

FROM SPECIALIST OBSERVATION TO PUBLIC VIEW

During the 1980s, there was a decided shift from largely academic/specialist interest to public attention, and ultimately government action. Aided by a flurry of environmental legislation in the 1960s and 1970s, a favorable public attitude toward protecting natural resources, along with formal programs dedicated to preserving wetlands, a coalition of academics, fishermen, environmental advocacy organizations, and public officials galvanized efforts to arrest coastal land loss. Popular concern with the Atchafalaya Basin, Louisiana's "river of trees," had fostered public concern with wetlands that was being drawn to the coastal marshes (Colten 2014b). And the maps of land loss provided a consistent visualization of the disappearing coast.

In 1987, *Newsweek* magazine ran an article on Louisiana's land loss and included a version of a map prepared by the Louisiana Geological Survey contrasting the "coastline today" with the "land area after erosion" (Gibney 1987, 54). The supporting article reports that the state was losing some sixty square miles a year or an acre every fourteen minutes. This nationally circulated illustration indicates that some of the efforts by Louisiana scientists were beginning to reach a wider audience.

The CRCL produced the first comprehensive overview of the coastal problem in 1989, along with recommendations for dealing with the situation. The report contained a modified version of the 1981 map by Gagliano and his associates. The document expressed land loss in four general categories, which included "severe" and "very severe." It indicated that the lower river delta, Lafourche and Terrebonne parishes were in dire circumstances. The report updated the life expectancy for the lower delta and projected it would disappear during the next two centuries. This landmark document sought to set out a "citizens' program for saving the Mississippi River delta region" (CRCL 1989). This effort took a deliberate approach to engaging with a broader public. By including wider participation, this document reveals a preliminary recognition that past management decisions had been divorced from key participants in the state's wetland culture and economy. It recruited comments and participation from environmental groups and fishermen, along with civic and faith-based organizations (CRCL 1989, Hanny 1983). While much of the report drew on scientific observations done by Gagliano and many others at the forefront of studying the problem, it sought to bring that knowledge to a wider audience to activate policy changes.

The report revealed, again, the frustration of the scientific community in its opening passage: "Few natural areas have been studied more with less result" (CRCL 1989, 1). At the same time, it declared this was a critical moment for taking steps to remedy the land loss while also elevating the problem to the national level by proclaiming Louisiana's wetlands constituted 40 percent of the country's coastal marsh (1).

The coalition and its report on the state's coastal situation contributed to action on the public policy front. Louisiana's congressional delegation had been active on coastal restoration legislation efforts in the 1980s, albeit with few accomplishments, but they were beginning to achieve greater success. Senator John Breaux's files contain numerous maps of wetland loss, including one prepared by the US Fish and Wildlife Service in 1989 and the CRCL plan (CRCL 1989, Breaux n.d.). Testifying before Congress, Paul Kemp, executive director of the CRCL, proclaimed that the coastal wetlands were a "national treasure" (Kemp in US House 1990, 270). A state senator, J. Bennett Johnston, warned that it was time to stop talking and time to take action (Johnston in US House 1990, 1). When passed, the Breaux Act specifically dedicated funds to coastal restoration and began a prolonged effort to delay the losses and reverse the receding coastline. The real accomplishment of Senator Breaux was the provision that dedicated 70 percent of the funds raised by CWPPRA to Louisiana wetland preservation and restoration with the balance being spent in other states (US Geological Survey, hereafter USGS 1994). Although there is no record of use of the maps in the testimony, the message from these cartographic depictions in Breaux's papers and the supportive studies, along with public involvement, were beginning to gain traction in policy deliberations.

Members of Congress drew on maps compiled by multiple branches of the Department of Interior since the late 1970s. Both the Fish and Wildlife Service (F&WS) and USGS issued land loss maps. Breaux consulted the F&WS's maps (Hanny 1983), and the USGS's recently created National Wetland Research Center in Lafayette began adding to the cartographic tracings of this process. Its 1990 map, which merges analysis of aerial photographs with digital satellite images, indicates that the basins in the Lafourche/Terrebonne coastal units were suffering the most severe land loss in the years 1956–90, as was the case in the 1956–78 period (Hanny 1983, USGS 1994). This report illustrates spatial variation across the coastal region and indicates that the rate of loss had been fairly consistent since the mid-1950s. But the cartographic presentation, which used large drainage basins with numbers superimposed on them, was not visually compelling to the public.

The CWPPRA legislation called for a task force to develop a "comprehensive approach to restore and prevent the loss of coastal wetlands in Louisiana" (LCWCRTF 1993, 1). Responding to this legislative mandate, the task force released a report in 1993 that reoriented cartographic presentations from historical land loss to land that would be lost. In addition, it displayed the disastrous future in bold red—without explaining its methods for projecting this loss (8). The report notes the value of the wetlands in terms of fisheries and flood protection, and observes that the loss of the littoral marshes would cost the American taxpayer (7). The task force also presents its restoration plan, which includes the familiar diversions, barrier island restoration, shoreline protection, and hydrologic modifications. The impact of restoration efforts, in terms of land gain or loss, remained completely imaginary at this point.

In 1994, Gagliano and his consulting firm prepared a status report on land loss with a blueprint for restoring the coast for the state of Louisiana. It contains a map that once again blends historical and projected losses (Gagliano 1994). This much-simplified version shows broad swaths of the coast experiencing land loss, and modest areas enjoying gain. The color presentation and the single categories for loss and gain do not reveal the variation in the pace of loss noted by the USGS, but they offer an unambiguous image of conditions beyond the view of most residents and embed an image in the collective mind of the state's citizens. And the report that contained this presentation advanced a more nuanced program for restoration that was attuned to the diverse environmental conditions across the coast. It outlined several options in addition to diversions. Among them were restoring barrier islands, managing wetlands and reefs, and also levees and "leaky barriers." There was no projection of how much land would be gained through restoration. The colorful treatment was partly a reflection of dropping costs of color reproduction, but it contributed to more effective and dramatic cartographic communication.

A landmark report released in 1998 solidified the depiction of projected land loss with its simple representation of what was anticipated by 2050 (LCWCRTF 1998; fig. 3.4). This report claimed to offer a new

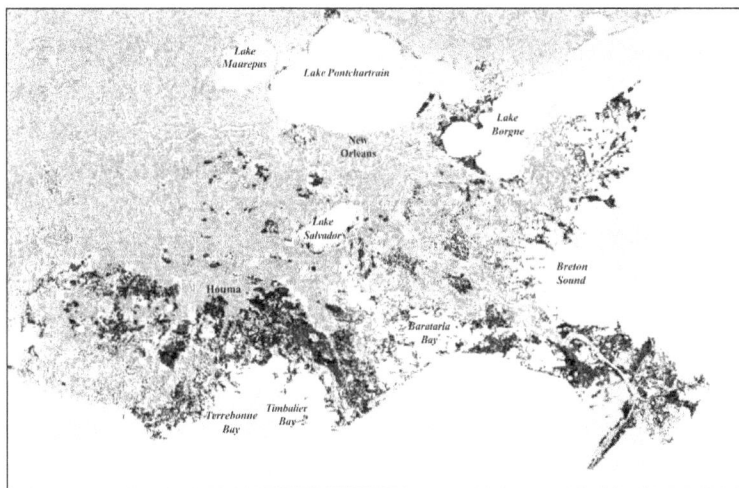

Fig. 3.4. Projected land loss, 1998. From *Coast 2050*, LCWCRTF 1998.

approach, to present a single unified plan for restoring the coast as a sustainable ecosystem that protects the environment, economy, and culture of the region. Yet the map of land loss, like most before it, fails to include the presence of people or economic activity. The absence of a human presence greatly simplifies the situation, and suggests that restoration is limited to manipulation of the biophysical environment. Its maps of restoration projects contain much more detail than previous efforts and seeks to maintain a coast-wide program.

For more than two decades, scholars and agency personnel had been presenting similar versions of a future that offered little hope for the coast's ecology and, to a lesser extent, residents of the region and their livelihoods. The USGS became a leading authority on mapping land loss and projecting future losses. By 2000, academics, agency personnel, and policy makers had embraced the basic concept of land loss. Conveying this to the public remained a challenge. The USGS and Louisiana officials sought a more comprehensible measure for public consumption. Around 2000, John Barras, a geographer with the USGS, calculated the rate of loss as approximately a football field per hour. While cautioning that this could oversimplify the situation, he acknowledged it could be useful in public outreach (Barras 2017). The Louisiana Department of Natural Resources used the rate in public discussions, and news media picked up on the catchy measurement.

In 2002, a coalition of businesses, foundations, and environmental organizations set out to elevate public concern with the land loss crisis and adopted the measure along with a campaign to retitle the coastal marshes as "America's Wetlands" (America's Wetland Foundation 2017). By inserting "America" for Louisiana, this public relations effort quite effectively asserted a national dimension to the problem—reflecting the 1990s congressional testimony that declared they were a national treasure. Merging the new title with the football-field metric captured wide public interest (Hardman 2015). When offering an updated land loss map in 2017, a USGS geographer pointed out that he continued using the measure, while also updating it, because the public could relate to it (Baurick 2017). The land loss conversation truly expanded to all levels of society when this terminology gained acceptance—with all its misconceptions. When an authority declares that the state is losing a football field an hour—which sounds like a threat to the sacred turf in Tiger Stadium on LSU's campus— it had a resonance previously unknown. No red-hued swaths of projected land loss could compare with this dire forecast for the stadium housing the state's premier football team.

Following Hurricane Katrina in 2005, Louisiana reorganized and centralized its coastal restoration efforts in the newly formed Coastal Protection and Restoration Agency (CPRA). This agency has produced a plan every five years, and its 2012 plan declares land loss as the "coastal crisis" and an "ongoing catastrophe" (fig. 3.5; CPRA 2012, 16, 21). While gaining strong legislative support, the plan acknowledges climate change as a factor, but does not foreground this process as a major factor in sea-level rise (CPRA 2012, 2017b). In a state with many influential climate skeptics, the agency's acknowledgment of this global situation might be surprising. Yet business interests tolerate it in part because the plan calls for governments to pay for restoration, and not the industries that were major contributors to the situation.

In its projection of future losses, based on modeling that considered a range of environmental uncertainties, not past land loss rates, CPRA used the dramatic red color to indicate land areas likely to disappear. The areas in red are truly alarming even to the casual viewer. The agency's pre-

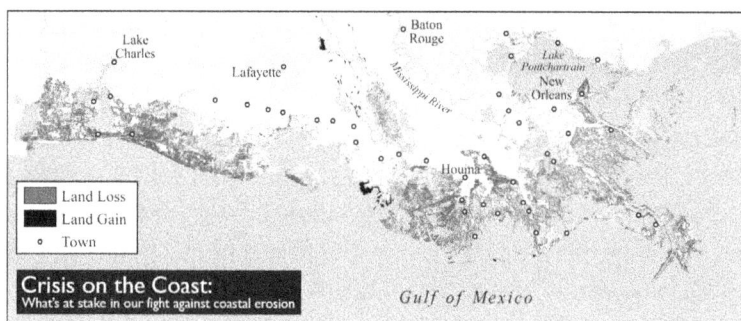

Fig. 3.5. Projected land loss, 2012. Map by Mary Lee Eggart, after CPRA 2012.

sentation of the restoration efforts is more comprehensible and visually appealing than prior depictions, but it fails to show the projected achievements of restoration projects and largely dismisses people. Despite asserting restoration as central to the coastal region's society and economy, the maps of future disappearance of coastal land reveal virtually nothing about social or economic losses (CPRA 2012, 2017b). In its 2017 plan, the state agency follows similar methods to achieve a consistent presentation of future losses: red to highlight the projected loss, and broad-stroke shading to show the placement of land restoration.

The remarkable cartographic transition that occurred over the decades since the first scientific measurements of land loss was the shift from historical loss to projected loss. The two most recent master plans report on the area of land loss in simple numbers, not as cartographic representations. The numbers are impressive. In 2012, the state reported that Louisiana had lost 1,880 square miles since 1930 (CPRA 2012, 16), and in 2017, the master plan observes that the state lost "more than 1,800 square miles between 1932 and 2010"—in effect discounting the total and not even updating it (CPRA 2017b, 2). In the two-page spread showing projected land loss, the plan projects that an additional 2,250 square miles could be lost in the coming fifty years. It spotlights the future threat, not the historical losses. This calls on readers to imagine a future that is even more perilous than the present. This has proven effective to secure funding from public bodies.

A prominent omission, or at least underrepresentation, on these maps of land loss was the presence of a human population. Great attention has been devoted to displaying the loss of coastal marshes and barrier islands, but there was never a comparable effort to depict the distribution of people in the littoral zone. Granted, most of the state's recent land loss maps designate the location of larger towns and cities. Small dots and labels are the only indication of where people live. Yet these depictions do not indicate the actual footprint of human settlement—urban and rural. Consequently, the threats of land loss tend to disguise the projected impacts on communities (CPRA 2012 and 2017b). A brief examination of the prospects for relocating coastal residents revealed the locations of threatened Native American communities (Dalbom, Hemmerling, and Lewis 2014). A more ambitious atlas of coastal Louisiana included multiple maps that revealed the footprint of human settlement, the distribution of multiple economic activities, and the relationship of land loss to these activities (Hemmerling 2017). Yet the state's restoration agency has not folded this valuable information into its plans.

DIGITAL VISUALIZATIONS

A number of interactive digital tools that display sea-level rise are available online, and most add important social and economic patterns missing from the traditional land loss maps for Louisiana. These tools use geographic information system (GIS) technologies to overlay projected sea-level heights with demographic and economic measures such as population, income, and vulnerability. Most of them include data for the entire United States but allow users to zoom in on an area of interest (CPRA 2015b, NOAA 2017, Climate Central 2017, Coastal Resilience 2017). Since Louisiana's coast is experiencing exceptionally high rates of relative sea-level rise because of its ongoing land loss that stems from subsidence, erosion, and other factors, these tools are of particular importance even if they do not depict the projected restorations. Most importantly, they address the issue of social and economic justice that the state master plan maps neglect and yet are central to the concept of sustainability. By enabling the visualization of social and economic issues in relationship to changing coastlines, these tools offer a model for more inclusive cartography.

The state's CPRA released its flood risk viewer in 2015 (CPRA 2015b).

It allows users to select different coverages to view the projected land loss, flood risk, and coastal vegetation at different points on a sliding timescale and with or without the proposed master plan projects. It also shows social vulnerability—those social characteristics that leave segments of society less able to respond to crisis—by fairly large geographic territories, but not by actual population distribution. It presents the one social measure in census blocks, which suggests vast areas with vulnerable people when few people live in some of those coastal tracts. By allowing the user to compare a future with the state's restoration efforts or without them, it is intended to highlight the value of the coastal master plan to people.

The National Oceanographic and Atmospheric Administration (NOAA) has a tool that allows public viewing of future sea-level rise risks. Users are able to overlay sea-level rise on social vulnerability (NOAA 2017). Climate Central, an independent NGO, developed a tool that allows users to select a future sea-level height, and it adjusts the categories of vulnerable coastal populations (Climate Central 2017). Both of these online tools allow users to adjust the future sea-level rise independent of a time dimension. By separating the height of sea level from a user's personal life expectancy, the tools lose immediacy. Nonetheless, they create alarming visualizations. A coalition of NGOs and government organizations have assembled a coastal resilience mapper which depicts at-risk economic assets and expected future damage at the county/parish level. This approach focuses on economic impacts of sea-level rise and not social issues, but it does show the types of biophysical/engineering solutions that can mitigate future risk—albeit not at a fine resolution (Coastal Resilience 2017). These digital tools enable public scrutiny of local risks in the future and insert social and economic measures into the visual landscape. Yet, by omitting concrete and unchallenged long-term historical losses, at least for Louisiana, they lessen their potential power as public visualizations.

The great accomplishment of the cartographic depictions of coastal land loss has been threefold. Representations of past loss pushed a largely unseen landscape into public view. It transformed a remote, unpopulated, and long-dismissed swath of coastal marsh into the foreground of multiple public discussions. Rising interest in remote wetlands as scenic resources along with attention to what we now refer to as "ecosystem services" has broadened public interest. Protection and restoration programs, aided by contemporaneous public policies that placed high value on protecting ecological resources and even restoring those that had been diminished by human action, became dominant outcomes that flowed from the mapping of a disappearing shore. This has been a step toward sustainable policies.

The second aspect was the elevation of coastal land loss as a national political issue by the state's congressional delegation and the successful passage of federal legislation in 1990. The federal legislation launched deliberate restoration projects funded by both state and federal programs and also spurred more investment in research on the processes that produced loss and those that could offset it. Presented as a process to protect and restore a valuable but disappearing ecosystem, and not a response to climate change, the ultimate objective aligns with current global climate-change concerns. Collectively, the research and restoration programs, along with expanding outreach efforts by local and national NGOs, sustained public interest and visibility. Sustainability has become a stated goal of the state's programs—although one subject to criticism due to the plan's huge costs, energy demands, and projected inability to stay apace with rising sea levels in the long run (Day and Erdman 2018).

Finally, both the maps of past loss and those of future loss made all too apparent that the coast was a dynamic landscape, even though they consistently eclipsed the coast's human geography. The digital versions, however, have largely dropped the historical views, while inserting some measure of a human presence in terms of vulnerability. The state's shore has been in constant change, and recognition of this situation spurred efforts to restore this susceptible setting. It also made clear that coasts, in an era of sea-level rise, are not solid, permanent foundations for society. Even if they are the basis for highly productive ecosystems that provide numerous resources, they are subject to degradation and loss. This is the ultimate message for the larger global climate-change community, and this underscores the need to pursue policies that promote and deliver sustainability.

Southern Florida, coastal Virginia, and the Houston metropolitan area, in particular, share similar, albeit not identical, characteristics. They are also home to much larger urban populations that face the threats associated with global climate change. Effective communication of risk using maps that portray a combination of projected physical losses, threats to social and economic systems, and their presentation over a prolonged period of time may prove effective in driving policies that embrace sustainability. While the Louisiana maps neglected social and economic landscapes, their visualizations provided a basis to impel policy makers to launch programs aimed at creating a more sustainable shore.

4

The Public in Public Works

Reworking the Mississippi River

An urban area can dominate local environmental management decisions, and this arrangement has certainly been the case in the Lower Mississippi River. New Orleans, the entrepôt city near the river's mouth, has had an outsized voice in navigation and flood-control policies, along with the numerous other environmental management strategies. At the insistence of urban politicians, risk has been displaced to more rural territories, as displayed in the maps of the disappearing coastal lands. After it became understood how these policies were contributing to degradation of the coastal wetlands, advocates for the city continued to demand the sacrifice of zones beyond the protective barriers surrounding the metropolis.

New Orleans is unquestionably a river city. Founded by the French in the eighteenth century to become the entrepôt for an expansive riparian hinterland, it owes its genesis to the presence of the Mississippi River and the colonial founders' notion that cities and rivers were essential partners. Nearly a century after the city's humble beginnings, and viewing it as a strategic port for America's emerging interior agricultural regions, President Thomas Jefferson launched efforts to purchase the city from France and ended up acquiring not only the Isle of Orleans in 1803, but also the river's entire western basin. Over the next half-century the arrival of steamboat-based commerce enhanced the city's role as an economic hub and solidified its position as the principal metropolis on the country's largest river. The river has clearly shaped the city's political and commercial history.

The city's landscape also has come to reflect the river's central role. Wharves and warehouses once lined the riverfront, which was constantly crowded with all manner of inland and marine vessels. Jackson Square, the most prominent social space, along with the main governmental and religious structures, face the waterway, and the residential districts of the wealthy hug the relatively narrow natural levee that offered some degree of elevation and security from flooding. Beginning in the 1720s, the French and all subsequent inhabitants have raised earthen embankments to hold back the river's seasonal high water. These levees, which follow the river's meandering course, now stand more than twenty feet high and obscure the river from view; they are arguably the most ubiquitous landscape feature in city. Historian Ari Kelman asserts they have acquired iconic status (2003, 161). But the levees do not end at the city limits, nor are they static features exempt from current social, political, and economic deliberations. They are at the nexus of safety and calamity, and conflict and coexistence. Indeed, not only the levees, but all of the other environmental management strategies have prioritized New Orleans. Whether offering flood protection, conserving wildlife for restaurants and urban sportsmen, restoring the wetlands to buffer storm surge, and even taking steps to reinforce sustainability, all of these strategies have given the lower river metropolis a commanding role in shaping policies that helped protect it and that enabled it to extract wealth from the region's resources.

New Orleans has had a complex relationship with the river and its broad floodplain and delta that the city has both relied on for its existence and constantly struggles to manage in order to survive. Public input has played a major role in the planning of Mississippi River projects during the twentieth century. Levees and flood control have been a prominent part of the city's enduring struggle to exist in a setting ill-suited to a major city—other than for its commercial potential. For nearly three centuries, New Orleans and its leaders have sought ways to fend off floods and, for the city's first hundred-plus years, have relied principally on structural protection. After the devastating 1927 flood, the city, which escaped inundation, quickly sought additional safeguards and readily advocated placing the cost of flood protection more firmly with the federal government and to implement a plan to deflect the floodwaters to other places and thus reduce the city's risk.

PUBLIC INPUT

A cornerstone of current environmental management is public involvement. It may come in many different forms and seek to open communication channels that allow a public dialogue at multiple stages in the planning process. It promises to permit the public to influence public works. Well before the advent of recent public involvement procedures, the public hearing, interagency review, letter-writing campaigns, and litigation afforded the insertion of public input into government-guided environmental management. The overwhelming tendency of major projects in the nineteenth century was for experts, such as the Corps of Engineers, to design projects; Congress would hold hearings and appropriate funds if the legislative branch agreed with the plans. Local interests often voiced their concerns at congressional or Corps hearings, but participants commonly were local politicians, local business boosters, or national organizations with vested interests in the proposed project. This process effectively privileged technical experts, local elites, and already influential businesses while neglecting input from common citizens and marginalized communities that might suffer adverse impacts. The hearings generally occurred after experts developed plans and often centered more on funding decisions than on reshaping plans. This process was certainly the case in the hearings about floodplain management in the lower Mississippi in the early twentieth century and was in accord with the science-based approach of progressive-era politics and conservation planning of the time.

The archival files of retired representatives and senators are full of letters sent by constituents on various issues of local importance. Even in the age before e-mail, the public would sometimes shower their elected officials with form letters or postcards appealing for a certain position on an upcoming vote. Volume often trumped substance. These campaigns were a vital tool for public input, even if representing a fairly narrow constituency. Additional input came via interagency review which allowed agencies with overlapping interest in an environmental management policy to weigh in on decisions. In finalizing floodplain policies, the Corps of Engineers might turn to the Fish and Wildlife Service and related state agencies for comment. Ultimately, the design decisions resided with the Corps and funding with Congress.

RIVER CITIES AND WATERWAY MANAGEMENT

Stéphane Castonguay and Matthew Evenden persuasively argue that in the industrial era "the river has not only changed its physical appearance, hydrology, and ecology, but its place and purpose in society and had also become the focus of political conflict" (2012, 1). The Mississippi River, a free-flowing giant in the eighteenth century, has become the object of persistent hydrological modifications that embroil those who live along its banks, and particularly residents in its traditional entrepôt, in ongoing political disputes that have enormous ramifications for the city and the entire lower river valley. Philip Scarpino made the case that the upper river underwent a major transformation as society tried to synchronize the river with the demands of an industrializing nation (1985, 13). Similar synchronization efforts characterize the projects to make the lower river more dependable for navigation and less risky for floodplain dwellers. Yet, according to Kelman, the relationship between New Orleans and the river has been reciprocal. His position aligns with that of Castonguay and Evenden, who claim that rivers contributed to urbanization, and in turn cities have exerted urbanizing influences on rivers (Kelman 2003, 8). The particulars of this reciprocal influence are singular to each city and river pair.

What is obvious in the lower Mississippi is that many of the modifications have been driven by the powerful influence of the metropolis near the river's mouth. The role of a city in shaping its neighboring river is contingent on numerous factors. Where is the city along the river? What are the political geographies of the watershed? How large is the waterway? What opportunities does the river offer, and what hazards does it pose (Colten 2012)? New Orleans is near the mouth of a massive river that drains more than 1.2 million square miles. Oceangoing ships reach the city's docks, and barge traffic from the Great Plains and the Midwest deliver cargo for export. The city endures the floods that flow from this gargantuan watershed, but it has relatively little direct environmental impact on the river in terms of water consumption and even pollution. Nonetheless, the city has been the centerpiece of huge investments in levees and upstream dams designed to protect this commercial center, and the environmental ramifications of these projects have been huge and extend well beyond the city's limits.

After a major flood in 1878, Congress acquiesced to lobbyists representing planters and commercial interests in Louisiana and Mississippi and created the MRC with responsibility to oversee the construction of a federally funded and consistently designed levee system. A central argument was that the river floods were a national problem that the lower river states could not afford to deal with alone. Yet in the post–Civil War era, the only way to secure such a federal investment in internal improvements in the deep South was to emphasize its value in supporting inland navigation and interstate commerce—not protecting the recently rebellious southern planters. A prevailing engineering theory held that a river confined between levees would scour a deeper channel. Thus, the federal policy, relying on scientific concepts, followed a "levees-only" approach to enhance navigation and not protect the plantation owners along the lower river. Although no appropriations were forthcoming for several years, when work finally began, both existing and new levees rose and closed off several natural distributaries. To accentuate the scouring potential and minimize the loss of valuable farmland, construction crews heaped up the earthen embankments near the river. A series of damaging floods in the early twentieth century prompted the MRC finally to concede that levees were for flood protection, and design specifications were altered in accord. Nonetheless, the design to confine the river was embedded in the massive engineering works and represents a grand example of path dependency (Cowdrey 1977, Camillo and Pearcy 2004, Colten 2005).

One distributary that remained connected to the main waterway was the Atchafalaya River (fig. 4.1). Diverging from the Mississippi upstream from Baton Rouge near where the Red River entered the Mississippi, this outlet could accommodate a portion of the overflow during spring floods

Fig. 4.1. Louisiana waterways, 2020. Natural distributaries include Bayou Manchac, Bayou Plaquemine, and Bayou Lafourche. Map by Mary Lee Eggart.

and thereby protect downstream cities and plantations during the early nineteenth century. In the 1830s, a human-made cutoff allowed a greater share of the Red River's discharge to flow down the Atchafalaya. With this increased flow came flotsam that accumulated during low river stages and effectively blocked navigation on the upper course of the Atchafalaya. To restore navigation, Louisiana authorized clearing the "raft." After successfully removing the obstruction by mid-century, an increasing portion of the Mississippi River's water flowed down the Atchafalaya (USACE 1951; Reuss 1998, 73; Barnett 2017). In effect, the distributary, which offered a deeper and more direct route to the Gulf, was capturing the main course of the Mississippi. With the increased discharge came higher floodwaters in the basin. Local levee districts regularly raised and extended levee protection after the flood of 1882 (US Congress, House 1919, 25).

This situation exposed both the value of the Atchafalaya as an outlet for floodwaters and the divergent interests of those who lived along the lower Mississippi and those who lived in the Atchafalaya Basin. Since the eighteenth century, powerful New Orleans interests have guided flood-protection efforts. During the colonial period, they deferred the cost of protection to rural planters. After statehood, parishes took primary responsibility for levee construction; later the state and levee districts assumed much of the responsibility; and in 1879, the federal government began a slow transition to develop a more consistent and federally financed levee system (Colten 2005, chap. 1). Securing additional financial support was central to the New Orleans flood-protection strategy, but displacement of risk also rose in importance. In the early twentieth century, deliberations about protecting New Orleans by diverting flood-waters down the Atchafalaya were a key point of contention.

During the second half of the twentieth century, with the Mississippi River largely confined between effective levees, hurricanes became the most perilous and uncontrolled risk, and the city secured federal assistance to erect barriers to hold back storm surge (Colten 2009). The biophysical impacts to the lower delta region from these dual efforts have been considerable. Starved of sediment, the delta is subsiding, and diversion of floodwaters to other locations produces episodic ecological disruptions. Thus, the decisions made to protect New Orleans have a regional impact. And currently, discussions about offsetting the rapid loss of coastal wetlands with land restoration projects have centered on displacing the environmental costs to those who live on the margins of the state's inhabitable land.

Historian Christopher Morris (2012) is one of several insightful scholars who have turned their attention to the Mississippi in recent years. While not focusing explicitly on the city-river relationship, he devotes considerable attention to the reworking of the vast wetlands created over the last fifteen thousand years by the Mississippi. Human endeavors over the past two centuries have persistently attempted to separate the river from swamps and marshes and make dry what was once wet. As Louisiana now turns its attention to restoring a small portion of the coastal wetlands, to counteract centuries of dewatering the floodplain, it faces strong opposition from coastal residents who have become acclimated to the conditions created by the reengineered lower delta. Natural resource–based activities are foundational livelihoods outside the city limits, and most fisherfolk can anticipate disruption of their current pursuits. Changes may come from the delivery of sediment that will bury oyster leases, which can be relocated, but at a cost. Addition of fresh water to the bays may alter salinity and drive bay shrimp and crabs farther from the small fishing ports and impose additional coasts on marginal fishing operations. Thus, those who have adapted to one set of transformations must consider how to adapt again. Meanwhile, those living behind the levees foresee little change, or perhaps are unwilling to consider it—even as sea level rises and diminishes the safety buffer provided by fixed infrastructure.

REDIRECTING RISK

Following the huge Mississippi River flood in 1882, a debate raged about the advisability of outlets as supplements to levees. The general course of action taken by the MRC was to build levees—largely a concession to navigation interests who feared shoaling if a major outlet was created (see Reuss 1998, chap. 3). Floods during the early years of the twentieth century accentuated the debates that shaped subsequent policy and flood-control practices and exposed sharp rifts between those living in the urban areas east of the Mississippi and the residents of parishes along the Atchafalaya. Following a spate of floods, the MRC launched a study in 1910 to determine the "necessity, urgency, and practicality of severing the two basins" (Board of Engineers in US Congress, House 1914, 3).

As part of this inquiry, the MRC held hearings that revealed contrasting positions in the debate that reflected divergent local interests. Most New Orleans political and business leaders opposed blocking flow through the Atchafalaya. Marshaling several arguments, their most consistent objection was that closing the Atchafalaya and forcing the entire flow by the city would raise flood stages at New Orleans. Furthermore, higher levees to enable this option would require massive investments in reworking New Orleans's waterfront infrastructure (fig. 4.2; Behrman [New Orleans Mayor] in US Congress, House 1914, 68; and Sanders [Chairman, New Orleans Board of Trade] in US Congress 1914, House 70–71, 48). Representatives of levee districts and parishes that straddled

Fig. 4.2. St. Joseph Street Landing in New Orleans, 1930s. Levee enlargement in New Orleans would have entailed massive reworking of the riverfront infrastructure, including elevating wharfs, warehouses, and levees. Photo from The Charles L. Franck Studio Collection at the Historic New Orleans Collection, Acc. No. 1979.325.3487.

the Atchafalaya reminded the MRC that the basin was a populated area with extensive agricultural development that would be dislocated if floods were allowed to flow down the distributary (Memorial Avoyelles Parish in US Congress, House 1914, 67; Gremillion [Red River and Bayou Des Glaises Levee and Drainage District] in US Congress, House 1914, 52). Their core argument was that closing the distributary would reduce flood risk for residents and planters in the basin, and beyond those benefits, they touted the potential for additional land reclamation in the basin (Memorandum from Port Allen in US Congress, House 1914, 51).

In his 1914 recommendation to the MRC, Colonel Frederic Abbot of the Corps of Engineers concluded, "The proposed work [cutting off the Atchafalaya] would result in gains or benefits to those living or having property in the Atchafalaya Basin due to a lowering of flood heights and a corresponding reduction in the cost of levees and development of lands, but, on the other hand it would entail losses and disadvantages to those living or having property along the Mississippi River because of increased flood heights and a corresponding increase in the cost of protecting lands that are already highly developed" (Abbot [Corps of Engineers] in US Congress, House 1914, 4). Ultimately, the Corps did not support separating the two waterways. Nonetheless, Abbot's observation highlights the contrasting positions between agricultural interests in the basin and commercial interests in New Orleans. Based on its study, the MRC decided the project was practicable, but not urgent, and took no direct action to separate the two waterways. Consequently, the Atchafalaya continued to serve as an outlet for the Mississippi's floods.

After the devastating 1916 flood, Congress directed the MRC to conduct a "survey of the Atchafalaya Outlet so far as may be necessary to determine the cost of protecting its basin from the floodwaters of the Mississippi River either by its divorcement from the Mississippi River or by other means" (Black [Chief of Engineers] in US Congress, House 1919, 2). At the time, conditions remained similar to previous years. Depending on the different stages of the various rivers, either all or a portion of the Red could flow down the Atchafalaya. When the Mississippi rose to high flood stages as in 1916, the Atchafalaya carried the entire discharge of the Red and a portion of the Mississippi's. Partial levees set back from the Atchafalaya directed the flow through the basin. In 1917, the Corps indicated that "the fullest measure of protection to the Atchafalaya Basin from both the Mississippi and the Red would be secured by closing the Atchafalaya at it head and allowing the Red to flow into the Mississippi" (Black in US Congress, House 1919, 2) Yet, while this option would reduce the flood risk in the Atchafalaya Basin, it would increase the flood volume in the Mississippi as well as the risk to New Orleans. Once again, when the MRC decided that separation of the Red and Atchafalaya was not necessary, it reached a conclusion that supported New Orleans interests (MRC in US Congress 1919, House 16).

Its decision was tested all too soon. In spring 1927, the Mississippi River rose to unprecedented heights. Levees failed along the river in the states of Mississippi and Arkansas, turbid floodwaters covered more than 25,000 square miles of land, and damaged more than 160,000 homes. The flood displaced some 900,000 floodplain residents, left more than 240 dead, and caused an estimated loss of $100 million in crops and livestock. As the levees failed upstream, tensions rose in New Orleans, and city leaders used the few days before the high water arrived to organize an effort to create an artificial outlet, or crevasse, in the levee system below the city. Drawing on the precedent of a natural crevasse in 1922 that lowered the river at New Orleans, they devised a plan to blast a hole in the levees and create what would amount to a second river mouth. In theory, by creating an additional opening, water would escape into the Gulf of Mexico faster and thereby lower the height of water at New Orleans (American National Red Cross 1929, Cowdrey 1977, Kelman 2003).

This plan was inequitable by design, and there was no formal public hearing on the matter. The city's business elite vigorously lobbied for the plan, which had as its primary objective to save the city of New Orleans from destruction (Barry 1998). In doing so, the diversion would flow across a fairly narrow swath of natural levee and into sprawling marshes that were the habitat of muskrats, which supported the world's largest fur-trapping enterprise, and other natural resources such as oysters. Business leaders from New Orleans assured the governor that residents of the impacted area would be cared for. Prior to the deliberate breach, officials ordered approximately 10,000 people, mainly farmer and trapper families, to evacuate. Not only were their livelihoods to be interrupted, but they were forced out of their homes for an undetermined period of time. Additionally, promises of compensation were not fulfilled (Kelman 2003, Gomez 2000).

On April 29, 1927, the Corps of Engineers blasted a hole in the levee several miles downstream from New Orleans (Cowdrey 1977). Creating a gap in some of the oldest and most formidable levees along the Mississippi took several detonations, but eventually water poured through the intentional breach and the torrent enlarged the gap into a sizable crevasse that remained open for months. Louisiana's chief engineer testified to the MRC that the opening effectively lowered the river at New Orleans by two and a half feet and its impact reached as far upstream as Donaldsonville (Schoenberger [Chief Engineer, Louisiana State Board of Engineers] in MRC 1927, 68). New Orleans did not flood, although the crevasse's actual role in protecting the city is questionable. Nonetheless, the use of an artificial outlet became a central tenet in the post-flood "rivers and outlets" flood-protection policy.

In the immediate aftermath of the flood, the MRC conducted hearings in the major cities along the river. After years of a more-or-less unified lobbying effort for federal levee funding, leaders in Mississippi, Arkansas, and Louisiana emerged from the 1927 flood with different opinions about how best to fix an obviously broken system. The levees-only policy had not worked, and spokespeople appealed to the commission for outlets, along with upstream reservoirs and other solutions (Louisiana State Board of Engineers 1929). During the Louisiana hearings in July, there was consensus on who should pay to repair the levees, including the artificial breach at Caernarvon. Officials from across the state argued for federal repairs to the many crevasses. Col. Marcel Garsaud from New Orleans asserted, "It is our opinion that the restoration of those levees should be at Federal expense and we urge it upon the Commission" (Garsaud [General Manager New Orleans Dock Board] in MRC 1927, 58).

A prominent fissure among those representing Louisiana appeared between those who sought protection for the state's leading city and those who felt that diverting water to rural agricultural areas unfairly favored New Orleans. General Dufor, representing the New Orleans Mayor's Flood Control Policy Committee, claimed, "Such means of control as spillways have been demonstrated and have given relief, and we will ask you, gentlemen, to favor a spillway policy . . . so that results will be in effect soon and we will be spared a recurrence of this awful disaster" (Dufor [New Orleans Mayor's Flood Control Policy Committee] in MRC 1927, 64). His claim rested on the effects of the still-open Caernarvon Crevasse and the belief that an engineered floodway could avert future calamities. The Louisiana chief engineer echoed the New Orleans position. George Schoenberger testified, "I, myself, and the majority of the members of the State Board of Engineers, and the levee boards, are of the opinion that the levees alone are inadequate to control the floods of the lower river and they should be supplemented by spillways. The flood of 1927 demonstrated that to me beyond a doubt" (in MRC 1927, 67). In contrast, Walter Kemper, head of the Atchafalaya Basin Protective Association, reflected on the dramatic impacts of the flood that flowed through the basin when upstream levees failed. Trying to fend off the argument for using the Atchafalaya as the principal floodway, he claimed: "The erroneous impression is that the Atchafalaya Basin is an immense tract of waste land through which flows a river of ample capacity to care for all the surplus water of the Mississippi River without danger of any great amount of damage being done. While a portion of the basin is swamp land the greater portion of it is in a high state of cultivation and comprises the principal portion of the 'Sugar Bowl' of Louisiana" (Kemper [Atchafalaya Basin Protective Association] in MRC 1927, 105).

Kemper acknowledged that New Orleans needed adequate protection, but revealed the sectional divisions when he asserted that Atchafalaya Basin residents were willing to take some of the water but would not sit by idly and watch all the water diverted down the Atchafalaya to protect the urban east bank of the river (in MRC 1927, 112).

In separate hearings before Congress, Andrew Gay, president of the Atchafalaya Basin Levee District, claimed that as many as million people would have to move if the federal government did not take responsibility for flood control. His large number seems to encompass the entire lower river valley, but he goes on to argue that use of the Atchafalaya as a floodway would destroy towns and villages and would "disarrange commerce of the region" (Gay in US Congress, House 1927a, pt. 3, 1303–4). Morgan City, a town of some 5,500 people, reliant on fishing and cypress, located near the mouth of the Atchafalaya, prepared a brief claiming that the city had faced only modest flood risks since its founding. Recent levee construction along the Mississippi that forced more water through the basin had changed that situation, and now it faced higher flood levels. Regular flooding "took tens of thousands of acres of sugar cane lands" (Morgan City 1927, 1). Morgan City opposed using the basin as a floodway and expressed its position in terms of equity: "The preponderance of the evidence goes to show that the Atchafalaya Basin has but few friends without the basin and even within the basin, those localities higher up are perfectly willing to gain relief at the expense of those below. . . . Morgan City hopes sincerely that the rest of the state will realize the enormity of the injustice to which it is proposed to subject her and parts of the Atchafalaya Basin" (fig. 4.3; Morgan City 1927, 2–3).

OUTLETS TO PROTECT THE CITY

Ultimately, Edgar Jadwin, the chief of engineers, recommended "that the Atchafalaya should be utilized to the limit of its capacity at flood stages to carry water to the Gulf" (in US Congress, House 1927b, 26). Using language that sounds similar to Dutch engineers promoting "making room for the river" in the early twenty-first century, Jadwin proclaimed, "Man

Fig. 4.3. Morgan City flooding, 1912. A small city near the mouth of the Atchafalaya River, Morgan City was subject to regular inundation, and it had no levees or floodwalls before the 1927 flood. Community leaders feared their city would endure worse flooding with the construction of the Atchafalaya Floodway. Courtesy of the City of Morgan City Archives.

must not try to restrict the Mississippi River too much in extreme floods. The river will break any plan which does this. *It must have the room it needs, and to accord with its nature must have the extra room laterally* [emphasis added]" (in US Congress, House 1927b, 4). This meant the broad expanse of the Atchafalaya as well as a second outlet just upriver from New Orleans at Bonnet Carré. He justified this decision declaring it unsafe to increase the levee heights along the lower river and asserted, "to afford proper protection to New Orleans, with its population of nearly half a million and property of over a billion dollars, a *special floodway upstream from the city is essential* [emphasis added]" (in US Congress, House 1927b, 7; also see US Congress, House 1927c, 4). In his thinking, it was less expensive to flood the Atchafalaya than to fortify the city's structural protection. As the basin's great entrepôt, New Orleans had interests that were aligned with the Corps of Engineers' and the MRC's fiscal concerns.

Adoption of the "levees and outlets" approach fundamentally altered the previous "levees only" policy, in service to the metropolitan center. The Corps made the case that these new structural features would protect New Orleans and largely ignored the populations living within the floodways' paths. Maps included in a 1927 letter to Congress show three potential "spillways": Bonnet Carré, Caernarvon, and Morganza (or the Atchafalaya) (fig. 4.4). Each map employs a simple cartography and shows only the bare alignment of the guide levees and the principal waterways the spillways will connect. Towns and cites outside the spillways appear as small dots on the map, suggesting that few residents would be affected (US Congress, House 1927c, after 28). The report observes that the Bonnet Carré Spillway, "while crossing some improved land, is so short as to involve but small property damage" (US Congress, House 1927c, 15). The discussion of the Atchafalaya indicated some levee alignments might need relocation to protect valuable (agricultural) lands and projected that the federal government would need to acquire "flowage rights" from lands that would be subjected to inundation, and major roads and railroads would need to be elevated. The analysis gave greater attention to fixed infrastructure owned by the state and corporations than to people and small properties. The Corps ultimately rejected the potential Caernarvon Spillway below New Orleans. Engineers concluded that the Bonnet Carré Spillway would adequately protect New Orleans and, by diverting water above the city and its extensive port facilities, would minimize the acceleration of river currents passing the city and reduce the risk of erosion undercutting the city's levees and wharfs (US Congress, House 1927c, 17).

Despite adoption of the Jadwin Plan, resistance to using the Atchafalaya as an outlet did not disappear. Subsequent hearings reveal the spillway proponents' pragmatic positions and the creative arguments of those representing landowners in the basin. Colonel Wooten, chairman of the Spillways Board, pointed out that Simmesport and Melville, two small communities on the Atchafalaya, "are the only two towns of any consequence at all which would have to be sacrificed." He added, "There is this little village of Atchafalaya, which consists merely of a house or two; nothing of any great consequence" (in US Congress, House 1927a, pt. 3, 1935).

Rebutting the Corps, Louisiana's state engineer, Harry Jacobs, acknowledged that use of the Atchafalaya seemed "unavoidable," but finally came to the aid of residents there and expressed interest in minimizing

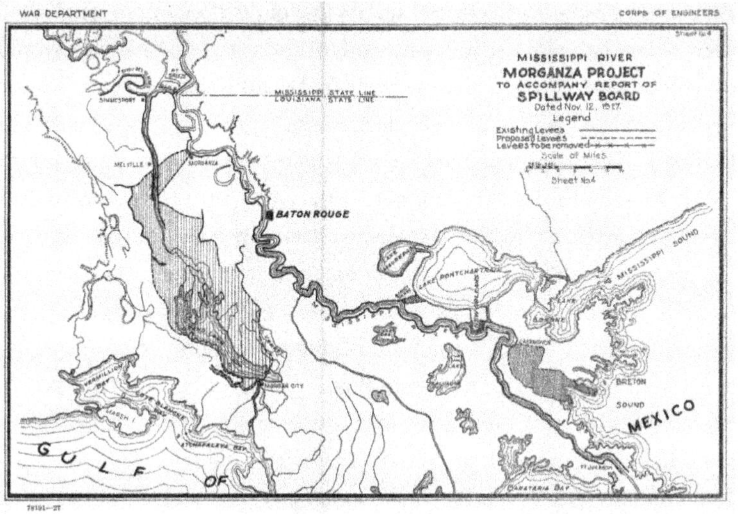

Fig. 4.4. US Army Corps of Engineers' proposed outlets following 1927 flood. USACE 1927.

disruption to landowners. He portrayed the basin as "developed" based on his observations that farmers had been abandoning land for the previous twenty years and that land referred to by the Corps as swamp was in cultivation twenty-five years before (in US Congress, House 1931b, 137–38). Two residents from Iberville Parish, midway down the basin, submitted an affidavit itemizing numerous plantations abandoned due to increasing heights of floodwaters through the Atchafalaya (Grace and Kleinpeter in US Congress, House 1931a, 139). They feared the Jadwin Plan would dislocate additional agricultural activities in the basin. A landowner from St. Martin Parish, further down the basin, claimed that much of the territory considered swamp at the time was productive cotton land in the nineteenth century. With increased reliance on the basin for flood control, "those people have been driven away from their homes" (Martin [basin resident] in US Congress, House 1930, pt. 1, 35). Yet these arguments revealed that abandonment of land had already taken place, thereby diminishing the potential for future damages.

The state countered the Jadwin Plan with a proposal to build reservoirs in Arkansas that would perforce dislocate farmers along the Arkansas River. Jacobs argued that Arkansas should have to bear a portion of the social costs for flood control since some of the floodwaters originated there. Expressing loyalty to his home state, he noted that his plan would only flood two or three small villages in Arkansas, and relocation costs likely would be low (Jacobs in US Congress, House 1931b, 26–27). Apparently, what was unacceptable for Louisiana residents was quite appropriate for those in the neighboring state. James Kemper, a New Orleans civil engineer, testified, "In the Atchafalaya Basin, by confining the flood to the upper river thousands of acres of the most productive lands in Pointe Coupee, Avoyelles, and St. Landry Parishes would be saved (in U.S. Congress, House 1931b, 115). In support of the state's claims of extensive development in the basin, the State Board of Engineers reported that in 1929 there were 1.7 million acres in the basin and that over 172,000 acres were in cultivation—about 10 percent—with a value of approximately $18.6 million (US Congress, House 1931a, 989). Beyond the direct value of land, Kemper also argued that damages to inundated property could reach $150 million (US Congress, House 1931b, 119). Advocates for protecting the basin sought to highlight the costs of using the spillway.

Absent a comparable conflict, work proceeded quickly on the smaller Bonnet Carré Spillway, and it reached completion in 1931 (fig. 4.5). There were a few large landowners displaced as well as some African American settlements. Meanwhile, the shrill opposition to the Jadwin Plan for use of the Atchafalaya prompted Congress to consider a revised option. The reworked design avoided impacting some of the best agricultural lands in the northern portion of the basin in Pointe Coupee Parish, introduced the construction of the Morganza Spillway near Old River to assure controlled flow of water into the basin, and called for the creation of an artificial outlet above Morgan City to protect that city and neighboring "improved lands" (US Congress, House 1941, 7; Arnold 1988). Absent adequate public participation in the initial planning, criticism from influential landowners prompted adjustments. The Overton Act of 1936 set this revised plan into motion. All in all, a lesser portion of the Atchafalaya would serve as a floodway, and Morgan City would receive new protection, but that did not alter the impacts to those who lived and worked in the basin itself. As a conciliatory action, Congress authorized payment of flowage easements to landowners in the basin (Reuss 1998, 188). While farmers received some compensation, the outlets in the new

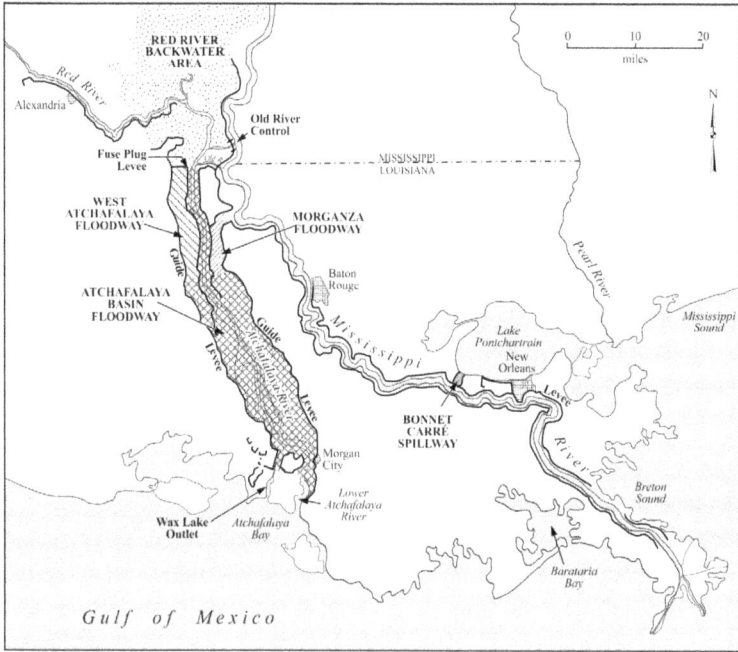

Fig. 4.5. Floodways and levees as constructed by the Corps of Engineers by the mid-1950s. Map by Mary Lee Eggart.

flood-control system displaced risk and initiated impacts to coastal fisheries when put into use. There was no concessions or compensation offered to the fisherfolk who were not heard from in the public hearings.

IMPACTS OF SPILLWAYS ON MARGINALIZED CITIZENS

The initial impact of the 1936 plan was that the Corps began acquiring easements for the Morganza and West Atchafalaya floodways. Louisiana residents retained ownership to their lands, but use restrictions discouraged development, although some livestock grazing continued. Work on the Atchafalaya Floodway structures moved forward fitfully, particularly as World War II re-prioritized federal spending (Reuss 1998, 199–203). Eventually the Morganza Floodway reached completion in 1955 (fig. 4.5).

The post-1927 flood-protection efforts that include the floodway and levee enlargement prompted several distinct arenas of population displacement that touched people outside New Orleans. Levee enlargement along the Mississippi River forced the dislocation of numerous rural and small-town residences and businesses. Bayou Goula, a rural settlement between the towns of Plaquemine and White Castle, had numerous structures in the path of the footprint for the broader levees. An inventory compiled by the Atchafalaya Levee District tabulated some ninety-two dwellings that would need to be moved along with sixteen stores, plus other barns, offices, churches, and a theater. This dislocation did not imply long-distance movement but re-situating structures outside the path of the new levees. Property owners feared that they would be unable to "re-establish" the building in their former condition and that ultimately they would have to demolish many of them. Owners of small agricultural tracts expressed concern that they would lose valuable acreage to the new levees. Taken together, the potentially displaced residents, both large planters and African Americans, pointed out that the destruction of taxable structures and productive farmlands would reduce the assessed value of land and undermine the Levee Board's income. They also argued that there was ample land on the river side of the levee where the wider footprint would not force dislocations, but for numerous reasons this argument was ignored (Bayou Goula Residents 1932). Partially as a result, Bayou Goula and other similar settlements are much smaller today than they were in 1927.

In the Atchafalaya Basin the impacts were both direct and immediate, but also protracted and indirect. Percy Viosca observed that the levees denied much of the adjacent wetlands of valuable nutrients and thus diminished an important food supply and economic pursuits (1927 and 1928). Small houseboat communities lined the larger bodies of water in the basin (fig. 4.6). Comprised of fluid populations, the communities had residents who fished, trapped, and made a living off nearby natural resources but did not own land. With increasing flow through the basin, Grand Lake, a water body formed by the Atchafalaya, began to fill with sediment, deposited as the river lost velocity when it entered still water. According to Jim Delahoussaye, who has interviewed numerous former residents, there were at least half a dozen houseboat communities around Grand Lake in 1920. By the late 1940s, the upper half of Grand Lake was largely a delta which continued to grow through the 1950s and completely severed

Fig. 4.6. Houseboat community near Morgan City, 1945. Fishing families commonly lived aboard houseboats on the margins of the inland lakes in the lower Atchafalaya Basin. Standard Oil (New Jersey) Collection, Acc. No. 25964, Archives and Special Collections, University of Louisville.

direct cross-lake transportation. With sedimentation, fish populations declined and livelihoods suffered. As an adjustment, fishing families began the arduous task of hauling their houseboats over the levee and establishing land-based communities. They continued to fish part-time with the use of outboard motors, and using automobiles they could find supplemental work in the sugar mills and oilfields (Delahoussaye 2010 and 2014). In addition to changing environmental conditions, public policy during the first half of the twentieth century tended to favor the propagation of sport fish and placed limits on commercial fishing (Colten 2014b). Thus, the marginalized fisherfolk who were well adapted to the fluvial environmental had to adapt to changes prompted by flood-protection and conservation policies.

The Bonnet Carré Spillway was functional by the mid-1930s, and the Corps opened it for the first time in 1937. The structure consists of a massive insert in the levee about thirty miles upstream from New Orleans. A series of large wooden panels, or "needles," can be raised to allow floodwaters from the Mississippi River to flow between a pair of "guide levees" into the Lake Pontchartrain Basin and from there into the Gulf of Mexico.

As much as 250,000 cubic feet per second can flow from the river when the system is fully opened. The initial test of the Bonnet Carré in 1937 allowed 81 percent of its capacity to pass through the lake toward the Gulf. When opened next in 1945, the Corps lifted all the needles and permitted the full 250,000 cubic feet per second to leave the river. This allowed fresh water to flood into the brackish lake and beyond into the Mississippi Sound off the coast of Mississippi. This area was a major oyster-harvesting territory, and oystermen complained that the combined effect of lower salinity and sediment deposition obliterated their cultivated bivalves (US Congress, House 1946b).

Politicians and scientists from Louisiana and Mississippi testified to Congress that the 1945 use of the Bonnet Carré was hugely detrimental to a thriving seafood industry. Biloxi mayor C. A. Delacruz reported that the oyster industry supported twenty-five canners and another sixty raw dealers. He claimed that the Bonnet Carré opening in 1945 "killed all our oysters" (Delacruz in US Congress, House 1946b, 21). The impact reduced production by 80 percent, he argued, and to restore the beds would take two to three years (23). A representative of the US Fish and Wildlife Service conducted a survey of the affected region which supported the mayor's comments with its findings of "practically 100 percent mortality" in the major oyster areas impacted by the release (Hopkins in US Congress, House 1946b, 26–27). A contrasting opinion offered by Percy Viosca, a highly respected government biologist, in reference to the 1937 opening of the spillway clouded the issue. He claimed that, in 1937, "The effect of the spillway was, on the whole, very beneficial because of its fertilizing effect on the waters of Lakes Pontchartrain and Borgne, and Mississippi Sound." He claimed that the fresh waters stimulated the organisms at the lower end of the food chain and this contributed to increased populations of mullet, menhaden, and shad: "The commercial shrimp crop taken in Lake Borgne and Mississippi Sound was the greatest since the shrimp trawl was introduced in 1917." Benefits, according to Viosca, were not limited to more mobile fish and shrimp. He reported a "fine set of oysters" in Mississippi Sound (Viosca [US Biological Survey] quoted in US Congress, House 1946b, 96). Of course the 1937 opening did not release as much fresh water as the 1945 event.

In addition, although not yet completed, the Morganza Floodway carried additional flow during the 1945 high water. Structures directed the Atchafalaya flow into coastal water bodies where local residents cultivated oysters. Freshwater destroyed these beds too. Louisiana officials estimated the losses in Terrebonne Parish at $331,000. Most of the oyster fishermen were "completely wiped out of the oyster business by these losses" (O'Neal [Louisiana Department of Wildlife and Fisheries] in US Congress, House 1946b, 79–81, quote at 81).

Louisiana Congressman Hale Boggs appealed for compensation this way: "the only question presented to this committee; whether or not an incident of national flood control which has fallen most heavily upon people who are least able to bear it should be borne by those people who are without funds and who are small operators, dependent upon their oyster crops form one season to the next, or whether it should be a problem for all of the people of the United States in connection with our great program of flood control" (in US Congress, House 1947, 8). This is an unusual entreaty for aid for the fisher families and may have used their hardships to extract more dollars for the full flood-protection system. Despite the pleas of Congressman Boggs, Congress denied any compensation to oyster fishermen following the event (Boggs to Stern 1949).

Flood-control practices continued to damage natural resources in order to protect urban populations and commercial activity with subsequent uses of the spillways. An exceptionally high river stage in 1973 prompted the first use of both the Morganza and Bonnet Carré spillways. A partial opening the Morganza Floodway allowed floodwaters from the Mississippi to inundate over 1 million acres in the basin. Water covered some 24,000 acres of agricultural land and caused an estimated $1.3 million in damage to crops, livestock, and pasture. The major cities and urban infrastructure escaped the high water. Only about 500 acres of developed urban and rural land suffered inundation, but the costs to urban land uses exceeded $15 million (excluding oil and gas industries, which were not included) (US Army Corps of Engineers, New Orleans District 1974, 126–28). The differential costs suggest that the emphasis on urban protection was cost effective.

Nonetheless, damage to the oyster beds by freshwater discharges from the outlets in 1973 was substantial and had profound impacts on family fishing operations and the small businesses that processed and distributed oysters. Reefs near the mouths of the Atchafalaya and Mississippi rivers suffered "serious mortalities," while "widespread mortalities resulted in the Mississippi Sound" according to one Corps of Engineers' sponsored research project (GSRI 1973, 44). A second report indicated that the combined discharges "had a disastrous effect on oyster grounds." The impacts were twofold: high mortality rates and closing of viable oyster beds and loss of income to oyster fishermen. Mortality rates were above 50 percent for the rich Lake Borgne beds. For the entire state's coastal areas, 70 percent of the oyster leases investigated suffered mortalities, with 45 percent reporting "heavy mortalities" (St. Amant 1973, 16–20). Downplaying the impact of the Morganza Floodway, researchers concluded that oyster mortality near the mouth of the Atchafalaya was already underway due to enlarged discharges by that distributary, but in reference to other commercial species it noted that "there is little evidence that flood conditions are detrimental to commercial catches in the area" (GSRI 1973, 55). Thus state officials largely dismissed the overall significance of the freshwater diversion while also pointing out that reliance on oysters was a recent adaptation to conditions created by the newly completed spillway—not traditional patterns (St. Amant 1973). To the oyster fishermen, damages to their livelihood, again, provided a powerful reminder that managing the river was not done with their interests at the forefront of decision-making. Looking for a helping hand, Louisiana's oyster growers sought federal disaster assistance but were turned down by Congress again (Vujnovich to Boggs 1975). It was not until 1994 that Congress authorized a disaster-declaration process for damages to fisheries due to natural hazards (Upton 2013).

Despite the lack of federal aid to restore the oyster beds, cultivating and harvesting these bivalves remained a prominent activity in the coastal waters during the 1970s and 1980s. Meanwhile, a major coastal infrastructure project moved forward to address changing environmental conditions and aid oyster production. Louisiana officials, with the backing of oyster fishermen, worked to install a freshwater diversion from the Mississippi River into Breton Sound near the site of the 1927 Caernarvon breach (fig. 2.2). The purpose was to deliver more fresh water, and to offset the increasing salinity in Breton Sound that was the result of coastal land loss and a contributing factor in declining oyster production. When put into operation in the early 1990s, it delivered sufficient fresh water to create favorable conditions in public oyster seed grounds and increase productivity there. However, the diversion lowered salinity in some private oyster leases and prompted the leaseholders to file suit against the state and later the federal government. Plaintiffs claimed that lowering salinity of their leases interfered with their livelihoods and was a "takings." The court ruled in favor of the oystermen, awarding damages of $48 million. A similar second suit resulted in a comparable ruling with awards to leaseholders totaling $662 million. The costs from these decisions looked disastrous for the state until the Louisiana Supreme Court reversed the lower court's ruling. The Louisiana Supreme Court sided with the state on the basis of "hold harmless" clauses contained in leases issued after 1989. In the eyes of the court, because the state had created and operated the leasing system, the insertion of clauses holding it harmless for changing environmental conditions exempted the state from liability. Legal scholars note that this decision indicates that there is now a precedent that could offer similar protection against environmental damages caused by coastal restoration projects (Keithly and Wilkins 2006; *Avenal v. State of Louisiana* 1999 and 2004).

High floodwaters flowed down the Mississippi River in 2011 and for only the second time prompted the opening of both the Bonnet Carré and the Morganza spillways. According to the Corps of Engineers, coastal areas affected by fresh water flowing out of Lake Pontchartrain into the Mississippi Sound and Breton Sound suffered oyster mortality rates of 85 percent. Estimates placed damage to the oyster industry in Mississippi at $60 million from that diversion (US Army Corps of Engineers 2012, v-22). To aid their fishing communities, both Louisiana and Mississippi officials requested a fisheries disaster declaration. Federal authorities determined that diversions from the Bonnet Carré did create a disaster for oyster and crabbing operations in Mississippi, but not for shrimping or fisheries in Louisiana (Barbour to Locke 2011, Barham to Locke 2011, and Upton 2013).

Impacts from the 2011 flood were also felt within the Atchafalaya Basin. Of the more than 600,000 acres inundated, over 94,000 acres of farmland suffered some damage, and Louisiana officials estimated losses at nearly $45 million (Carlson et al. 2012, 14). Even though over six hundred residences and nine hundred camps were subject to inundation when the spillway was opened in 2011, relatively few saw significant damage (24–25). Nonetheless, evacuation orders prompted many residents to depart for several days. There were additional damages to government and private-sector structures and facilities, but the totals were less than feared (Carlson et al. 2012). New Orleans faced virtually no threats and no damages with the use of the two artificial outlets.

Large-scale infrastructure projects have enduring legacies. Not only do they create path dependency on a historically chosen option, but they have lasting impacts on environmental conditions and people and society. In the lower Mississippi, the city's interests shaped flood protection for New Orleans and riverside industries and agriculture, and these structures have been remarkably effective. The levees, revetments, and outlets, along with ongoing maintenance, have afforded reliable protection from river floods. Yet the environmental impacts have extended into the Atchafalaya Basin, across the coastal wetlands, and into habitats that support marine fisheries. For commercial fishermen in the Atchafalaya Basin, flood-protection systems effectively displaced riverboat communities and prompted families to seek alternate livelihoods. When the Army Corps of Engineers opens outlets, fresh water from the river damages the fixed oyster-farming operations in the Gulf of Mexico. There were accommodations made in planning the Atchafalaya Floodway for farmers, but nothing for the freshwater fishermen. Oyster farmers have been better organized and able to win government assistance in the form of siphons and freshwater diversions to mitigate saltwater intrusion. Nonetheless, river-management decisions have placed the burden of adaptation on those pursuing natural-resource livelihoods and have permitted life in New Orleans, in the large agricultural operations, and for the large industries to continue with fewer demands to adapt.

5

The Public in Public Works
Coping with the Coastal Crisis

Through multiple phases of managing the environment, Louisiana has privileged certain perspectives. Economic interests, allied with engineering experts, dominated the public hearing process and guided the design and construction of the river levees. Local political and economic interests were the primary influences in the decisions to breach the levee in 1927 and to install outlets. Again in 1947 and 1965, demands from local leaders at public hearings drove the planning for hurricane-protection levees for the New Orleans region. In the 1950s, Louisiana fishermen had to do an end run around uninterested state officials in order to mobilize an interstate pollution investigation and hearing (Colten 2006). A vigorous campaign by small-town officials prompted this federal intervention. As the state and the nation expanded their attention to protecting the environment in the 1960s and thereafter, new protocols for public engagement opened new opportunities for input from citizens. The environmental impact statement requirement in the National Environmental Protection Act (NEPA) of 1970 offered new opportunities for citizen and local government involvement in planning projects using federal funds. Since that time there have been additional stages of public engagement/ participation that moved from stakeholder engagement to public participation. Opportunities for public involvement in Louisiana's coastal management efforts have evolved since 1970.

Prior to the passage of NEPA and its expansion of input into federal projects, Louisiana had a history of highly selective input into environmental management decisions. This reflected political and economic disparities rooted in social inequities and racial segregation, poor education, and political cronyism. While federal policy opened new channels, Louisiana's political culture and the burdens arising from social inequities mitigated, but did not deny, their use or attempts to move beyond the initial opportunities.

NEPA required a multistage environmental impact statement (EIS) procedure that involved interagency review along with public involvement throughout (Greenberg 2013, 3, 5–6). Early implementation of the NEPA process was fraught with problems. Planning for some projects was well underway when the new law went into effect, and some agencies which had previously had little interest in environmental protection undertook the EIS procedures with less enthusiasm than some of their counterparts. It was a new, complex, and sometimes costly step in carrying out an agency's mission that staff sometimes resisted initially (Mazmanian and Nienaber 1979). Not surprisingly, public objections to EIS findings became a common outcome, and in the 1990s the federal government created a conflict resolution procedure to deal with struggles that ensued from an approved EIS. Ultimately the courts became, and remain, the final arbiter (Greenberg 2013, 7). Criticisms of the EIS process have been compiled in several forums. One point of criticism has been its failure to fully incorporate public comments (Anastasia 2001). This imperfect system framed public involvement in environmental management projects into the twenty-first century.

During the rollout of the National Environmental Protection Act's EIS procedures, Louisiana found itself in the midst of controversies with the still-evolving public involvement procedures. One of the early test cases of the EIS process sparked controversy over the hurricane-protection levees planned for the New Orleans area after Hurricane Betsy in 1965. Design work had begun before the passage of NEPA, and the EIS was an add-on well into the process. The Corps's 1974 environmental impact statement contained reviews by related agencies and approved a design for a levee and a pair of gates across the eastern end of Lake Pontchartrain. Fishermen opposed the "barrier plan" and argued that the Corps inadequately addressed their concerns and feared that the structures would alter water quality in the brackish water body and diminish the fisheries there. Residents in the parish north of the lake took the position that the barriers would deflect storm surge into their communities. This led to a court battle and a decision by the Corps to revamp the design and eliminate the barriers. The Lake Pontchartrain legal battle was not a consensus-building process. Subsequent battles over the federal hurricane-levee system for the west bank of New Orleans encountered stiff opposition from local governments, centering on wetland protection, and greatly delayed the completion of the hurricane protection system there (Colten 2009). These local conflicts reflect the foibles in the process as federal agencies attempted to put a policy into action. Local authorities and citizens have embraced the process when it allows them to bend federal projects to their own design. It also allows local political leaders to chastise organizations such as the Corps of Engineers when projects do not mesh with local economic objectives.

National-level assessments of the EIS procedure point out that, beyond the technical challenges, a key sticking point remains achieving a public consensus. Values, beliefs, and convictions among diverse stakeholders often contribute to more vexing challenges than technical or scientific issues (Vicente and Partidario 2006, Person 2006). While retrospective reviews laud the basic purposes of the legislation and support public comment (Council on Environmental Quality 1997), the process has been under fire in conservative political circles as an unnecessary and costly delay. As a deeply conservative state, Louisiana has a mixed history with the EIS process. It has provided a tool to local leaders to reorient federal projects—such as the hurricane-protection levees for southeast Louisiana. Additionally, it has offered cover for state political leaders who sought to deflect popular dissatisfaction with federal projects. A former Louisiana CPRA head, Garret Graves, was well known for his savage criticisms of all things done by the Corps of Engineers. In many cases, his critiques shrouded the state's preceding advocacy for the very efforts he criticized, and that brought substantial federal investment to the state. Nonetheless, the EIS procedure provided a more formalized public involvement process with implications for Louisiana's environmental management procedures.

At the national level, frustration with the EIS process prompted the rise of "stakeholder engagement." This term erupted in the lexicon in the 1980s, and the process seeks to correct shortcomings of the traditional and often legally mandated public involvement, or formal events that allowed comments on plans that for all intents and purposes were final—or nearly so. Engagement sought to enable a dialogue earlier in the process of developing plans and policies. In addition, stakeholder engagement deliberately seeks to bring multiple constituencies into the planning procedure to help guide the selection of priorities and ensure public buy-in. Yet, in the public hearing, EIS, and stakeholder engagement procedures, experts have controlled the science and engineering that underlies planning and implementation of projects. Experts shaped the technical components of the plans and which served as the basis for ensuing conversations. In the engagement process, an additional layer of expertise is commonly used. Task forces and advisory committees, composed of specialists and paid advocates, play prominent and clearly defined roles in reviewing plans as different stages of development. Yet these support groups often bypass or underrepresent marginalized citizens. Restricting the input on the meaningful phases of plan development to experts minimizes public understanding and public critique. Technical experts have often called for better science education to address the public's inability to grasp some details, while ignoring their responsibility to communicate effectively to those without their technical backgrounds and to bring them into the planning process more fully.

One of the general weaknesses of the NEPA protocol was its tendency to rely heavily on experts and neglect the general public, although it allowed activists with expertise to inject their concerns into the discussions. Advocates for a more inclusive process have pushed for methods that fall under the label of public participatory or collaborative participation since the 1990s (Innes and Booher 2004; O'Brien and McIvor 2007; Yang and Callahan 2007; Kindon, Pain, and Kesby 2010; DeLyser and Sui 2014). These methods seek more than mere attendance at public forums, selection of priorities from a suite of options in the scoping process, or comments on draft documents. Eric Higgs, specifically addressing ecological restoration, notes that reliance on technological expertise moves restoration away from collaborative approaches (2003). As long as the forum for public engagement remains in the domain of science, technical expertise is privileged and diminishes robust and meaningful public participation. This concern is one reason Superfund remediation procedures sometimes provided funding for local communities to hire their own experts to bridge the technical expertise gap.

By definition, a robust and fully collaborative, participatory method strives to bring citizens into the process at the earliest stages of environmental management decision making (before decisions are made), use direct dialogue between specialists and citizen groups to educate the public to the technical nuances of the projects, build institutional capacity for citizen groups, and regard citizen input as crucial to defining the goals and outcomes of public investments in environmental management (Innes and Booher 2004). The federal government sought to enlarge public participation opportunities in planning to restore the Florida Everglades beginning in the 1990s (US Government Accounting Office 1995). Louisiana's coastal management agencies, too, have sought to expand participatory methods in its recent plans (CPRA 2012, 2017b). Although present, these methods have been used modestly. Nonetheless, engagement and belated participation have expanded over the years.

An auxiliary component of both public engagement and public participatory methods has been public comment. This process offers a phase where the public can submit comments on a near-final plan. In some of Louisiana recent master plans the pages devoted to reprinting public comments exceeds the plans themselves, while the influence of these after-the-fact comments is negligible. Public comment assumes an informed and already engaged population willing to wade through draft reports. Comments often reflect the observations of experts excluded from the initial planning. An additional shortcoming is that public comments seldom facilitate a dialogue and offer a window dressing for participation. The state touts its receipt of comments, which tend to reveal highly localized self-interest and less concern for the wider plan (CPRA 2017b, comments section appendix).

THE PUBLIC AND THE LAND LOSS CRISIS

Early measurements of coastal land loss by geographers and geologists occurred as early as the 1950s (see chap. 3; Morgan and Larimore 1957), but by the 1970s and 1980s persuasive maps illustrated an on-going process (Gagliano, Meyer-Arendt, and Wicker 1981). Interest in the process was most acute within the coastal science community, particularly at Louisiana State University. Despite Louisiana's jaded history with public input, local environmental advocates sought to expand the emerging knowledge about and involvement with the coastal land loss issue and efforts to protect it. Mapping the process had been funded by state and federal dollars, but mobilizing public awareness lagged behind the discoveries. With little incentive to expose this situation based on their past management practices, government bodies did not mobilize to inform the public. The ad hoc CRCL, quite contrary to prior efforts, took on that task. It recruited a diverse group of individuals and organizations to join what eventually became a formal organization in 1988 (Hanny 1995 and CRCL 1989). Initially guided by a group of lawyers working on environmental litigation for national NGOs and tapping the expertise of scientists, its initial roster included several national environmental groups such as the Sierra Club, the National Wildlife Federation, and local Audubon Club chapters.

Most of these groups and their leaders had been involved with coastal issues already. Several religious organizations participated, along with a local Native American group, several Louisiana state agencies, fishermen's organizations, and coastal scientists (CRCL 1987). The objective was to build a team of technical experts, experienced environmental advocates, and grassroots representatives. Absent from this group were representatives of the oil and gas industry, shipping, and owners of large wetland territories. As recounted by David Hanny, it sought to deploy science in the service of public policy and to push reluctant state agencies to take more assertive actions to restore the coast (Hanny 1995, 78). It stands out in that it did not mirror some of the strategic goals of national environmental groups, although drawing on their existing talents and institutional strengths. It also brought to the fore coastal scientists frustrated with inaction by government bodies. This alliance, along with deeper public involvement, represented a new approach to addressing the land loss issue.

In 1987, the incipient organization released a draft of its goals for coastal restoration, and the subtitle clearly asserted that it was "A Citizens' Program for Saving the Mississippi River Delta Region." The draft represented the research and experience of more than two dozen scientists and laypersons and had been through a round of comments from "governments, fishermen's associations, research institutions, environmental and conservation clubs, civic clubs, religious organizations, coastal landowners, scientific consulting firms and private businesses and industry" (CRCL 1987, ii). Although presented as a grassroots movement, the authors were primarily experienced, professional environmental advocates working with scientists based in area universities with research programs focused on the state's coastal setting. Nonetheless, CRCL deliberately involved local constituencies that had been overlooked in more traditional public hearings—namely faith-based groups and fishermen's organizations. The document appeared in a final form in 1989 (CRCL 1989) and indicated, once again, that its contents reflected the input of the same groups noted in the draft, along with "industry." It called for action by the state, the federal government, and citizens. In particular, the document declared that "environmental and civic groups, churches, commercial and sports fishing organizations, hunting and trapping organizations, landowners and coastal businesses, and industry organizations must play a central role in the design and implementation of a comprehensive and effective state and federal plan" (22). This statement suggests the CRCL sought a collaborative and fully participatory approach, and its origins reflect a bottom-up and more inclusive process than traditional public hearings. Nonetheless, it was an informal process compared to other more recent public engagement procedures (Kemp 2017).

Although the coalition reached out to industry and landowners for comments on its draft, and its plan attributed land loss to natural subsidence of the delta, it noted the relatively recent increase in the land loss rate was due to "man-induced" factors. It squarely placed responsibility on economic pursuits in the coastal zone, namely navigation, flood control, and oil and gas production. The document identifies two major causes of the existing rate of land loss: "dramatic reduction in inputs of Mississippi River sediment into the coastal zone" (due to levees that induce sediment starvation) and the cumulative effect of "the construction of navigation and access canals" which contributed to saltwater intrusion, accelerated erosion, and impoundment of marsh land (CRCL 1989, 16). This blunt assignment of culpability to the shipping and mineral industries, and the Corps of Engineers that oversaw the levee system, was a bold statement that reflected almost no input from the state's two leading economic powers. The three core goals of the plan were to: use diversions to enhance sediment and fresh water to the coastal zone, use dredged material for repair or restoration of wetlands, and drastically reduce and phase out canal construction or expansion (17). These goals rested on scientific research more than on public opinion, but public acceptance of this science was critical to the coalition's efforts and its subsequent role in advancing legislation.

As the state moved forward with legislation on coastal protection and congressmen pushed legislation at the federal level, the CRCL's influence was obvious, particularly in terms of the causes of coastal damage. In an effort to demonstrate its commitment to the state's perilous situation, the legislature passed the Coastal Wetlands, Conservation, Restoration, and Management Act, or Act 6, in 1989. It dedicated state dollars to restoration projects and made a portion of state funds available for cost sharing with state/federal restoration projects. In order to support these efforts, the legislature directed a portion of the state's revenue from oil and gas to a wetlands trust fund, which won popular support as a constitutional amendment in 1989 (Hanny 1995, 119). This was not a new tax or an increase, but a redirection of funds already being collected. Although the tax raised only a modest sum that sharply declined over the ensuing years, the statewide vote in support of the amendment illustrates the effectiveness of the coalition's experts in educating the public and the persuasiveness of its appeal. The oil and gas industry were also alerted to the prospect of legislators eyeing mineral revenues to fund the process to correct damage this industry had contributed to (without a new tax on the industry). The general population had a powerful voice in the process. Also of note, the legislation created a Wetlands Conservation and Restoration Task Force which opened the door for more direct participation by those accused of creating the problem in the first place: oil and gas and shipping interests (Hanny 1995, Hebert 1997, 1171–72). The task force's mandated responsibility was to develop a "comprehensive approach to restore and prevent the loss of coastal wetlands in Louisiana" (LCWCRTF 1993, v).

Moving beyond the state, Senator John Breaux worked for several years to pass federal legislation that would aid the state's efforts. A core of this strategy was elevating a local problem to a national concern. Testimony by Louisiana's delegation hammered home this theme that recalled the strategy used to garner national support for flood control (O'Neill 2006, Reuss 1998). In their congressional testimony, Louisiana's elected officials noted three major causes for wetland loss. Two of them were cast as directly related to the national economy. River management for navigation and flood control as well as oil and gas development had implications beyond the lower river territory (US Congress, House 1990, testimony by Breaux 3–4, Tauzin 12–14, Boggs 6–7). According to Louisiana spokespersons, the state was sacrificing its wetlands to advance national economic prosperity. The third cause identified by Congressman Tauzin was human-caused climate change and sea-level rise (US Congress, House 1990, 12). The elected officials had embraced and articulated the key causes identified by the CRCL. Paul Kemp represented the CRCL in this congressional hearing, and he made the case that Louisiana's wetlands were a "national treasure"—indirectly equating them to the Florida Everglades, which had earned designation as a national park (McCally 1999, Colten 2014b). He also emphasized that wetland restoration was about preserving lives, livelihoods, and ways of life (US Congress, House 1990, Kemp 26–27). Inexplicitly, at this stage no representatives from shipping, mineral, or landowners testified. Congress passed the CWPPRA in 1990 and established a funding stream from non-mineral-related sources that complemented the state's dedicated funds. It also established a technical task force that has met regularly since 1991 (USACE 1991–2017). Nationalizing the problem proved effective in gaining public support.

By 1993, the Coastal Conservation and Restoration Task Force had assembled its initial plan with input from the legislated federal agencies (Corps of Engineers, Environmental Protection Agency, Department of the Interior, Department of Commerce, Department of Agriculture) and the Louisiana Governor's Office. Constituted this way, the primary expertise resided in the federal agencies staffed with scientists and engineers and with a technical expert from the governor's office. In addition, the task force explicitly created a process for "public participation." It provided for involvement of local officials, landowners, farmers, sportsmen, commercial fishermen, oil and gas developers, navigation interests, and environmental organizations (LCWCRTF 1993, 3). Among the groups were the CRCL and its diverse membership, but also on a similar level were two oil and gas associations and two groups representing navigation (LCWCRTF 1993, appendix J, 1). The Citizen Participation Group was created to "promote citizen participation and involvement in formulating Priority Project Lists and the restoration plan" (3). Several stages of public meetings were conducted during the planning process in locations across the coastal parishes. The 1993 plan touts that the task force held sixty-five public meetings leading to the document's preparation. The public forums allowed seventeen organizations in the Citizen Participation Group to receive briefings on projects developed by the task force, and they helped prioritize projects. The next step enabled more direct public involvement through "scoping meetings" to identify specific wetland problems and to solicit solutions to them. "Nearly all of the ideas presented in those meetings" reportedly were incorporated into the plan (appendix J, 1–2).

Subsequent meetings included intensive three-day meetings for the task force to formulate a viable plan, and it was in these gatherings that ideas from the scoping meetings were folded into the plan. Still another round of public meetings followed, and the task force solicited public comments on the plans. In an era of increasing attention to "stakeholders," the term appears only once in five-hundred-page document, even though the organizations that participated were in fact stakeholders. Finally, a formal public hearing was held to review the environmental impact statement prepared for the plan. The plan contents reflect a dominant influence of the technical experts with an intended audience of technical experts. This type of content was essential, but there was no companion document for the general educated population, although the task force assembled a program for ongoing public interaction (LCWCRTF 1993, exhibit 2, 6).

With an emphasis on land loss as a national concern and the more prominent role of economic interests in the engagement process, a subtle shift in land loss culpability emerges. The task force's document presents the economic infrastructure as an important local asset threatened by land loss and as worthy of protection as the ecological resources. Modest mention of cultural resources, mainly as a tourism asset, also appears (LCWCRTF 1993, 19–22). The report notes, "The primary causes of wetland loss in coastal Louisiana have been understood for some time; they include subsidence, global sea-level rise, sediment deprivation, and hydrologic alteration" (24). The authors present subsidence and sea-level rise as "natural" processes and soften the terminology associated with the diversion of sediment (from starvation to deprivation) and canal building to hydrologic alteration. In its more detailed descriptions, the report points out that there is a natural component to these processes and turns to passive voice to obscure the responsibilities. Specifically, sediment deprivation "*is affected* by development of continuous river levee systems that prevent overbank flooding and crevasse development." And hydrologic alteration "*is affected* by thousands of miles of dredged channels and associated levees that alter hydrology, sedimentation, and salinity regimes" (25; emphasis added). The reason behind this shift in tone is not known, but while acknowledging levees and canals, the reports does not tie particular organizations or industries to these actions as prior reports had done.

The next landmark document in the coastal restoration effort was *Coast 2050* (LCWCRTF 1998). It reflected growing concern, rising to the level of alarm, with the "catastrophic proportions" of land loss. Despite its shrill warning, it takes a less aggressive stance towards oil and gas and shipping. In the opening passages it states that the causes were the "effects of natural processes like subsidence and storms" and reduces "human actions" to secondary status. It also presented sea-level rise as less certain: "The loss could be greater, especially if worst-case scenario projections of sea-level rise are realized" (1). By asserting there was "no single cause" for land loss, it aligned itself with previous studies, but ultimately softened the accusations of earlier reports and congressional testimony. Subsidence receives extensive discussion and frames the core cause as a natural, not human-induced, process. The report acknowledges the processes of sediment capture in upstream impoundments and also deprivation of sediment to the marshes due to levees, but does not specify that human actions are the primary and underlying causes. Faulting and sealevel rise appear as related natural processes contributing to subsidence

(33–39). Storms are cast as a separate contributing factor and another "natural" force particularly damaging to barrier islands. Canals, identified in previous plans as a dominant cause, receive the designation of "hydrologic alterations." While this is a more inclusive term for a host of related human influences, the report offers very little detailed information on the extent of this factor (40). The issue of canals and navigation remained prominent concerns among advocacy groups but receded in the official document. This adjustment reflects a major deviation from prior publications and public interests and suggests the rising influence of oil and gas and shipping interests in framing the issue. By broadening participation to more directly include the major economic interests, the document's language became more general in terms of the primary influences and emphasized natural processes.

The 1998 plan proclaimed to offer a new approach by integrating the numerous efforts and plans that preceded it. At its core, however, it perpetuated an approach dedicated to ecosystem restoration, relying on technical expertise (LCWCRTF 1998, 2). As with the earlier efforts, expertise included participation from the local academic science community with decades of experience in Louisiana's coastal ecology. The report acknowledged the importance of ecosystems to society but did not elevate social processes into its planning to the same level as its efforts to manage biophysical processes. It also inserted the term "sustainable" into the title, suggesting human actions to restore the coast would produce a viable, long-term, and self-perpetuating ecology.

The document presented a more fully articulated public engagement process and emphasized the importance of consensus building and the involvement of diverse interests. More than the CRCL document and even more so than the 1993 task force plan, government agencies played a central role in shaping the technical content, and they constituted the Strategic Working Group. Parish and other local organizations made up the Coastal Zone Management Working Group. And there were four Regional Planning Teams to develop plans for different coastal regions. A series of public meetings were offered at different stages of the planning process and mirrored in many respects the early 1990s gatherings. In effect, technical experts shared their understanding of the situation and ongoing processes, and the public helped determine which issues were most important. The public also provided input on the draft plan (LCWCRTF 1998, 11–18). While allowing ample opportunity for public engagement, the planning process centered on ecosystem management—a technical enterprise. With the initial planning housed in government agencies, the process privileged experts and their representations of ecosystem processes. In this round of planning, the mantle of "objectivity" naturalized the processes that were creating the crisis and withdrew the accusing fingers formerly pointed at oil and gas, shipping, and the Corps of Engineers. This discursive adjustment is the most significant change in the communication of the land loss situation at this stage.

In the early years of the twenty-first century, a deliberate attempt to elevate the coastal crisis to the national level took shape. Louisiana Governor Mike Foster appointed a committee to recommend changes and new approaches to existing restoration methods. Its 2002 report made the explicit case that a comprehensive plan for the entire coast, rather than piecemeal projects, was essential, and implicitly it provided a rationale for greater involvement by key economic interests in the discussion. It did so by fundamentally by recalibrating which resources were at stake. Although it borrowed the "national treasure" term used by Paul Kemp in congressional testimony in reference to the state's coastal wetlands, it emphasized the wetlands' economic value or ecosystem services and the activities their preservation would sustain. In particular the report devoted attention to storm protection, communities and infrastructure, oil and gas networks, transportation networks, water quality, and fisheries before mentioning the "unique ecosystems" (Committee for the Future of Coastal Louisiana 2002). This focus contrasted with prior reports that had foregrounded wetland ecology.

Following this 2002 report, Louisiana political and business leaders formed a group called America's Wetland Foundation. Relabeling Louisiana's wetlands as "America's" was a deliberate statement to frame the coastal land loss issue as one of national significance and to present economics as the primary reason for preserving the coast. The foundation's members and partners included a wide array of local booster organizations, coastal restoration organizations, and local communities. It sought to translate the technical science of land loss into economic terms in order to mobilize business and industry support for restoration efforts.

Among its most prominent sponsors were oil and gas corporations. Its goal was "to transcend historic and parochial differences for the higher good of saving national environmental and economic assets that support the U.S. economy and provide for domestic energy security" (America's Wetland Foundation 2017). In its basic language, the statement placed saving economic assets on the same plane as environmental ones, but by including "domestic energy security," it clearly revealed its underlying support. It also sought to expand the discussion of coastal restoration to the other Gulf Coast states and coined the phrase "America's Energy Coast," further underscoring the national implications of offshore mineral resources (America's Wetland Foundation 2013). While a prominent force in exposing the land loss crisis, the organization disbanded in early 2020. Throughout its existence, it supported restoration paid for by the government and not by the oil and gas industry.

Into the early years of this century, each successive stage of restoration planning provided for public input and also sought to consolidate the process. Public input remained a form of stakeholder engagement with the planning largely carried out by technical experts in government agencies with assistance from academic scientists and consulting companies. With the exception of the early 1980s efforts by the CRCL, full participatory efforts were absent or anemic. As a follow-up to the *Coast 2050* report, a joint Corps of Engineers and Louisiana effort led to the production of the Louisiana Coastal Area: Ecosystem Restoration Study (USACE, New Orleans District 2004). For more than two years, the agencies charged with preparing the study participated in a multiphase public engagement process. The process allowed for public scoping meetings, stakeholder roundtable discussions, and comments on the draft report (5-1–5-3). The report tabulated the public concerns, and the district engineer offered a set of priority projects based on environmental, social, and economic factors (6-1).

Tragic and massive flooding caused by the failure of protection levees during Hurricanes Katrina and Rita in 2005 inundated about 80 percent of New Orleans and seriously damaged over 105,000 residences of the 188,000 occupied residences (Liu, Fellowes, and Mabanta 2006). The urban responses to that event included bolstering the existing structural protection surrounding New Orleans, but more influential urban-based organizations have voiced even stronger support for projects to restore the state's coastal wetlands. Within the city's protective perimeter, an initial effort to impose an expert-driven plan ran into harsh public backlash, and the city revamped its strategy to allow for a more inclusive, if fragmented, neighborhood-driven planning (Nelson, Ehrenfeuct, and Laska 2007; Olshansky and Johnson 2010). Also in the wake of the 2005 floods, a group of coastal specialists developed a comprehensive strategy labeled "multiple lines of defense" for the wider region. The plan promotes use of natural landscape features such as barrier islands and marshes as initial defenses. Human-made features, including highways and levees, provide additional protection. Raising houses in the coastal areas and within levee rings is another line of defense (Lopez et al. 2005). Even in the wake of the devastating storms, the option to elevate houses has received modest implementation within the New Orleans levee system. In 2015, the city received some 4,200 permit applications to elevate houses or a total equivalent to about 4 percent of the seriously damaged homes (New Orleans Dept. of Safety and Permits 2015). A decade after the storm, many homes remained susceptible to flood damage if water were to top the levees again. The commitment to the multiple lines of defense in order to buffer the city prevails. It defers most costs to the state and adaptive measures to those outside the levees.

Another response within New Orleans's levee system was a revamped water plan. Orchestrated by the Louisiana Office of Community Development and funded with federal grants, a group of experts sought to rethink the city's dilemma of having to pump every drop of water up and out of the city. Drawing on the Dutch concept of "living with water" and aligning with the multiple-lines-of-defense strategy, the plan envisions major alterations to the city's drainage system. The plan calls for retaining water in the soil, to inhibit subsidence, and making room for the storm runoff in the form of wetland and recreational spaces. Launched with great fanfare, this ambitious effort emerged from the collaboration of an impressive group of local, national, and international water management and urban design specialists (Waggoner and Ball 2013). Thus it reflects the expert-driven approach to managing environments and engages with the state restoration plans by virtue of its fundamental reliance on effective coastal wetland restoration beyond the city's defenses.

The devastating impacts of the 2005 hurricanes prompted two important actions at the state level that began a shift toward more robust participatory practices. The Louisiana legislature, in response to federal wishes to consolidate coastal restoration and flood-control activities, reconfigured the state's Wetland Conservation and Restoration Authority into the Coastal Protection and Restoration Authority (CPRA 2017a). Additionally, responding to outside pressure to deploy a rational plan to the recovery efforts and responsibly spend federal recovery dollars, the state launched Louisiana Speaks. It was a considerable outreach program that directly engaged the public in a series of more than one hundred meetings and assembled the results of thousands of surveys to formulate a regional recovery plan for the region (Louisiana Recovery Authority, hereafter LRA 2007). Led by a group of planners, the project assembled several computer-modeled scenarios for future social and ecological conditions. The public engagement allowed "citizens to weigh in on how South Louisiana should approach economic development, which coastal protection and restoration strategies to prioritize, which pattern of future growth and development the region should pursue, and how to balance individual rights with community risk" (LRA 2007, 26). This process allowed them to select among the scenarios projected by the expert teams. In the words of the technical team, citizens were given "clear choices about their future" (18). This endeavor represented a considerable expansion of public engagement, but one that allowed a response to options presented by expert teams. Ultimately, these efforts, along with other studies and reports, contributed to the state's first master plan for a sustainable coast (CPRA 2007).

Creation of the CPRA after Katrina brought staff who had been dispersed among several state agencies with restoration responsibilities under a single administrator. The newly formed state agency received a mandate to prepare a revised comprehensive coastal master plan every five years. Its staff has met that charge with a series of master plans approved by the legislature in 2007, 2012, and 2017 (CPRA 2007, 2012, 2017b). Each contained multiple stages of public input in alignment with such practices elsewhere and a commitment to display a degree of transparency but, like their predecessors, no fully participatory methods shaped the plans.

The 2007 master plan casts the causes underlying land loss as a set of human-induced "changes" that provided specific "benefits," but that also had some "tradeoffs" (or costs). In particular, it noted that levees, canals and channels, and wetland drainage provided flood protection, floodplain development, navigational opportunities, and oil and gas exploration and extraction, and expanded territory for agriculture, industry, and cities. In the past, the desire to boost economic activities justified the changes which produced "unintended effects" (CPRA 2007, 12–13). The tradeoffs were destabilized coastal landscapes, accelerated land loss, and ultimately the shrinking of land area and an increased number of people at risk. This framing of the situation withdraws the accusatory finger and suggests a benign set of actions taken to bolster the state's economy without the recognition of the unintended impacts, even though a state scientist had pointed out some of the problems associated with severing the river from the floodplain in the 1920s (Viosca 1928).

In the wake of the massive 2005 hurricanes, flood protection rose dramatically as a justification for coastal restoration planning. The 2007 master plan's development began with an integrated planning team consisting of nine agency personnel. It conducted public workshops and drafted a report that was subject to the Corps of Engineers for review and was the topic discussed at Louisiana Speaks meetings and fifty stakeholder gatherings (CPRA 2007, 42). Subsequently, state personnel held a workshop that included partner agencies, science advisors, and NGO representatives. One group that was nudged out of this process was university-based scientists who had been deeply involved in prior efforts (Day 2020). Workshops considering a follow-up plan formulation led to the composition of a draft plan that underwent further public review and comment by technical review panels made up of external academic and government scientists, followed by public hearings. This process was far more thoroughly documented than early public engagement efforts (CPRA 2007, appendices B, H). Comparable, although refined and expanded, methods guided the master planning process for the 2012 and 2017 documents (CPRA 2012 and 2017b).

In advance of its 2017 plan, CPRA hosted twenty "community conversations," gave 115 briefings to fifty-five advisory groups, which were followed by four public hearings that included opportunity for conversations with attendees. There was a wide array of public participation among the numerous focus groups, including communities, fisheries, landowners, energy, and navigation interests (CPRA 2017b, 165–67). Separate focus groups for key businesses outnumbered the representation of communities and fisheries. The 2012 and 2017 plans relied heavily on predictive models to project possible changes in the coast and to identify the most cost-effective restoration and protection projects (CPRA 2012, 63). Using a modeling approach, it could project changing conditions either with or without the projects. This technique, along with the various technical boards and advisory committees, provided technical rationales for projects and their costs and framed all public discussions within this scientific context (CPRA 2012 and 2017b). The 2017 plan asserts it is more community focused even while continuing to privilege science and engineering (CPRA 2017b, 28).

The most recent plan once again relied heavily on expert knowledge to formulate options and to model future conditions. These projections framed the public discussions (see CPRA 2017a, appendix B). It also conceded that sustainability was not a true goal, noting that, even with its numerous projects, more land would be lost than restored. This reality prompted a shift in the emphasis from wetland restoration to risk reduction. Although there were numerous junctures where public input was possible, true participatory methods were largely absent. While the distinction between public involvement and participation might seem merely semantic, it reflects the scientific orientation of both the CPRA staff and their methods. The absence of professionals equipped to invigorate a full-fledged participatory process inhibits the agency's abilities in this methodological arena.

OUTSOURCING PUBLIC PARTICIPATION

From its inception, CPRA has accommodated different forms of pubic feedback to expert-developed plans. This follows similar practices across the country and reflects the proliferation and growing professionalization of environmental advocacy groups to counter professional lobbyists for business and industry organizations (Spears 2020, O'Brien and McIvor 2007). Academics and practitioners have come to realize and recommend effective public participation at the outset to diminish conflict during the unveiling of a final plan. The CPRA allows for public audiences to respond to carefully assembled documents and selective predictive models. True public participation with the experts at the earliest stages has been absent. Despite staff with diverse scientific talents, CPRA does not have a team with comparable expertise and experience in participatory methods. Hence, it has outsourced direct participatory projects while other independent organizations have also launched efforts intended to feed into the master planning process. These efforts typically have omitted most of Louisiana's coastal science experts on the numerous panels.

A group of scholars, applied scientists, and coastal residents participated in a "sci-tek" (scientific/traditional ecological knowledge) project to integrate local ecological expertise into the coastal restoration process. Funded by CPRA, the technical team worked with local fisherfolk to translate their "traditional ecological knowledge" into a GIS format that would be usable by the state's technical experts. This project sought to address the shortcomings of mere stakeholder engagement. The authors and the local fisherfolk even took the state experts out on their boats to offer what amounted to a floating seminar for the normally office-bound scientists. This process was to enable a direct transfer of local expertise to agency experts and transfer local stakeholders' priorities to government officials (Bethel et al. 2011).

Additional projects include a set of nonstructural policy recommendations, developed in part to inform the CPRA process for its 2017 master plan. A critique of the 2012 master plan was its emphasis on structural projects as well as marsh building while omitting attention to human habitation and community persistence outside the structural systems. The Center for Planning Excellence (CPEX), a Baton Rouge planning group, secured external funding to solicit options for nonstructural projects from coastal residents intended to aid the 2017 planning process. Its report—based on interviews, polls, and focus groups with coastal residents—noted that residents and local leaders wanted greater coordination and alignment between their nonstructural efforts and state and federal programs. In other words, they were frustrated with what they saw as an emphasis on structural projects. While not funded by CPRA, this project directly sought to influence the master planning process (CPEX 2015). As

CPEX was engaged it its extensive research and community engagement, a team at the independent research institute, the Water Institute of the Gulf (TWIG), used CPRA funding to carry out a pair of scenario-building workshops. This effort sought to allow local experts to project future scenarios rather than using external technical experts and computers. Using a method developed by the US Department of the Interior, TWIG staff assembled groups of citizens, local government officials, businesspeople, landowners, and other stakeholders to lay out what they foresaw as social and economic changes that would unfold with or without coastal restoration projects. These interactions used proposed CPRA restoration projects as the starting point for discussion, but the projects considered biophysical conditions and the publicly developed scenarios focused on future social and economic conditions. A central concern expressed by participants was the desire for local input in restoration planning (Colten 2014a). As with the CPEX effort, this participatory process sought to feed into the CPRA planning process.

Seeking to build on the sci-tek project, a Water Institute team conducted a series of community workshops and participatory mapping exercises to enable the dual-directional transfer of technical expertise and traditional knowledge among the different communities. Using a grant from Louisiana Sea Grant (an NOAA-funded entity), the workshops focused on the exchange of ecosystem expertise, and the participatory mapping enabled community members to identify places of value (Carruthers et al. 2017). Once again, local participants voiced frustration with absence of local knowledge in the restoration planning process (43).

Louisiana's CPRA has focused on ecosystem management and has not raised human dimensions to a comparable level in its three plans. Seeking to address this oft-criticized shortcoming, the Louisiana Office of Community Development (LOCD) launched an ambitious participatory process aimed at fostering a set of adaptive strategies for the future (LOCD 2017) They refer to it as a "co-design" process. Without pre-determined scenarios, the LA SAFE project carried out a multistage process to identify local goals, needs, and opportunities to achieve those goals, to be followed by the development of desired outcomes. Each of these elements will be built on local community input and ultimately will be used to draft long-term strategies for an adaptation plan. While seeking original input, the process uses CPRA maps of land loss and its various projects to guide discussion. OCD seeks to integrate its community-informed efforts with CPRA's three general adaptation strategies: flood proofing, elevation, and voluntary acquisition (LOCD 2017). In doing so, it inserts CPRA framing into its activities. Funding, however, is coming from a federal grant, not CPRA. Community participation has been robust and reflects citizen willingness to lend their time and expertise to the larger goals. While this process is more complex and time-consuming than expert-driven stakeholder engagement, it avoids the democratic deficit some describe in the absence of true participatory methods (Vanclay 2012).

Louisiana folded many aspects of the multiple-lines-of-defense strategy, unveiled after Hurricane Katrina, into its coastal master plan that seeks to mitigate the impacts of coastal land loss and sea-level rise (CPRA 2012). This ambitious and expensive plan calls for a number of efforts to restore portions of the disappearing coastal wetlands. As of 2012, a major portion of the $50 billion budget targeted restoration—an estimated $28.5 billion. While the strategy includes elevating houses to ensure flood proofing within the levee system, the initial emphasis has been on coastal restoration. The 2012 master plan included some $10 million in its budgetary projection for "non-structural" projects which would include elevating residences and other buildings. State officials reported that the planning for this procedure remained to be done (CPRA 2012, 36 and appendix F). In the long run, coastal restoration and structural approaches will require less adaptation and investment in nonstructural improvements by those within the urban levees. There are small communities that are outside the projected structural systems, and restoration projects will likely disrupt natural-resource-based economic activities that have evolved with the current levees and outlet system. Once again, the dominance of region's largest city has had a powerful influence on the direction of protection from environmental hazards, and the orientation of protective systems continues to displace risk beyond the urban pale and places the responsibility to adapt to those who have adapted to the existing human-environment conditions.

*   *   *

In anticipation of the 2017 master plan, the Center for Planning Excellence, a Baton Rouge–based organization with support from several charitable foundations, conducted an extensive survey to reveal public concern with the plan's nonstructural elements. Nonstructural includes such options as elevating houses and other flood-proofing practices, and also relocation to safer locations—"voluntary acquisition" in the language of the master plan. The authors note that restoration and structural protection alone could not "provide a complete solution to flood risk" (CPEX 2015, 5). The report observes that, despite the creation of a subcommittee on nonstructural topics and an advisory group dedicated to resilience, there remained much to be accomplished on the nonstructural front. The study revealed a lack of capacity at the parish level to plan and implement much of the nonstructural agenda. It also recommended a dedicated funding stream for nonstructural projects. There were numerous other recommendations for enhancing the nonstructural component in the 2017 plan and for strengthening local capacities and developing best practices for flood mitigation beyond the structural approaches (9–10).

During the comment period prior for the draft 2017 plan, a common theme in both oral testimony at public hearings and in written form was the need for stronger support for nonstructural work. Community and environmental organizations called for a fortified nonstructural budget (see Sierra Club, Gulf Restoration Network, Bayou Interfaith, and New Orleans Resilience Office in CPRA 2017b, appendix G, attachments G1, G2A, G2B, and G2C). An overwhelming amount of the public input sought structural fixes to local concerns, particularly when projects in the 2012 plan disappeared from the 2017 version. Planning for two major sediment diversions were a prominent part of the 2017 plan and will serve largely to restore wetlands in major bays downstream from New Orleans. They have support from the city, numerous scientists, and the state, but are opposed by fishing families (Save Louisiana Coalition 2020). Indeed, fishermen in the areas where sediment will cover oyster leases and push shrimp further out toward the Gulf have voiced the strongest opposition to the master plan. They admit that they are not against sediment diversions, only large ones such as those in the 2017 plan (Save Louisiana Coalition 2020), and they feel as if their voices are not heard.

During the spring of 2021, the Army Corps of Engineers released its draft environmental impact statement for the first of the major diversions. It noted that the regulations guiding these reviews require an early and open process for public involvement (USACE 2021, 7-1). The document reports that over 280 people signed attendance logs for the various scoping meetings, and that the Corps received 871comments in the course of its public engagement. While these numbers are impressive, the process did not undertake robust public participatory methods. The Corps basically took on the task of environmental review as required prior to permitting. Louisiana's CPRA had laid out its plan for a diversion into Barataria Bay prior to the launching of this stage. Consequently, the possibility for early public involvement had long passed. The Corps got involved midstream. Their belated, albeit legal and ambitious, public engagement program was not directed toward guiding the design. That responsibility resided with CPRA, but it had largely set aside the advice of a report it commissioned in 2014 to outline methods for adequately allowing public participation for Mid-Barataria diversion planning. That report recommended following the international principles of social impact assessments, which call for public participation before the planning begins (Colten and Hemmerling 2014).

While the draft EIS contains an essential evaluation of potential socioeconomic impacts of the diversion, it finds one of the chief benefits will be to prevent infrastructure damage from future storm surge and sea-level rise (USACE 2021, appendix H). In other words, it will protect itself, other structures, and the New Orleans urban areas by building a marsh buffer. Those residents expected to contend with the greatest adverse impacts are low-income fishing families. The EIS notes that they might be able to move to other locations to continue their traditional livelihoods (USACE 2021, appendix H, sec. 3.14). It makes no mention of any consideration to provide community relocation assistance or even voluntary buyouts. Individual relocation contributes to cultural erosion, which is not considered as a potential impact. The same people who felt voiceless in 2017 are the people who will be asked to adapt once again as the diversion sends sediment into the bay and disrupts the ecology that commercial and subsistence fisherfolk rely on.

The first and highly influential organization devoted to addressing Louisiana's land loss was built around a coalition of environmental activists and coastal scientists. It included citizen, faith-based, and fishing organizations and thus had a broad public base. This organization sought to avoid some of the pitfalls of the environmental impact statement and the stakeholder engagement processes and allow for grassroots input from the outset. As concern with land loss gained government agency attention and funding, more formalized public involvement took form. Opportunities included the organization of focus groups and technical review panels that consisted of representatives from various stakeholder categories. Major economic interests had their focus groups for their particular activities, and this gave additional heft to the input from those organizations, which outnumbered the single focus group for "communities." The major economic interests also benefited by being able to dispatch professionals to the meetings, which small communities were unable to do. Despite numerous community meetings, scoping meetings, and other forums, there remained a tendency for public input to respond to draft plans and not to help shape the plan from the outset. Sometimes with CPRA funding and sometimes with outside assistance, several organizations have undertaken activities that exhibit a more robust type of participation, but their ultimate influence remains modest at best. There is no question that the state has expanded its efforts to include input from the public, but it has also opened the door for specialized and technical experts to shape and dominate the conversation.

Conclusions
The Erasure of Coastal People

There is an unlikely congruence between the early French maps of the Louisiana coast and the most recent projections of impending land loss (CPRA 2017b). Both depict a coastal region largely devoid of people (see fig. I.1). The colonial-era cartographers were most attentive to shorelines, navigational hazards, freshwater supplies, and routes to the interior. They did not venture into the soggy wetlands. Human settlements, both indigenous and Euro-African, along the Mississippi River appear on maps from the early eighteenth century. The coastal marshes remained largely a *terra incognita* with vague cartographic detail. Recent visualizations also reveal few physical or human specifics in the interest of highlighting the entire coast and emphasizing one thing: the immediate threat of land loss. This cartographic omission reflects larger conceptual omissions in the plans to restore the cultures and societies of the state's littoral region.

Much has changed in the three centuries since European mappers charted the coast. Multiple waves of migrants displaced indigenous groups as Europeans, Africans, and Asians have settled more widely across the region. They established deep and firm attachments to a land overlooked by many outside observers. Certainly, Louisiana's traditional fishing and hunting folk along with its legendary sportsmen made expeditions throughout the wetlands, but their presence was temporary and seasonal. The lure of mineral resources drew others into the coastal wetlands. As experts began predicting land loss, they sought to emphasize the threat by plotting the lands that had or would go beneath the Gulf's waters. Towns and cities, if shown at all, were small dots on the map to orient the viewer. The overall erasure of people and the foregrounding of the biophysical setting have contributed to a chronic dismissal or neglect of social and cultural concerns. While science provided powerful and detailed insights about ecological, hydrological, and geomorphological change, there has been no corresponding full-blown inquiry into the processes at work in human communities. There have been no coordinated efforts to examine the numerous social and cultural processes and how they have and might interact with environmental change. Granted, numerous scholars have dedicated their careers to examining the human coast and provided vital insights on nature-society relations (Laska 2020), but without the support or overarching coordination provided to the physical sciences. For the master plan to be truly sustainable, which in principle includes equity and justice, it must afford people the same consideration as plants, animals, waterways, climate, and soil.

Society has been neglected in the development of the state's coastal restoration plans. As a corollary, by slighting people in the planning process, the plan's temporal scale, based in rates of change in the biophysical realm, largely dismisses the pace of social and cultural change. This creates a fundamental disjunction between how society and nonhuman ecology respond to rising seas and restoration projects.

ADAPTATIONS OR TRANSITIONS

Each phase of human settlement, environmental management, mapping land loss, and public policy making exhibited adaptations to perceived threats or opportunities. Yet piecemeal or disarticulated adaptations have produced unintended, albeit foreseeable, consequences. Cloaked in the mantle of an "objective" science, the adaptations become divorced from the social processes that created them. Adaptations introduced prior to the adoption of the concept of sustainability are burdened with consequences of underlying unsustainable programs. Furthermore, inherent resilience, practices carried out at the local and family level, have proven effective in helping communities recover from traumatic situations, but top-down formal resilience programs seldom integrate with these grassroots practices. It is the locally based practices that have endured over time and possess potential connection points for fostering a more sustainable approach for the long term. The integration of inherent and formal practices offers an opportunity for "re-articulating" adaptations (Jesse 2020) and thereby moving towards an adaptive transition.

With coastal planning focused on a fifty-year horizon, planners seldom peer beyond the temporally constrained horizon and into the scale of human life in the coastal region. Nor do they appear to consider the assembly of multiple adaptations that might add up to create an adaptive transition. Social processes operate at a different pace than diversions or marsh-creation projects, and planners have yet to investigate the human timescales and how the plan might take advantage of social processes. The predication that twenty years will provide sufficient time for human adaptation to the master plan's projects reveals the failure to consider the pace of human adaptations in coastal Louisiana (CPRA 2017a, 4).

An adaptive transition requires thinking beyond the coast as currently configured and the land area that will be lost. To deal with displacement of society, the planning process should expand its horizon to inland parishes. These locations will eventually have to accommodate those who depart their coastal homes while also facing greater risk from extreme tropical weather and inland flooding as sea levels rise and the base level of streams rises in accord. Granted, this goes beyond the current scope of the state's definition of the coastal region, in both biophysical and social terms, but the coast is moving inland. The master plan should adjust to accommodate the future coast visualized in its land loss maps.

Louisiana coastal residents have been moving inland for more than a century, and resettlement is an obvious option (Hemmerling 2017, Simms 2017a). Young people are leaving their home towns and relocating to urban centers farther from the coast (Simms 2017b). This has been a slow, multigenerational process without government assistance. After Hurricane Katrina, there was considerable relocation away from some of the most severely damaged neighborhoods in New Orleans (Zaninetti and Colten 2012). Additionally, the "immovable industries"—minerals, fishing, and shipping—no longer rely solely on local employees. Workers on offshore platforms commonly commute from states well removed from the coast. Fishing and shipping employees, likewise, can drive longer distances than in the past, even if just from neighboring parishes. As some families retreat landward, there is new investment in expensive "camps"—raised houses for use by wealthy sportsmen. The demographics of the coast are changing, and the need to fortify the coast is declining. Louisiana's Office of Community Development has outlined an adaptation strategy that situates relocation as an important activity to ensure safety to at-risk populations (LOCD 2019). The changing coastal demographics and the work of LOCD should cause planners to recalibrate priorities from structural protections to assisted community transplants—helping whole communities find safe ground where they can reconstitute themselves. Ample scholarship also points toward the need to raise coordinated resettlement on the priority list (Koslov 2016, Siders et al. 2019, US Government Accountability Office 2020). So far, the master plan contains only a "voluntary acquisition" component that will foster atomistic departures and community fragmentation. It does not reflect the stated goal of cultural protection, but functions as a voluntary ethnic cleansing.

RESILIENCE AND OVERLAPPING DISASTER RECOVERIES

People have lived and adapted to changing conditions in Louisiana's coastal region for centuries. Adaptations have provided a set of resilient practices that have enabled their persistence in place. Yet resilience has been tested repeatedly. In some cases local capacities proved sufficient to allow communities to rebound; in other situations this was less so. Resilience can be fragile and transitory. Increasing reliance on formal procedures tends to diminish the locally based inherent practices. The rapid-fire series of disasters in coastal Louisiana since 2001 has strained both inherent and formal resiliency. This situation poses a serious challenge to the viability of coastal cultures coping with the slow-moving land loss crisis.

The resilience curve (fig. C.1) effectively illustrates how resiliency may cushion a society that encounters a traumatic event. The sharp downward curve represents the impacts of an acute disruption. A resilient community will not descend as far as one that is less resilient, and it will have a shorter recovery climb (CARRI 2011, 15). Yet it portrays a situation where there is a single disaster and not successive events that compound the initial impacts. Machlis and McNutt (2010) have observed that a secondary

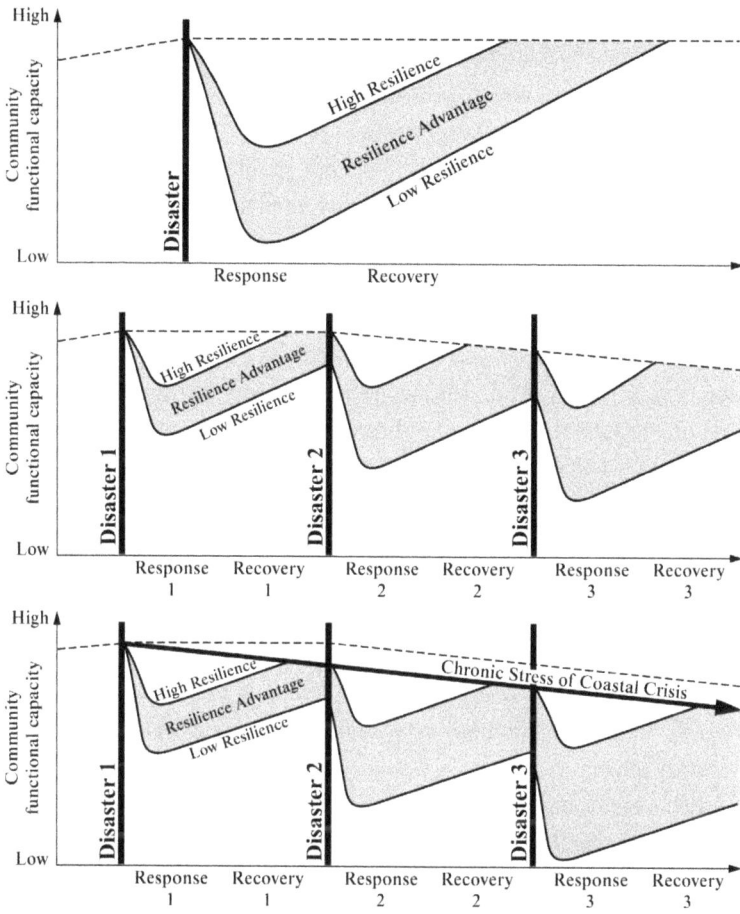

Fig. C.1. Resilience curve and the cumulative impacts of sequential disasters and an ongoing crisis. Adapted from model developed by Community and Regional Resilience Institute and Machlis and McNutt (2010). Graphs by Mary Lee Eggart.

shock can disrupt a long-term recovery and plunge a society into deeper turmoil. Louisiana's coastal region has endured multiple rapid-onset disasters in its recent history, all the while grappling with the slow-motion land loss crisis for over half a century. The 9/11 attacks on New York and Washington in 2001 disrupted air travel nationwide and abruptly decreased tourism in New Orleans for a few years. As the state was reestablishing tourism revenue, Katrina ravaged all aspects of coastal Louisiana's economy and society, which led to a multiyear recovery effort, aided by substantial external funds.

The Great Recession of 2008 was not as devastating to Louisiana as to other parts of the country, but it caused economic turmoil and seriously strained the state's budget as the governor pushed for tax cuts. The BP oil spill in the Gulf of Mexico in 2010 disrupted oil and gas activity along with marine fisheries, although in the long run, payments from BP and the other responsible parties have been a windfall to the state, particularly in restoration funding. Ever present, even if in the background of these more dramatic disasters, coastal land loss has captivated the attention of state and local officials and weighed heavily on the state's budget. The hurricanes of 2020 damaged restoration projects which now need repairs with federal funds. Each of these disruptions has strained community resilience in different ways, but consistently disadvantaged populations have endured the greatest relative impacts. Service workers in the tourism sector faced temporary unemployment after 9/11 and Katrina, and to some extent after the BP spill. Fisher families and those living in exposed coastal communities endured a mix of declining catches, limited fishing seasons, and damages to personal property and the resources they rely on. They have commonly expressed a sense of neglect in government recovery efforts.

Recovery from each disaster has overlapped to some extent with the following events. Although some sections of New Orleans appeared to be functioning normally after Katrina, numerous recovery efforts were still underway when the Deepwater Horizon gusher and explosion occurred. Indeed, efforts were still in motion in 2020 to assess and devise a plan for the storm-damaged Charity Hospital, and vast sections of eastern New Orleans remained only partially redeveloped. Oil spill recovery funds have underwritten studies of ecological damage and paid for restoration projects, but ecological harm persists in the deep Gulf. These concurrent recovery trajectories are overlaid upon the long-term coastal restoration efforts. When a new disaster turns the upward tail end of a preceding event's recovery downward again, the impacts befall a society with diminished resiliency (fig. C.1). Each successive blow drives a community lower on the resilience curve and extends the recovery climb. Recovery projects begin to compete with limited financial resources, setting in motion contests over access to limited resources. In Louisiana, with a strong political orientation toward fiscal restraint, dollars are always tight. This situation is heightened by the long-term commitment to a $50+ billion coastal restoration effort. Dedicated state funds reduce the state's flexibility to respond to each new disaster. Granted, Louisiana has proven adept at securing external funds for levee building, hurricane recovery, and oil spill damages. An increasing resistance in Congress to respond to local disasters may diminish such external funding in the future. Tensions over how and where to spend limited state dollars can result in inequitable treatment of politically disenfranchised citizens.

Mississippi River flood risks have become amplified this century and present an additional disruptive influence. The pace and duration of floods is exemplified by use of the Bonnet Carré Spillway, upstream from New Orleans. Since the spillway's completion in the 1930s, the Corps of Engineers has opened this outlet fifteen times—seven times between 2000 and 2020. Recent use included an unprecedented two openings in 2019 when the river ran above flood stage for 211 days, a record stretch of high water. The quickening pace of high river stages triggering the openings reflects increased precipitation and runoff in the upper basin that is associated with climate change. The extended high river in 2019 pushed more fresh water into the Gulf of Mexico and reduced the state's shrimp landings. Additionally, use of the Bonnet Carré twice that year diverted fresh water into the oyster beds in Mississippi Sound. The flood-protection system continues to send ripple effects through the natural resource–based livelihoods of coastal residents, creating an additional overlapping recovery curve.

Beyond the dramatic localized twenty-first century events, the cataclysmic circumstances unleashed by the novel coronavirus pandemic in 2020, the related oil price drop, and the disruption caused by Hurricanes Laura and Delta have the region facing a trio of exceptional recovery challenges. Models for the state's coastal future did not factor in these events. Widespread unemployment in the hospitality trades during the state-imposed pandemic response, coupled with the loss of jobs in the mineral sector, and damage caused by a powerful hurricanes present a fiscal catastrophe for families and the state. Federal bailout funds helped the state minimize cuts for its 2020–21 budget. With a resurgence in COVID-19 cases during the summer and fall of 2020, lingering low oil prices, and economic disruption caused by the hurricanes, state revenues may fall further from the budgeted demands for 2021. These fiscal conditions may mean the climb up the resilience curve will be steeper and slower than hoped for. Additionally, these conditions can complicate and prolong the pandemic / oil crash / hurricane recovery overlaid on the coastal crisis.

This situation is not just a Louisiana concern. Threats of hurricanes and floods remain realities in the midst of the pandemic. As more people depend on federal levees than half a century ago and rely on federal disaster aid, the competition for recovery assistance becomes a truly national issue. The spate of hurricanes in 2017 severely taxed FEMA's resources, and the pandemic in 2020 has shown the burden a single nationwide calamity can impose on emergency response capabilities designed to deal with more localized disasters. The president's executive order in August 2020 to deploy FEMA emergency funds to underwrite unemployment payments, on the eve of the hurricane season's most active period, exemplifies the competition for limited resources. Competition for pandemic, wildfire, and hurricane recovery funds in late 2020 exemplifies the challenges legislative leaders face. With more responsibility for coping with disasters shifted to the federal government, recoveries from multiple, sequential events, even for resilient communities, may be extended.

The chronologies of adaptations and resilience are tied in part to tragic events that motivate both local and large-scale responses. Inherent resilience practices are set into motion in the immediate aftermath of an extreme event, and persist for the full recovery. Governments and corporations mobilize formal resilience actions shortly after disasters, and they tend to fade away in the early stages of long-term recovery. Formal mitigation efforts, such as levees and coastal restoration, take decades to implement, and often public support for these costly and slow-moving initiatives decays over time. As we consider public support for the state's master plan, we must take into account the temporal dimension of adaptations that enhance resiliency as well as the interconnections among multiple disruptive events and the recovery efforts. Is there alignment between the adaptations and longer-term transitions and the steps taken to manage and alter environmental conditions?

BY WAY OF SUMMATION

Society, Culture, Adaptation, and Resilience

People from a range of backgrounds and geographic locations settled coastal Louisiana over the past several millennia. They adapted to an unfamiliar environment and passed down the lessons learned to their descendants, who have found ways to survive. Inherent resilient practices that arose from these adaptations along with deep attachments to place enabled an enduring presence in a perilous place. Coping with disasters over the years prompted some landward geographic relocations. Formal disaster-mitigation systems, such as levees and programs that provide assistance in emergency response and recovery, gradually supplanted some of the socially embedded, traditional practices. These external resilience measures were not attached to the locally based inherent practices. The tragic failure of river and hurricane protection levees demonstrated that scientific expertise is not a complete substitute for local knowledge and resilience. Without integration of the inherent and formal resilience, opportunities to amply both have been missed. The neglect of local resilient practices and expertise continued in the planning for coastal restoration. Reliance on structural systems has allowed river floods and storm surges that exceed their design limits to inflict horrendous damages. These disasters should remind us to fortify inherent resilience, to incorporate community-guided resettlement into the state's plans, and perhaps to even rely less on levees.

Planners have adopted a fifty-year timescale for biophysical restoration and assume that twenty years is adequate for society to adjust while largely ignoring the multigenerational temporal scale of past human adaptations and the longer-term adaptive transitions. By focusing on engineering a restored ecology, geomorphology, and hydrology, they failed to imagine the full range of cascading consequences that could occur over time. Their research did not delve into social transitions as a set of long-term processes that involve changes in culture, economics, politics, and technology. The scientific approach was to provide answers to hard questions, but did not consider the even harder questions involving values and meaning that are rooted in culture.

One of the more obvious points of departure from a human-centered approach has been the omission of an assisted resettlement strategy. Numerous groups in the coastal region arrived by way of traumatic diasporas. They have exhibited the capacity to relocate in a gradual process, without assistance, following past disasters. Mobility is embedded in their cultural DNA. The state master plan barely touches on "voluntary acquisition" as assistance for those who live beyond the structural protections to sell their dwellings and relocate inland. No extensive analysis compares economic costs of resettlement versus restoration projects. No maps portray the potential culture loss arising from the restoration of the biophysical environment. Society has shouldered many of the impacts unleashed by the unintended consequences of human-induced environmental change. Migration has been one way of adapting and perpetuating culture that the master plan has not explored in any detail. Assisted resettlement could function to restore culture.

Managing Environments

The neglect of people in a series of schemes to manage Louisiana's coastal territory was not necessarily deliberate, but it became a customary part of how things were done with lingering impacts. Granted, the first major actions to manipulate the coastal environment served to protect people, their property, and settlements. Prehistoric midden mounds heaped up in the marsh provided solid ground for wetland dwellers. French leaders set in place policies to require landowners to build levees to fend off annual inundations along the lower Mississippi River. Thus began a series of disarticulated policies to manage the environment for human benefit, but without accounting for the social ripple effects of the multiple public works. Each successive phase of environmental management neglected to fully address the enduring legacies of its predecessors. Levees constitute the most durable component of environmental manipulations. Government bodies have consistently funded and improved these visible landscape features. They have provided protection for riparian residents, but they also have had profound impacts on the coastal region by way of diverting sediment into the deep Gulf and greatly restricting deposition on the delta and the floodplain. Relying on them for protection from variable-track hurricanes has provided inconsistent benefits. Levees are a key factor in coastal land loss, but they remain a largely untouchable fixture in future plans. Consequently, with an eye to maintaining the current control of the river, both the beneficial and deleterious impacts will continue even with the completion of the controversial sediment diversions.

Conservation policies sought to protect wildlife for sportsmen and commercial hunters and fishermen. Outlawing hunting birds of plume and waterfowl for diners caused the displacement of commercial hunters, but policy makers saw it as a social and ecological benefit. The establishment of leases for oyster fishermen sought to guarantee a sustainable yield for harvesters and consumers. The social consequences of confining oyster fishermen to fixed waterbottom leases was given little thought in terms of potential disruptions like hurricanes, freshwater floods, or pollution. Policy makers did not examine the possible ripple effects that could follow policies that forced adaptations on those engaged in traditional pursuits. As leaseholders, oyster gatherers now want protection from the impacts of freshwater diversions for their immobile operations. Conservation sought to manage wildlife and other biological communities through science. It treated dwindling waterfowl and fish populations as a problem with a scientific remedy. Conservation also addressed mineral extraction and sought to implement policies that would extend the life of subterranean petroleum resources. While unspoken, the remedies would benefit a select segment of society that was engaged in natural resource pursuits. But conservationists did not see their mission as addressing preexisting social conditions or those that arose from mineral extraction.

Likewise, wetland reclamation projects transferred thousands of acres from a public commons into private use and restricted hunters and trappers from areas were they had made their living or sought subsistence. Some of the wetland reclamation efforts permanently damaged sizable marsh areas, rendering them useless for agriculture; they became places available to urban sportsmen but not to those engaged in traditional resource-based livelihoods.

With the advent of environmental protection and ecological restoration, once again science remained the dominant approach. Environmental protection broadened the scope of its mission to a national and international scale and treated water and air as common resources necessary to all citizens. Yet the preexisting flood-protection and conservation policies remained in place and did not always mesh with the new agendas. Hemmerling, Barra, and Bond (2020) refer to coastal projects in the era before Hurricane Katrina (2005) as "piecemeal." That is, they were not fully integrated and represented discrete adaptations, without transitional goals.

Restoration science, which provided a framework for management since the 1980s, prioritized the reconstitution of ecological functions to damaged landscapes. It operated with an underlying assumption that these efforts would benefit society, but there was no contemporaneous examination of the interrelated biophysical and social processes and human responses to environmental changes set in motion by restoration. There was no detailed review of the sociology or the culture of science as a human enterprise in pursuing restoration goals. Sustainability, at its core, seeks to manage resources into the future in ways that will be equitable and just. Yet in Louisiana, older management policies, with inequitable foundations, protrude into current management efforts. Path dependencies and incompatible economic priorities complicate the achievement of truly sustainable goals. Indeed, the previous management regimes, with their unsustainable characteristics, undermine the long-term viability of current plans by forcing them to accommodate flood-control levees and their continuing impacts along with the scars of oil extraction activities. The state's fifty-year time horizon reflects an unspoken concession to both an uncertain future and the plans' unsustainability. It also largely excludes addressing the most basic factors contributing to climate change-driven land loss: reliance on fossil fuels and greenhouse emissions. A Louisiana congressman raised this issue in testimony in 1990, but it has been allowed to fade from most state documents (Randolph 2018). While the most recent plan seeks a more regional and coordinated approach to coastal restoration projects than most previous regimes, it still lacks a transitional scope, remains a collection of piecemeal adaptations that omit most social concerns, and fails to address renewable energy options. The timescale of restoration does not mesh with either the pace of social adaptation or the temporal horizon of sustainability. The master plan will not be comprehensive until it fully incorporates social change writ large.

Mapping Change without People

For more than half a century, coastal scientists and cartographers have portrayed the geography and pace of Louisiana's land loss. The first maps reflected a concern with retreating shorelines and their impact on oil revenues within the state's territorial waters. Subsequent maps shifted to portraying land loss as a threat to the vital coastal ecology which supported numerous traditional livelihoods. The economy certainly factored into the motivation for these cartographic exercises. Yet the large-area, small-scale maps tended to remove human communities and populations. The choices behind what to exclude were in part for cartographic convenience and legibility. Not everything could be presented in the maps designed to show land loss across the breadth of the state's coast, but in narrative form the same constraints did not exist. Nonetheless, the texts of reports on the emerging crisis mentioned local culture lightly, and these narratives did not fully compensate for the inadequate cartographic portrayal of the cultural landscape patterns and how they might change within the frightening realignment of the littoral territory.

Consequently, the science of restoration and public investments that followed addressed what was visible in dramatic visualizations. The biophysical environment, the domain of the scientists, took precedence and garnered the most dollars for research and projects. Cost-benefit accounting prioritized larger population centers such as New Orleans and Houma. Vulnerability as a measure of social conditions appears in various online interactive maps well after the plans acquired a rigid form. Investments based on cost-benefit do not reflect social vulnerability. I am convinced that the erasure of people from the multiple generations of maps contributed to their neglect in current planning. Maps deliberately made land loss visible, but not culture loss.

Public in Public Works

Traditional public hearings provided an opportunity for residents to voice their concerns with large-scale public works projects. Hearings were not the first or only opportunity, but they were a key component in justifying expenditures for expensive government undertakings. In the lower Mississippi River Valley, local leaders commonly lobbied Congress for federal investment in levees and other flood-control works. The conduit for this input was directly to elected representatives via correspondence or during hearings. After federal legislators approved flood-mitigation efforts, the Corps of Engineers proceeded to design structures and occasionally held further public hearings. Yet both the lobbying and testimony to Congress and subsequent hearings privileged the voices of elected officials and influential business interests. The exclusion of fisher families and others who were most affected by the post-1927 outlets stands as a prime example. These families were not among those able to speak at the hearings, and they have endured the brunt of the impacts when the outlets have been opened. Thus, public hearings were only partially public.

As stakeholder engagement became formalized in project reviews, opportunities expanded for broader public input. With each iteration of the master plan, the state has expanded opportunities for public input (Hemmerling, Barra, and Bond 2020). Yet numerous groups feel neglected in the process, and the number of formal stakeholder groups is weighted in favor of business interests and not communities. Local expertise, typically brought in late in the process, can complement the essential science and engineering. The major economic enterprises and their trade associations can dispatch professionals to make their case, while citizen groups may or may not have well-paid spokespeople. Various programs that truly seek broad-based public participation have been carried out, but not within the agency charged with implementing the restoration and protection plan. As a result, these outsourced efforts are not fully integrated into the master planning process. In the absence of a truly participatory process from the outset of planning, the plan remains deficient in terms of social justice for those families living on the state's geographic and economic margins. Consequently, it does not adequately incorporate the fundamental goals of a sustainable transition. Populations, living on the state's physical and social margins, have expressed disenchantment with their opportunities to influence the planning process. And they are often the ones expected to adapt to new conditions.

The Louisiana master plan for a sustainable coast seeks to guide a remarkable undertaking for a remarkable place. It is one of only a very few such efforts to directly address long-term coastal issues associated with rising seas at the state scale. While I have pointed out a remarkable and obvious omission—the human coast—it is not too late to begin a more full-fledged integration of the work being done by sister agencies and NGOs and incorporating humanities and social science perspectives into the planning process. These other organizations have carried out remarkable projects that consider the long-term future of coastal people. There is also a growing body of humanities and social science scholarship available. So a solid foundation exists that can be built on. Making an adjustment to integrate what have been largely disconnected efforts, which necessitates more robust public participatory methods, would open the door for a truly sustainable master plan for all residents of the Louisiana coast.

REFERENCES CITED

Abramson, David M., Lynn M. Grattan, Brian Mayer, Craig E. Colten, Farah A. Arosemena, Ariane Bedimo-Rung, and Maureen Lichtveld. 2015. "The Resilience Activation Framework: A Conceptual Model of How Access to Social Resources Promotes Adaptation and Rapid Recovery in Post-disaster Settings." *Journal of Behavioral Health Services & Research* 42, no. 1: 42–57.

ABS Group. 2018. *City of New Orleans Drainage System Root Cause Analysis.* New Orleans: Sewerage and Water Board.

Adamson, George C., Matthew J. Hannaford, and Eleonora J. Rohland. 2018. "Rethinking the Present: The Role of a Historical Focus in Climate Change Adaptation Research." *Global Environmental Change* 48: 195–205.

Adelson, Jeff. 2013. "Levee Board Appointments May Let Jindal Interfere with Suit." *Baton Rouge Advocate,* August 23. theadvocate.com/news/6834770–123/levee -board-appointments-may-allow.

Adger, W. N. 2000. "Social and Ecological Resilience: Are They Related?" *Progress in Human Geography* 24, no. 3: 347–64.

Adger, W. N., J. Barnett, F. S. Chapin III, and H. Elemor. 2011. "This Must Be the Place: Underrepresentation on Identity and Meaning in Climate Change Decision Making." *Global Environmental Politics* 11, no. 2: 1–25.

Adger, W. N., Jon Barrett, Katrina Brown, Nadine Marshall, and Karen O'Brien. 2013. "Cultural Dimensions of Climate Change Impacts and Adaptation." *Nature Climate Change* 3: 112–17.

Adger, W. N., S. Dessai, M. Goulden, M. Hulme, I. Lorenzoni, D. R. Nelson, L. O. Naess, J. Wolf, and A. Wreford. 2009. "Are There Social Limits to Adaptation to Climate Change?" *Climatic Change* 93, no. 3: 335–54.

Adger, W. N., T. P. Hughes, C. Folke, S. R. Carpenter, and J. Rockström. 2005. "Social-ecological Resilience to Coastal Disasters." *Science* 309, no. 5737: 1036–39.

Airriess, Christopher, et al. 2007. "Church Based Social Capital, Networks and Geographical Scale: Katrina Evacuation, Relocation, and Recovery in a New Orleans Vietnamese American Community." *Geoforum* 39, no. 3: 1333–46.

Alexander, B. 2015. "St. Bernard Council Adopts Resolution Opposing Proposed Sediment Diversions." *New Orleans Times-Picayune,* April 21. www.nola.com/politics/index.ssf/2015/04/proposed_sediment_diversions_0.html.

American National Red Cross. 1929. *The Mississippi Valley Flood Disaster of 1927: Official Report of the Relief Operations.* Washington, DC: American National Red Cross.

American Society of Civil Engineers, Hurricane Katrina External Review Panel. 2007. "The New Orleans Hurricane Protection System: What Went Wrong and Why: A Report, 2007." www.asce.org/uploadedfiles/publications/asce_news/2009/04_april/erpreport.pdf.

America's Wetland Foundation. 2013. "Beyond Unintended Consequences." www.futureofthegulfcoast.org/AmericasWETLANDFoundation_Beyond.pdf (accessed June 2017).

———. 2017. "Who We Are." www.americaswetland.com/custompage.cfm?pageid=280 (accessed June 2017).

Anastasia, Orestes. 2001. "The National Environmental Policy Act of 1969: Thirty Years of Experience." *Proceedings of Seminar on Environmental Impact Assessment,* Hutovo Blato, Bosnia and Herzegovina, November 26–27, 1999, 25–66.

Arnold, Joseph L. 1988. *The Evolution of the 1936 Flood Control Act.* Fort Belvoir, VA: US Army Corps of Engineers, Office of History.

Avenal v. State of Louisiana. 1999. 757 So.2d 1.

Avenal v. State of Louisiana. 2004. 886 So. 2d 1085.

Bacon-Blood, Lattice. 2013. "St. Charles Parish Approves $5.8 Million Levee Project." *New Orleans Times-Picayune,* November 18. www.nola.com/politics/index.ssf/2013/11/st_charles_parish_approves_58.html.

Balee, W. 1998. *Advances in Historical Ecology.* New York: Columbia University Press.

Bankoff, G. 2010. "No Such Thing as Natural Disasters." *Harvard International Review* 23 (August). hir.harvard.edu/article/?a=2694.

Banta, Brady. 1981. "The Regulation and Conservation of Petroleum Resources in Louisiana, 1901–1940." PhD diss., Louisiana State University.

Barbour, Haley (Governor of Mississippi), to Gary Locke (US Secretary of Commerce). 2011. Correspondence, June 22. www.fisheries.noaa.gov/national/fund

ing-and-financial-services/fishery-disaster-determinations#numbers-53-16
-(2010-2000).

Barham, Robert (Secretary of Louisiana Dept. of Wildlife and Fisheries), to Gary
Locke (US Secretary of Commerce). 2011. Correspondence, May 6. www.wlf
.louisiana.gov/news/34123.

Barnes, S., C. Bond, N. Burger, K. Anania, A. Strong, S. Weiland, and S. Virgets.
2015. *Economic Evaluation of Coastal Land Loss in Louisiana.* Baton Rouge:
Coastal Protection and Restoration Agency.

Barnett, James F., Jr. 2017. *Beyond Control: The Mississippi River's New Channel to
the Gulf of Mexico.* Jackson: University Press of Mississippi.

Barras, John. 2017. Personal communication. December 18.

Barry, John, 1998. *Rising Tide: The Great Mississippi Flood of 1927 and How It Changed
America.* New York: Simon and Schuster.

Bates, F. L., C. W. Fogelman, W. J. Parenton, R. H. Pittman, and G. S. Tracy. 1963.
*The Social and Psychological Consequences of a Natural Disaster: A Longitudinal
Study of Hurricane Audrey.* Washington, DC: National Academy of Sciences.

Baurick, Tristan. 2017. "Is Louisiana Really Losing a Football Field of Land per
Hour?" *New Orleans Times-Picayune,* May 29. www.nola.com/environment
/index.ssf/2017/05/is_louisiana_losing_a_football.html (accessed December
2017).

Bayou Goula Residents. 1932. "Petition to Atchafalaya Levee District." Bayou
Goula folder, Atchafalaya Levee District Archives, Port Allen, LA.

Beck, Robert E. 1994. "The Movement in the United States to Restoration and
Creation of Wetlands." *Natural Resources Journal* 34: 781–822.

Berkes, F., J. Colding, and C. Folke. 2003. *Navigating Social-ecological Systems:
Building Resilience From Complexity and Change.* Cambridge, UK: Cambridge
University Press.

Bethel, M. B., L. F. Brien, E. J. Danielson, S. B. Laska, J. B. Trougman, M. W.
Boshart, M. J. Giardino, and M. P. Phillips. 2011. "Blending Geospatial
Technology and Traditional Ecological Knowledge to Enhance Restoration
Decision-support Processes in Coastal Louisiana." *Journal of Coastal Research*
27, no. 3: 555–71.

"Betsy a Big One but Wound not Deep." 1965. *New Orleans Times-Picayune* 11 September, 12.

Blake, N. M. 1980. *Land into Water—Water into Land: A History of Water Management in Florida.* Tallahassee: University Press of Florida.

Blakely, Edward. 2012. *My Storm: Managing the Recovery of New Orleans in the
Wake of Katrina.* Philadelphia: University of Pennsylvania Press.

Boggs, Hale, to Percival Stern. 1949. Correspondence, March 15. Hale and Lindy

Boggs Papers, MS. Collection 1000, box 522, folder 5, Tulane University Special Collections, New Orleans.

Boudreaux, C. 2015. "Fishermen Oppose River Diversions to Fix Louisiana Coast." *Lafourche Gazette*, August 7. www.tlgnewspaper.com/fishermen-oppose-river -diversions-to-fix-louisiana-coast.

Brázdil, R., C. Pfister, H. Wanner, H. V. Storch, and J. Luterbacher. 2005. "Historical Climatology in Europe – The State of the Art." *Climate Change* 70: 363–430.

Breaux, John B. N.d. Papers. Louisiana State University Libraries Special Collections, MSS 4922, box 217, folders 3, 18, and 19; box 230, folder 20.

Brookings Institution and Greater New Orleans Community Data Center. 2007. *The New Orleans Index: Tracking Recovery of New Orleans and the Metro Area.* New Orleans: Brookings Institution and Greater New Orleans Community Data Center.

Burby, Raymond J. 2006. "Hurricane Katrina and the Paradoxes of Government Disaster Policy: Bringing About Wise Governmental Decisions for Hazardous Areas." *Annals of the American Academy of Political and Social Science* 604, no. 1: 171–91.

Burley, David M. 2010. *Losing Ground: Identity and Land Loss in Coastal Louisiana.* Jackson: University Press of Mississippi.

Burley, David M., P. Jenkins, S. Laska, and T. Davis. 2007. "Place Attachment and Environmental Change in Coastal Louisiana." *Organization and Environment* 20: 347–66.

Butzer, K. 2012. "Collapse, Environment and Society." *Proceedings of the National Academy of Sciences* 109, no. 10: 3632–39.

Camillo, C. A., and M. T. Pearcy. 2004. *Upon Their Shoulders: A History of the Mississippi River Commission.* Vicksburg: Mississippi River Commission.

Carlson, Douglas, Marty Horn, Thomas Van Biersel, and David Fruge. 2012. *2011 Atchafalaya Basin Inundation Data Collection and Damage Assessment Project. Report of Investigations,* no. 12–01. Baton Rouge: Louisiana Geological Survey.

Carruthers, T. J. B, S. Hemmerling, S. A. Barra, T. A. Saxby, and L. Moss. 2017. *"This Is Your Shield, This Is Your Estuary": Building Community and Coastal Resilience to a Changing Louisiana Coastline through Restoration of Key Ecosystem Functions.* Baton Rouge: Water Institute of the Gulf.

Castonguay, Stéphane, and Matthew Evenden. 2012. "Introduction." In *Urban Rivers: Remaking Rivers, Cities, and Space in Europe and North America,* ed. Castonguay and Evenden, 1–16. Pittsburgh: University of Pittsburgh Press.

Castree, Noel, et al. 2014. "Changing the Intellectual Climate." *Nature Climate Change* 4: 763–68.

Chmutina, K., and J. von Meding. 2019. "A Dilemma of Language: 'Natural Disasters' in Academic Literature." *International Journal of Disaster Risk Science* 10: 283–92. doi.org/10.1007/s13753-019-00232-2.

"City's Hurricane Loss Light." 1947. *New Orleans Times-Picayune,* September 20, 2.

Climate Central. 2017. "Surging Seas Risk Zone Map." ss2.climatecentral.org/#9 /29.6928/-90.7141?show=sovi&projections=0-K14_RCP85-SLR&level=5& unit=feet&pois=hide (accessed December 2017).

Coalition to Restore Coastal Louisiana. 1987. "Coastal Louisiana: Here Today and Gone Tomorrow?" Draft. Baton Rouge: Coalition to Restore Coastal Louisiana.

———. 1989. *Here Today, Gone Tomorrow: A Citizen's Program for Saving the Mississippi River Delta Region to Protect Its Heritage, Economy, and Environment.* Baton Rouge: Coalition to Restore Coastal Louisiana.

———. 2017. *Our Coast, Our Future.* www.crcl.org/about-us/about-crcl.html (accessed June 2017).

Coastal Protection and Restoration Authority. 2007. *Louisiana's Comprehensive Master Plan for a Sustainable Coast.* Baton Rouge: Coastal Protection and Restoration Authority.

———. 2012. *Louisiana's Comprehensive Master Plan for a Sustainable Coast.* Baton Rouge: Coastal Protection and Restoration Authority.

———. 2017a. "History." coastal.la.gov/about/history/ (accessed June 2017).

———. 2017b. *Louisiana's Comprehensive Master Plan for a Sustainable Coast.* Baton Rouge: Coastal Protection and Restoration Authority.

Coastal Protection and Restoration Authority of Louisiana. 2015a. "CPRA Recommends Advancing Two Mississippi River Sediment Diversions." Press Release, October 21. coastal.la.gov/wp-content/uploads/2015/10/FINAL-SedimentDiv ersionsRecommendation-2.pdf.

———. 2015b. "Flood Risk and Resilience Viewer." cims.coastal.louisiana.gov /masterplan (accessed December 2017).

———. 2016. *Working Together.* coastal.la.gov/a-common-vision/2017-master-plan -update/technical-analysisteam/.

Coastal Resilience. 2017. "Flood and Sea Level Rise, Mapping Portal." maps.coastal resilience.org/network/ (accessed December 2017).

Coastal Wetlands Planning, Protection, and Restoration Act. 2015. lacoast.gov/new /About/.

Colten, Craig E. 2005. *Unnatural Metropolis: Wresting New Orleans from Nature.* Baton Rouge: Louisiana State University Press.

———. 2006. "Contesting Pollution in Dixie: The Case of Corney Creek." *Journal of Southern History* 72, no. 3 (2006): 605–34.

———. 2009. *Perilous Place, Powerful Storms: Hurricane Protection in Coastal Louisiana.* Jackson: University Press of Mississippi.

———. 2011. "Floods and Inequitable Responses: New Orleans Before Katrina." In *Environmental and Social Justice in the City: Historical Perspectives,* ed. R. Roger and G. Massard-Guilbaud, 113–29. Cambridge, UK: White Horse Press.

———. 2012. "Forgetting the Unforgettable: Losing Resilience in New Orleans." In *American Environments: Climate–Cultures–Catastrophe,* ed. Christof Mauch and Sylvia Mayer, 159–76. Heidelberg: Universitätsverlag.

———. 2014a. *Scenario Building Workshops.* Baton Rouge: Water Institute of the Gulf.

———. 2014b. *Southern Waters: The Limits to Abundance.* Baton Rouge: Louisiana State University Press.

———. 2015. "Historic City with a Poor Memory." In *The Katrina Effect: On the Nature of Catastrophe,* ed. William M. Taylor, Michael P. Livine, Oenone Rooksby, and Joely-Kym Sobott, 305–30. London: Bloomsbury.

———. 2017. "Environmental Management in Coastal Louisiana: A Historical Review." *Journal of Coastal Research* 33, no. 3: 699–711.

———. 2018. "Raising New Orleans: Historical Analogs and Future Environmental Risks." *Environmental History* 23, no. 1: 135–42.

———. 2019. "Adaptive Transitions: The Long Term Perspective on Humans in Changing Coastal Settings." *Geographical Review* 109, no. 3: 416–35.

Colten, Craig E., and Alexandra Giancarlo. 2011. "Losing Resilience on the Gulf Coast: Hurricanes and Social Memory." *Environment: Science and Policy for Sustainable Development* 53, no. 4: 6–19.

Colten, Craig E., A. A. Grismore, and J. R. Z. Simms. 2015. "Oil Spills and Community Resilience." *Geographical Review* 105, no. 4: 391–407.

Colten, Craig E., J. Hay, and A. Giancarlo. 2012. "Community Resilience and Oil Spills in Coastal Louisiana." *Ecology and Society* 17, no. 3. dx.doi.org/10.5751/ES -05047–170305.

Colten, Craig E., and S. A. Hemmerling. 2014. *Social Impact Assessment Methodology for Diversions and other Louisiana Coastal Master Plan Restoration and Protection Projects.* Baton Rouge: Water Institute of the Gulf.

Colten, Craig E., R. W. Kates, and S. Laska. 2008. *Community Resilience: Lessons from New Orleans.* Oak Ridge, TN: Oak Ridge National Laboratory.

Colten, Craig E., Jessica R. Z. Simms, Audrey A. Grismore, and Scott A. Hemmerling. 2018. "Social Justice and Mobility in Coastal Louisiana, USA." *Regional Environmental Change* 18, no. 2: 371–83.

Colten, Craig E., and A. Sumpter. 2009. "Social Memory and Resilience in New Orleans." *Natural Hazards* 48, no. 3: 355–64.

Comeaux, Malcolm L. 1972. *Atchafalaya Swamp Life: Settlement and Folk Occupation.* Baton Rouge: Louisiana State University, School of Geosciences.

Committee for the Future of Coastal Louisiana. 2002. *Saving Coastal Louisiana: A National Treasure.* Baton Rouge: Governor's Office of Coastal Activities.

Community and Regional Resilience Institute. 2011. "Community Resilience System Initiative (CRSI) Steering Committee Final Report." s31207.pcdn.co/wp-content/uploads/2019/08/CRSI-Final-Report.pdf.

Corthell, E. L. 1897. "The Delta of the Mississippi River." *National Geographic Magazine* 8: 351–54.

Corthell, E. L., et al. 1852. "Discussion on Reclamation of River Deltas." *Transactions of the American Society of Civil Engineers* 54, paper 990: 83–87.

Council on Environmental Quality. 1997. *The National Environmental Policy Act: A Study of Its Effectiveness After Twenty-five Years.* Washington, DC: Council on Environmental Quality, Executive Office of the President. ceq.doe.gov/docs/ceq-publications/nepa25fn.pdf.

Cowdrey, Albert E. 1977. *Land's End: A History of the New Orleans District Corps of Engineers.* New Orleans: US Army Corps of Engineers.

Cutter, S. L. 1996. "Vulnerability to Environmental Hazards." *Progress in Human Geography* 20, no. 4: 529–539.

Cutter, S. L., L. Barnes, M. Berry, C. Burton, E. Evans, E. Tate, and J. Webb. 2008. "A Place-based Model for Understanding Community Resilience to Natural Disasters." *Global Environmental Change* 18, no. 4: 598–606.

Dahl, Thomas E. 1990. *Wetland Losses in the United States, 1780s to 1980s.* Washington, DC: US Dept. of the Interior, Fish and Wildlife Service.

Dalbom, C., S. A. Hemmerling, and J. Lewis. 2014. *Community Resettlement Prospects in Southeast Louisiana: A Multidisciplinary Exploration of Legal, Cultural, and Demographic Aspects of Moving Individuals and Communities.* New Orleans: Tulane Institute on Water Resources Law & Policy.

Darby, William. 1817. *A Geographical Description of the State of Louisiana.* New York: James Olmstead.

Data Center. 2014. *Coastal Index, 2014.* New Orleans: Data Center.

Dauber, M. L. 2013. *The Sympathetic State: Disaster Relief and the Origins of the American Welfare State.* Chicago: University of Chicago Press.

Day, John. 2020. Interview, August 14.

Day, John, and Jori Erdman, eds. 2018. *Mississippi Delta Restoration: Pathways to a Sustainable Future.* Cham, Switzerland: Springer.

"Delacroix Island Village Battens Down for Storm." 1947. *New Orleans Times-Picayune,* September 19, 6.

Delahoussaye, Jim. 2010. *A James Delahoussaye Collection of Atchafalaya River Basin Recordings.* Library of Congress, Washington, DC.

———. 2014. Personal interview. December 22.

DeLyser, D., and D. Sui. 2014. "Crossing the Qualitative-Quantitative Chasm III: Enduring Methods, Open Geography, Participatory Research, and the Fourth Paradigm." *Progress in Human Geography* 29, no. 2: 294–307.

Desbiens, Caroline. 2013. *Power from the North: Territory, Identity, and the Culture of Hydroelectricity in Quebec.* Vancouver: University of British Columbia Press.

De Vorsey, Louis. 1988. "La Salle's Cartography of the Lower Mississippi: Product of Error or Deception?" *Geoscience and Man* 25: 5–23.

Dorst, Neal M. 2007. "The National Hurricane Research Project." *Bulletin of the American Meteorological Society* 88, no. 1: 1566–88.

Dyer, C., and R. L. Leard. 1994. "Folk Management in the Oyster Industry in the U.S. Gulf of Mexico." In *Folk Management in the World's Fisheries,* ed. C. L. Lyer and J. R. McGoodwin, 55–89. Denver: University Press of Colorado.

Edwards, Jay D. 2011. "Upper Louisiana's French Vernacular Architecture in the Greater Atlantic World." *Atlantic Studies* 8, no. 4: 411–45.

Elliott, D. O. 1932. *The Improvement of the Lower Mississippi River for Flood Control and Navigation.* Vicksburg, MS: US Army Corps of Engineers, Waterways Experiment Station.

Estaville, L. 1986. "Mapping the Louisiana French." *Southeastern Geographer* 26: 90–113.

Filipich, Judy, and Lee Taylor. 1971. *Lakefront New Orleans: Planning and Development, 1926–1971.* New Orleans: Louisiana State University in New Orleans, Urban Studies Institute.

Fogelman, C. W. 1958. "Family and Community in Disaster: A Socio-psychological Study of the Effects of a Major Disaster upon Individuals and Groups within the Impact Area." PhD diss., Louisiana State University.

Freudenburg, William, Robert Gramling, Shirley Laska, and Kai Erikson. 2007. "Katrina: Lessons Unlearned." *World Watch* 20, no. 5: 14–19.

———. 2009. *Catastrophe in the Making: The Engineering of Katrina and the Disasters of Tomorrow.* Washington, DC: Island Press.

Frierson, Ruthie. 2014. "Guest Commentary: Levee Board Reforms Could Be Washed Away." *Baton Rouge Advocate,* May 2. theadvocate.com/news/opinion /8993757–123/guest-op-ed-levee-board-reforms.

Gagliano, Sherwood. 1994. *An Environmental-Economic Blueprint for Restoring the Louisiana Coastal Zone: The State Plan.* Baton Rouge: Governor's Office of Coastal Activities.

Gagliano, Sherwood, K. J. Meyer-Arendt, and K. M. Wicker. 1981. "Land Loss in the Mississippi River Deltaic Plain." *Transactions, Gulf Coast Association of Geological Societies* 31: 295–300.

Gagliano, Sherwood, P. Light, and R. E. Becker. 1973. "Controlled Diversions in

the Mississippi Delta System: An Approach to Environmental Management."
Baton Rouge: Louisiana State University, Center for Wetland Resources.

Gagliano, Sherwood, and J. L. van Beek. 1970. "Geological and Geomorphic Aspects of Deltaic Processes, Mississippi Delta System." Baton Rouge: Center for Wetland Resources, Louisiana State University.

Garde-Hansen, J., L. McEwen, A. Holmes, and O. Jones. 2017. "Sustainable Flood Memory: Remembering as Resilience." *Memory Studies* 10, no. 4: 384–405.

GC-Harms Interviews. 2016. Conducted by Jessica R. Z. Simms as part of the GC-Harms Project, 2015–16.

Giancarlo, Alexandra. 2011. "The Lower Ninth Ward: Resistance, Recovery, and Renewal." MA thesis, Louisiana State University.

Giblett, Rod. 2016. *Cities and Wetlands: The Return of the Repressed in Nature and Culture.* London: Bloomsbury.

Gibney, Frank Jr. 1987. "Louisiana's Bayou Blues." *Newsweek* 109 (June 22): 54–55.

Glantz, Michael H. 1988. "Introduction. " In *Societal Responses to Climate Change: Forecasting by Analogy,* ed. Michael H. Glantz, 1–8. Boulder, CO: Westview Press.

Gomez, G. M. 1998. *A Wetland Biography: Seasons on Louisiana's Chenier Plain.* Austin: University of Texas Press.

———. 2000. "Perspective, Power, and Priorities: New Orleans and the Mississippi River Flood of 1927." In *Transforming New Orleans and Its Environs: Centuries of Change,* ed. C. E. Colten, 109–20. Pittsburgh: University of Pittsburgh Press.

Gorman, H. S. 2001. *Redefining Efficiency: Pollution Concerns, Regulatory Mechanisms, and Technological Change in the U.S. Petroleum Industry.* Akron, OH: University of Akron Press.

Gramling, R., and R. Hagelman. 2005. "A Working Coast: People in the Louisiana Wetlands." *Journal of Coastal Research* 44: 112–33.

Greater New Orleans Community Data Center. 2013. *The New Orleans Index at Eight.* New Orleans: Greater New Orleans Community Data Center.

Green, Timothy, and Robert Olshansky. 2012. "Rebuilding Housing in New Orleans: The Road Home Program after the Hurricane Katrina Disaster." *Housing Policy Debate* 22, no. 1: 75–99.

Greenberg, Michael R. 2013. *The Environmental Impact Statement after Two Generations: Managing Environmental Power.* New York: Routledge.

Greer, A. 2012. "Commons and Enclosure in the Colonization of North America." *American Historical Review* 117, no. 2: 365–86.

Grismore, Audrey. 2018. "Natural Resources–Based Conflicts in Coastal Louisiana: A Multi-faceted Social and Ecological Setting." PhD diss., Louisiana State University.

Guerrini, A., and J. E. Dugan. 2010. "Informing Ecological Restoration in a Coastal Context." In *Restoration and History: The Search for A Usable Environmental Past,* ed. C. W. Finkl and S. M. Kahlil, 131–42. New York: Routledge.

Gulf South Research Institute. 1973. *Flood of '73: Post Flood Report: Fish and Wildlife Supplement.* Baton Rouge: Gulf South Research Institute.

Hall, Marcus, ed. 2010. *Restoration and History: The Search for a Usable Environmental Past.* New York: Routledge.

Hanny, David D. 1995. "Interest Group Formation through Resource Mobilization: The Case of the Coalition to Restore Coastal Louisiana." PhD diss., University of Oklahoma.

Hardin, Garrett. 1968. "Tragedy of the Commons." *Science* 162: 1243–48.

Hardman, Jesse. 2015. "Why Do We Measure Wetlands Loss in Football Fields." WWNO Radio, March 3. www.wno.org/post/why-do-we-measure-wetlands-loss-football-fields (accessed December 2017).

Harrison, R. W., and W. M. Kollmorgen. 1947. "Past and Prospective Drainage Reclamation in the Coastal Marshlands of the Mississippi River Delta." *Journal of Land and Public Utility Economics* 23, no. 3: 297–320.

Hays, S. P. 1959. *Conservation and the Gospel of Efficiency: The Progressive Conservation Movement, 1890–1920.* Cambridge, MA: Harvard University Press.

Hebert, M. C. 1997. "Coastal Restoration under CWPPRA and Property Rights Issues." *Louisiana Law Review* 57: 1165–1211.

Hemmerling, Scott A. 2017. *A Louisiana Coastal Atlas: Resources, Economies, and Demographics.* Baton Rouge: Louisiana State University Press.

Hemmerling, Scott A., Monica Barra, and Rebecca H. Bond. 2020. "Adapting to a Smaller Coast: Restoration, Protection, and Social Justice in Coastal Louisiana." In *Louisiana's Response to Extreme Weather,* ed. Shirley Laska, 113–46. Cham, Switzerland: Springer.

Higgs, Eric. 2003. *Nature by Design: People, Natural Processes, Ecological Restoration.* Cambridge, MA: MIT Press.

———. 2010. "Restoring Dirt under the Fingernails." In *Restoration and History: The Search for a Usable Environmental Past,* ed. Marcus Hall, 309–14. New York: Routledge.

Holm, Poul, Joni Adamson, Hsinya Huang, Lars Kirdan, Sally Kitch, Iain McCalman, James Ogude. 2015. "Humanities for the Environment—A Manifesto for Research and Action." *Humanities* 4, no. 4: 977–92.

Holm, Poul, and Verena Winiwarter. 2017. "Climate Change Studies and the Human Sciences." *Global and Planetary Change* 156: 115–22.

Holmes, Andrew, and Lindsey McEwen. 2020. "How to Exchange Stories of Local

Flood Resilience from Flood Rich Areas to the Flooded Areas of the Future." *Environmental Communication* 4, no. 5: 1–17.

Horowitz, Ben. 2014. *Our Changing Demographic Landscape: Map Collection.* New Orleans: Data Center, 2014.

Houck, O. A. 2015. "The Reckoning: Oil and Gas Development in the Louisiana Coastal Zone." *Tulane Environmental Law Journal* 28, no. 2: 187–296.

Iberville, Pierre Le Moyne. 1661–1706. 1981 ed. *Iberville's Gulf Journals,* trans. R. G. McWilliams. University: University of Alabama Press.

Innes, Judith E., and David E. Booher. 2004. "Reframing Public Participation: Strategies for the 21st Century." *Planning Theory & Practice* 5, no. 4: 419–36.

Jesse, Nathan. 2020. "Community Resettlement in Louisiana: Learning from Histories of Horror and Hope." In *Louisiana's Response to Extreme Weather,* ed. Shirley Laska, 147–84. Cham, Switzerland: Springer.

Kasemir, B. 2003. *Public Participation in Sustainability Science: A Handbook.* New York: Cambridge University Press.

Kates, R. W., W. C. Clark, R. Corell, J. M. Hall, C. C. Jaeger, I. Lowe, J. J. McCarthy, H. J. Schellnhuber, B. Bolin, N. M. Dickson, and S. Faucheux. 2001. "Sustainability Science." *Science* 292, no. 5517: 641–42.

Kates, R. W., Craig E. Colten, Shirley Laska, and Stephen P. Leatherman. 2006. "Reconstruction of New Orleans after Hurricane Katrina: A Research Perspective." *Proceedings of the National Academy of Sciences* 103, no. 40: 14653–60.

Kates, R. W., William R. Travis, and Thomas J. Wilbanks. 2012. "Transformational Adaptation When Incremental Adaptations to Climate Change Are Insufficient." *Proceedings of the National Academy of Sciences* 109: 7156–61.

Keim, Barry D., And Robert A. Muller. 2009. *Hurricanes of the Gulf of Mexico.* Baton Rouge: Louisiana State University Press.

Keithly, Walter R., and James G. Wilkins. 2006. "Compensable Property Interests and Takings: A Coast Study of the Louisiana Oyster Industry." *American Fisheries Society Symposium Proceedings,* 587–97.

Kelman, Ari. 2003. *A River and Its City: The Nature of Landscape in New Orleans.* Berkeley: University of California Press.

———. 2009. "Even Paranoids Have Enemies: Rumors of Levee Sabotage in New Orleans's Lower 9th Ward." *Journal of Urban History* 35, no. 5: 627–39.

Kemp, G. Paul. 2017. Interview with author. June 21.

Kidder, Tristam R. 2000. "Making the City Inevitable: Native Americans and the Geography of New Orleans." In *Transforming New Orleans in Its Environs: Centuries of Change,* ed. Craig E. Colten, 9–21. Pittsburgh: University of Pittsburgh Press.

Kindon, S., R. Pain, and M. Kesby, eds. 2010. *Participatory Action Research Approaches and Methods: Connecting People, Participation and Place.* Abingdon, UK: Routledge.

Kmen, Harry. 1957. "New Orleans's Forty Days in 1849." *Louisiana Historical Quarterly* 40: 25–45.

Kniffen, F. B. 1936a. "Louisiana House Types." *Annals of the Association of American Geographers* 26, no. 4: 179–93.

———. 1936b. "Preliminary Report on the Indian Mounds and Middens of Plaquemines and St. Bernard Parishes." *Louisiana Geological Survey Bulletin* 8: 407–22.

———. 1965. "Folk Housing: Key to Diffusion." *Annals of the Association of American Geographers* 55, no. 4: 549–76.

Kniffen, F. B., Hiram F. Gregory, and George A. Stokes. 1994. *The Historic Indian Tribes of Louisiana: From 1542 to the Present.* Baton Rouge: Louisiana State University Press.

Kniffen, F. B., and M. Wright. 1963. "Disaster and Reconstruction in Cameron Parish." *Louisiana Studies* 2: 74–83.

Knowles, Scott G. 2014. "Learning from Disaster: The History of Technology and the Future of Disaster Research." *Technology and Culture* 55, no. 4: 773–84.

Koslov, Liz. 2016. "The Case for Retreat." *Public Culture* 28, no. 2 (79): 359–87.

Krebs, B. 1923. "Coast Sea Food Interests Favor Spillway Plan." *New Orleans Times-Picayune,* November 6, 1–2.

Lake, R. W., ed. 1987. *Resolving Locational Conflict.* New Brunswick, NJ: Center for Urban Policy Research.

Lamb, H. H. 1982. *Climate, History, and the Modern World.* London: Methuen.

Landphair, Juliet. 2007. "'The Forgotten People of New Orleans': Community, Vulnerability, and the Lower Ninth Ward," *American Historical Review* 94, no. 2: 837–45.

Laska, Shirley, ed. 2020. *Louisiana's Response to Extreme Weather: A Coastal State's Adaptation Challenges and Successes.* New York: Springer Nature.

Laska, Shirley, George Woodell, Ronald Hagelman, Robert Gramling, and Monica Teets Farris. 2005. "At Risk: The Human, Community and Infrastructure Resources of Coastal Louisiana." *Journal of Coastal Research* 44: 90–111.

Lerner, S. 2005. *Diamond: A Struggle for Environmental Justice in Louisiana's Chemical Corridor.* Cambridge, MA: MIT Press.

Liu, Amy, Matt Fellowes, and Mia Mabanta. 2006. *Katrina Index: A One-Year Review of Key Indicators of Recovery in Post-Storm New Orleans.* Washington, DC: Brookings Institution.

Livingston, David. 2010. *Putting Science in Its Place: Geographies of Scientific Knowledge.* Chicago: University of Chicago Press.

Lockett, Samuel H. 1874. *Louisiana As It Is: A Geographical and Topographical Description of the State.* Baton Rouge: Louisiana State University Press, 1969.

Lopez, John A., John Day, Greg Miller, Sue Hawes, Cindy Brown, Paul Keddy, and Carlton Dufrechou. 2005. *The Multiple Lines of Defense Strategy to Sustain Louisiana's Coast.* New Orleans: Lake Pontchartrain Basin Foundation.

Lorovich, Frank M. 1967. "The Dalmatian Yugoslavs in Louisiana." *Louisiana History* 8, no. 2: 149–64.

Louisiana Civil Defense Agency. 1957. *Louisiana Survival Plan: Reception and Care—Resources Study.* Baton Rouge: Louisiana Civil Defense Agency.

Louisiana Coastal Wetlands Conservation and Restoration Task Force. 1993. *Louisiana Coastal Wetlands Restoration Plan: Main Report and Environmental Impact Statement.* New Orleans: US Army Corps of Engineers, New Orleans District.

Louisiana Coastal Wetlands Conservation and Restoration Task Force and the Wetlands Conservation and Restoration Authority. 1998. *Coast 2050: Toward a Sustainable Coastal Louisiana.* Baton Rouge: Louisiana Dept. of Natural Resources.

Louisiana Commission for the Protection of Birds, Game and Fish. 1912. *Report of the Board of Commissioners for the Protection of Birds, Game and Fish.* Baton Rouge: Louisiana Commission for the Protection of Birds, Game and Fish.

Louisiana Commission of Birds, Game and Fish. 1910. *Report of the Commissioners of Birds, Game and Fish.* Baton Rouge: Louisiana Commission of Birds, Game and Fish.

Louisiana Department of Natural Resources. 2001. *Coastal Restoration Division: Annual Project Reviews.* Baton Rouge: Louisiana Dept. of Natural Resources.

———. 2005. *Coastal Restoration Division: Annual Project Reviews.* Baton Rouge: Louisiana Dept. of Natural Resources.

Louisiana Governor's Office of Homeland Security and Emergency Preparedness. 2008. *After-Action Report and Improvement Plan: Hurricanes Gustav and Ike.* Baton Rouge: Louisiana Governor's Office of Homeland Security and Emergency Preparedness.

———. 2012. *Hurricane Isaac After Action Report and Improvement Plan.* Baton Rouge: Louisiana Governor's Office of Homeland Security and Emergency Preparedness.

Louisiana Military Dept. 1949. *Disaster Relief Plan for Greater New Orleans Area.* Baton Rouge: Louisiana Military Dept.

Louisiana Office of Community Development. 2017. *LA SAFE: Louisiana's Strategic Adaptations for Future Environment.* lasafe.la.gov/ (accessed June 2017).

———. 2019. *Our Land and Water: A Regional Approach to Adaptation.* s3.amazonaws.com/lasafe/Final+Adaptation+Strategies/Regional+Adaptation+Strategy.pdf.

Louisiana Office of Community Development Disaster Recovery Unit. 2015a. "LA SAFE: Louisiana's Strategic Adaptations for Future Environments." Baton Rouge: Louisiana Office of Community Development Disaster Recovery Unit.

———. 2015b. "Resettlement as Resilience Strategy: And the Case of Isle de Jean Charles." Baton Rouge: Louisiana Office of Community Development Disaster Recovery Unit.

Louisiana Recovery Authority. 2007. "Louisiana Speaks: Vision and Strategies for Recovery and Growth in South Louisiana." static1.squarespace.com/static /536d55f1e4b07afeea8cef61/t/54500a8de4b0d2e64620a808/1414531725899 /LA_Speaks_FINAL.pdf (accessed June 2017).

Louisiana State Board of Engineers. 1929. *Flood Control in the Lower Mississippi Valley.* Baton Rouge: Louisiana State Board of Engineers.

Ludwig, D., R. Hilborn, and C. Walters. 1993. "Uncertainty, Resource Exploitation, and Conservation: Lessons from History." *Science* 260 (April): 17, 36.

Maass, A. 2014. "Adapting Resilience to a New Hazard: Oil and Oysters in Coastal Louisiana." MS thesis, Louisiana State University.

Machlis, G. E., J. E. Force, and W. R. Burch Jr. 1997. "The Human Ecosystem Part I: The Human Ecosystem as an Organizing Concept in Ecosystem Management." *Society & Natural Resources,* 10, no. 4: 347–67.

Machlis, G. E., and Marcia K. McNutt. 2010. "Scenario-building for the Deepwater Horizon Oil Spill." *Science* 329, no. 5995: 1018–19.

MacKinnon, Danny, and Kate Driscoll Derickson. 2013. "From Resilience to Resourcefulness: A Critique of Resilience Policy and Activism." *Progress in Human Geography* 37, no. 2: 253–70.

Maldonado, J. K. C. Shearer, R. Bronen, K. Peterson, and H. Lazrus. 2013. "The Impact of Climate Change on Tribal Communities in the U.S.: Displacement, Relocation, and Human Rights." *Climatic Change* 120, no. 3: 601–14.

Mandelman, Adam. 2020. *The Place with No Edge: An Intimate History of People, Technology, and the Mississippi River Delta.* Baton Rouge: Louisiana State University Press.

Manning-Broome, C., J. Dubinin, and P. Jenkins. 2015. *View from the Coast: Local Perspectives and Policy Recommendations on Flood-Risk Reduction in South Louisiana.* Policy Report. Baton Rouge: Center for Planning Excellence. static1. squarespace.com/static/536d55f1e4b07afeea8cef61/t/57d84991ff7c5058ba5e cda8/1473792452625/VFTC_final.pdf.

Marks, B. 2012. "The Political Economy of Household Commodity Production in the Louisiana Shrimp Fishery." *Journal of Agrarian Change* 12, nos. 2–3: 227–51.

Marshall, Bob. 2014. "Experts: New N.O. Levees Built at Lower Standards." *Baton Rouge Advocate,* May 19, pp. 1 and 3.

Martin, Laura J. 2015. "Natural and National Recovery: The Rise of Ecological Restoration in the United States, 1930–1975." PhD diss., Cornell University.

Mazmanian, Daniel A., and Jeanne Nienaber. 1979. *Can Organizations Change? Environmental Protection, Citizen Participation, and the Corps of Engineers.* Washington, DC: Brookings Institution.

McCally, David. 1999. *The Everglades: An Environmental History.* Gainesville: University of Florida Press.

McGuire, T. R. 2008. "Shell Games on the Water Bottoms of Louisiana: Investigative Journalism and Anthropological Inquiry." In *Against the Grain: The Vayda Tradition in Human Ecology and Ecological Anthropology,* ed. B. Walters, B. McCay, P. West, and S. Lees, S., 117–34. Lanham, MD: Rowman and Littlefield.

McIlhenny, E. A. 1918. Correspondence to M. L. Alexander (President of the Louisiana Conservation Commission), April 10. McIlhenny Collection, acc. # 3534, folder 268, Louisiana State University.

———. 1928. "The Creating of the Wild Life Refuges in Louisiana." *Ninth Biennial Report of the Department of Conservation of the State of Louisiana,* 133–39. New Orleans: Dept. of Conservation.

McLeman, R. 2014. *Climate and Human Migration: Past Experiences, Future Challenges.* New York: Cambridge University Press.

McMichael, R. N. 1961. "Plant Location Factors in the Petrochemical Industry in Louisiana." PhD diss., Louisiana State University.

McNeill, W. H. 2001. "Passing Strange: The Convergence of Evolutionary Science with Scientific History." *History and Theory* 44, no. 1: 1–15.

Miller, David C. 1989. *Dark Eden: The Swamp in Nineteenth-Century American Culture.* New York: Cambridge University Press.

Miller, G. B. 1997. "Louisiana's Tidelands Controversy: The United States v. State of Louisiana Maritime Boundary Cases." *Louisiana History* 38, no. 2: 203–21.

Mississippi River Commission. 1927. *Public Hearings of the Mississippi River Commission (July 7, 1927–August 20, 1927).* Vicksburg: Mississippi River Commission.

Moore, H. F. 1899. *Report on the Oyster-beds of Louisiana.* Washington, DC: US Government Printing Office.

Morgan, J. P., and P. B. Larimore. 1957. "Changes in the Louisiana Shoreline." *Gulf Coast Association of Geological Societies* 7: 303–10.

Morgan City, Louisiana. 1927. *A Brief Stating the Position and Policy of Morgan City, Louisiana with Reference to Flood Control.* Morgan City: King Hannaford.

Morris, Christopher. 2012. *The Big Muddy: An Environmental History of the Mississippi River and Its Peoples from Hernando De Soto to Hurricane Katrina.* New York: Oxford University Press.

———. 2016. "Disturbing the Mississippi: The Language of Science, Engineering, and River Restoration." *Open Rivers* 2. https://editions.lib.umn.edu/openrivers /article/disturbing-the-mississippi-the-language-of-science-engineering-and -river-restoration/.

National Oceanographic and Atmospheric Administration. 2017. "Sea Level Rise Viewer." coast.noaa.gov/slr/#/layer/vul-soc/4/-50294420.54465331/3503029 .693527597/8/satellite/none/0.8/2050/interHigh/midAccretion (accessed December 2017).

National Research Council. 1999. *Our Common Journey: A Transition Toward Sustainability.* Washington, DC: National Academies Press.

———. 2012. *Disaster Resilience: A National Imperative.* Washington, DC: National Academies Press. doi.org/10.17226/13457.

Nelson, Marla, Renia Ehrenfeuct, and S. Laska. 2007. "Planning, Plans, and People: Professional Expertise, Local Knowledge, and Governmental Action in Post–Hurricane Katrina New Orleans." *Cityscape* 9, no. 3: 23–52.

Nesbitt, D. M. 1885. *Tide Marshes of the United States.* Washington, DC: US Dept. of Agriculture, Special Report 7.

New Orleans, City of. 2007. *The Unified New Orleans Plan.* New Orleans: City of New Orleans.

New Orleans Department of Safety and Permits. 2015. Elevation Permits, August 29, 2005–January 18, 2015.

"New Orleans Is Exemplar of Resiliency: Editorial." 2013. *New Orleans Times-Picayune,* December 13, www.nola.com/opinions/index.ssf/2013/12/new _orleans_is_an_exemplar_of.html.

"New Orleans Scrambles to Repair Drainage System After Severe Flooding." *New York Times,* August 11. www.nytimes.com/2017/08/11/us/new-orleans-repair -pumping-system-flooding.html.

Norgress, R. E. 1947. "The History of the Cypress Lumber Industry in Louisiana." *Louisiana Historical Quarterly* 30, no. 3: 1–83.

O'Brien, W., and J. A. McIvor. 2007. "Is There Anything Good about the Everglades Restoration?" *Environments* 35, no. 1: 1–20.

Office of the President. 2006. *The Federal Response to Hurricane Katrina: Lessons Learned.* Washington, DC: Office of the President.

O'Keefe, Phil, Ken Westgate, and Ben Wisner. 1976. "Taking the Naturalness out of Natural Disasters." *Nature* 260: 566–67.

Okey, C. M. 1914. *Wetlands of Southern Louisiana and their Drainage.* Washington, DC: US Dept. of Agriculture, Bulletin 71.

"Old Bucktown Folk, Undaunted, Rise to Rebuild Ruined Homes." 1915. *New Orleans Times-Picayune* October 1, 13.

Olshansky, Robert, and Laurie Johnson. 2010. *Clear as Mud: Planning for the Rebuilding of New Orleans.* Chicago: American Planning Association.

Olson, Sherry H. 1971. *The Depletion Myth: A History of Railroad Use of Timber.* Cambridge, MA: Harvard University Press.

O'Neill, K. M. 2006. *Rivers by Design: State Power and the Origins of U.S. Flood Control.* Durham, NC: Duke University Press.

Orleans Levee Board. 1954. *Building a Great City.* New Orleans: Orleans Levee Board.

Orleans Levee District. 1950. *Report on Flood Control and Shore Erosion Protection for the City of New Orleans.* New Orleans: Bedel and Nelson.

Owens, J. A. 1999. "Holding Back the Waters: Land Development and the Origins of Levees on the Mississippi, 1720–1845." PhD diss., Louisiana State University.

Oxfam. 2014. "Integrating Social Science and Gulf Coast Restoration." www .oxfamamerica.org/socialscience.

Pabis, George S. 1998. "Delaying the Deluge: The Engineering Debate over Flood Control on the Lower Mississippi River, 1846–1861." *Journal of Southern History* 64, no. 3: 421–54.

Parker, Charles, et al. 2009. "Preventable Catastrophe? The Hurricane Katrina Disaster Revisited." *Journal of Contingencies and Crisis Management* 17, no. 4: 206–20.

Parsons, James J. 1983. "The Migration of Canary Islanders to the Americas: An Unbroken Current since Columbus." *Americas* 39, no. 4: 447–81.

Paskoff, Paul. 2007. *Troubled Waters: Steamboat Disasters, River Improvements, and American Public Policy, 1821–1860.* Baton Rouge: Louisiana State University Press.

Pelling, Mark. 2011. *Adaptation to Climate Change: From Resilience to Transformation.* New York: Routledge.

Pelling, Mark, Karen O'Brien, and David Matyas. 2015. "Adaptation and Transition." *Climatic Change* 133: 113–27.

Penland, S. and R. Boyd. 1981. "Shoreline Changes in Louisiana Barrier Coast." *Oceans* 81: 209–29.

Person, J. 2006. "Theoretical Reflections on the Connection between Environmental Assessment Methods in Conflict." *Environmental Impact Assessment Review* 26: 605–13.

Petterson, J. S., L. D. Stanley, E. Glazier, and J. Philipp. 2006. "A Preliminary Assessment of Social and Economic Impacts Associated with Hurricane Katrina." *American Anthropologist* 108, no. 4: 643–70.

Peyronnin, N., M. Green, C. P. Richards, A. Owens, D. Reed, J. Chamberlain, D. G. Groves, W. K. Rhinehart, and K. Belhadjali. 2013. "Louisiana's 2012 Coastal

Master Plan: Overview of a Science-based and Publicly Informed Decision-making Process." *Journal of Coastal Research* 67, no. 1: 1–15.

Plaquemines Parish Council. 1970. "Minutes of Meetings." Belle Chasse, LA.

Platt, R. 1999. *Disasters and Democracy: The Politics of Extreme Natural Events.* Washington, DC: Island Press.

Priest, Tyler. 2008. "Claiming the Coastal Sea: The Battles for the 'Tidelands,' 1937–1953." In *History of the Offshore Oil and Gas Industry in Southern Louisiana,* vol. 1, ed. D. Austin, B. Carriker, T. McGuire, J. Pratt, T. Priest, and A. G. Pulsipher, 67–91. New Orleans: US Dept. of the Interior, Minerals Management Service.

Prince, Hugh. 2008. *Wetlands of the American Midwest: A Historical Geography of Changing Attitudes.* Chicago: University of Chicago Press.

Randolph, Ned. 2018. "License to Extract: How Louisiana's Master Plan for a Sustainable Coast Is Sinking It." *Lateral: Journal of the Cultural Studies Association* 7, no. 2. csalateral.org/randy-martin-prize/license-to-extract-louisiana-master-plan-sustainable-coast-randolph/.

Reed, Denise, and Alison Plyer. 2019. "Toward Holistic Planning for Community Adaptation on the Louisiana Coast: Workshop Report." Unpublished report. New Orleans.

Rehder, J. 1999. *Delta Sugar: Louisiana's Vanishing Plantation Landscape.* Baltimore: Johns Hopkins University Press.

Reid, Robert. 2013. "Defending New Orleans." *Civil Engineering* 83, no. 11 (November): 48–83.

Reuss, M. 1998. *Designing the Bayous: The Control of Water in the Atchafalaya Basin, 1800–1995.* Alexandria, VA: US Army Corps of Engineers, Office of History.

Roberts, Harry H. 1997. "Dynamic Changes of the Holocene Mississippi River Delta Plain: The Delta Cycle." *Journal of Coastal Research,* 13, no. 3 : 605–27.

Roberston, Morgan M. 2000. "No Net Loss: Wetland Restoration and the Incomplete Capitalization of Nature." *Antipode* 32, no. 4: 463–93.

Rockefeller Foundation. 2013. "100 Resilient Cities: Centennial Challenge." 100resilientcities.rockefellerfoundation.org/cities.

Rodrigue, J. C. 2001. *Reconstruction in the Cane Fields: From Slavery to Free Labor in Louisiana's Sugar Parishes.* Baton Rouge: Louisiana State University Press.

Rohland, E. 2018. *Changes in the Air: Hurricanes in New Orleans from 1718 to the Present.* New York: Berghan Books.

Rosner, David, and Gerald Markowitz. 2002. *Deceit and Denial: The Deadly Politics of Industrial Pollution.* Berkeley: University of California Press.

Russell, Edmund, James Allison, Thomas Finger, John K. Brown, Brian Balogh, and W. Bernard Carlson. 2011. "The Power of Nature: Synthesizing the History of Technology and Environmental History." *Technology and Culture* 52, no. 2: 246–59.

Russell, R. J. 1936. "Physiography of the Lower Mississippi River Delta." In "Lower Mississippi River Delta," *Louisiana Geological Survey Bulletin 8.*

Save Louisiana Coalition. 2020. "The Save Louisiana Coalition." www.thesavelou isianacoalition.com/.

Scaife, W. W., R. E. Turner, and R. Costanza. 1983. "Coastal Louisiana: Recent Land Loss and Canal Impacts." *Environmental Management* 7: 433–42.

Scarpino, Phillip. 1985. *Great River: An Environmental History of the Upper Mississippi, 1890–1950.* Columbia: University of Missouri Press.

Schleifstein, M. 2013. "Louisiana Could Begin Building Mid-Barataria Sediment Diversion by Late 2015." *New Orleans Times-Picayune*, September 18. www.nola .com/environment/index.ssf/2013/09/louisiana_could_begin_building.html.

———. 2014. "Louisiana's Top Coastal Official May Explore Lawsuit to Block Levee Board Suit Against Energy Companies." *New Orleans Times-Picayune*, February 14. www.nola.com/environment/index.ssf/2014/01/coastal_author ity_chairman_may.html.

Schlesselman, G. W. 1955. "The Gulf Coast Oyster Industry in the United States." *Geographical Review* 45, no. 4: 531–41.

Siders, A. R., Miyuki Hino, and Katharine J. Mach. 2019. "The Case for Strategic and Managed Climate Retreat." *Science* 365, no. 6455: 761–763.

Simms, Jessica Rose. 2017a. "Grounds for Displacement: Issues of Migration on Louisiana's Disappearing Coast." PhD diss., Louisiana State University.

———. 2017b. "'Why Would I Live Anyplace Else?': Resilience, Sense of Place, and Possibilities of Migration in Coastal Louisiana." *Journal of Coastal Research* 33, no. 2: 408–20.

Smit, B., and J. Wandel. 2006. "Adaptation, Adaptive Capacity and Vulnerability." *Global Environmental Change* 16, no. 3: 282–92.

Spears, Ellen G. 2020. *Rethinking the American Environmental Movement post-1945.* New York: Routledge.

St. Amant, Lyle. 1973. Testimony to Congress. In US Congress, Senate, *Damage to Oyster Beds Due to Federal Action, Hearing Before the Subcommittee on Water Resources.* 93rd Cong., 1st Sess., 16–23.

St. Bernard Parish Police Jury. 1970. "Minutes of Meetings." Chalmette, LA.

Steinberg, Ted. 2000. *Acts of God: The Unnatural History of Natural Disasters in America.* Oxford, UK: Oxford University Press.

Steller-McDonald, Karen, Lee Sischinger, and Gregor Auble. 1990. *Wetland Creation and Restoration: Description and Summary of the Literature.* Buffalo, NY: Amherst Systems.

Stevenson, J. 2000. "Louisiana's Oyster Lease Relocation Program: A Step Toward Common Ground." *Southern University Law Review* 28, no. 1: 19–43.

Stine, Jeffrey K. 2008. *America's Forested Wetlands: From Wasteland to Valued Resource.* Durham, NC: Forest History Society.

Swanton, J. R. 1946. *The Indians of the Southeastern United States.* Washington, DC: Smithsonian Institution, Bureau of American Ethnology.

Swyngedouw, E. 1996. "The City as a Hybrid: On Nature, Society and Cyborg Urbanization." *Capitalism Nature Socialism* 7, no. 2: 65–80.

Theriot, J. P. 2014. *American Energy, Imperiled Coast: Oil and Gas Development in Louisiana's Wetlands.* Baton Rouge: Louisiana State University Press.

Thibodeaux, Ron. 2012. "Hurricane Isaac Floodwaters Take LaPlace and Slidell by Surprise." *New Orleans Times-Picayune,* August 30. www.nola.com/hurricane /index.ssf/2012/08/hurricane_isaac_floodwaters_ta.html.

Thompson, Richard. 2013. "Army Corps Reconfirms St. John Parish Levee Route." *Baton Rouge Advocate,* November 30. theadvocate.com/news/neworleans/new orleansnews/7691823–123/army-corps-reconfirms-preference-for.

———. 2014. "Work Begins on Levee System for St. Charles Parish's West Bank." *Baton Rouge Advocate,* January 25. theadvocate.com/news/neworleans/neworleans news/8172364–123/work-begins-on-levee-system.

Törnqvist, T. E., K. L. Jankowski, Y.-X. Li, and J. L. González. 2020. "Tipping Points of Mississippi Delta Marshes due to Accelerated Sea-level Rise." *Science Advances* 6, no. 21. eaaz5512. doi.org/10.1126/sciadv.aaz5512.

"Tropical Storm Expected to Hit Near River Mouth." 1915. *New Orleans Times-Picayune,* September 29, 1.

Tulian, E. A. 1921. Correspondence to E. A. McIlhenny, July 25. McIlhenny Collection, acc. # 3534, folder 696, E. A. Hill Memorial Library, Louisiana State University.

Turner, R. Eugene, and Giovanna McClenachan. 2018. "Reversing Wetland Death from 35,000 Cuts: Opportunities to Restore Louisiana's Dredged Canals." *PLoS ONE* 13, no. 12: e0207717. doi.org/10.1371/journal.pone.0207717.

Tzoumis, Kelly A. 1998. "Wetlands Policymaking in the U.S. Congress from 1789–1995." *Wetlands* 18, no. 3: 447–59.

United Nations. 2015. *Sustainable Development Goals.* www.un.org/sustainablede velopment/sustainable-development-goals/.

Upton, Harold. 2013. *Commercial Fishery Disaster Assistance,* CRS Report RL34209. Washington, DC: Congressional Research Service.

US Army Corps of Engineers. 1951. *The Atchafalaya River Study: A Report Based upon Engineering and Geological Studies of the Enlargement of Old and Atchafalaya Rivers.* Vicksburg: Mississippi River Commission.

———. 1991–2017. "Technical Task Force Meeting Minutes." www.mvn.usace.army
.mil/Missions/Environmental/CWPPRA/Meeting-Documents/ (accessed June
2017).

———. 2012. *2011 Post-Flood Report.* Vicksburg: US Army Corps of Engineers, Mississippi Valley Division.

US Army Corps of Engineers, New Orleans District. 1965. *Report on Hurricane
Betsy.* New Orleans: US Army Corps of Engineers.

———. 1974. *Flood of 1973: Post-Flood Report.* Vol. 1. New Orleans: US Army Corps
of Engineers.

———. 2004. *Louisiana Coastal Area: Ecosystem Restoration Study,* vol. 1. New Orleans: US Army Corps of Engineers, New Orleans District.

———. 2021. *DRAFT: Environmental Impact Statement for the Proposed Mid-
Barataria Sediment Diversion Project—Plaquemines Parish, Louisiana.* New Orleans: U.S. Army Corps of Engineers, New Orleans District.

US Congress, House of Representatives. 1914. *Separation of the Red and Atchafalaya Rivers from the Mississippi River.* House Doc. 841, 63rd Cong., 2nd Sess.

———. 1919. *Atchafalaya River, Louisiana, and Related Basins.* House Doc. 288,
66th Cong., 1st Sess.

———. 1927a. *Flood Control: Hearings before the Committee on Flood Control.* 70th
Cong., 1st Sess. November 7 to November 22.

———. 1927b. *Flood Control in the Mississippi Valley.* House Doc. 90, 70th Cong.,
1st Sess.

———. 1927c. *Spillways on the Lower Mississippi.* House Doc. 95. 70th Cong., 1st Sess.

———. 1930. *Flood Control on the Mississippi River: Hearings before the Committee
on Flood Control.* Pt. 1. 71st Cong. 2nd Sess.

———. 1931a. *Control of Floods in the Alluvial Valley of the Lower Mississippi River.*
House Doc. 798, 71st Cong., 3rd Sess.

———. 1931b. *Flood Control on the Mississippi River: Hearings before Subcommittee
of the Committee on Flood Control.* 71st Cong., 3rd Sess.

———. 1941. *Flood Control on the Lower Mississippi River.* House Doc. 359, 77th
Cong., 1st Sess.

———. 1946a. "Lake Pontchartrain, La." House Doc. 691, 79th Cong., 2nd Sess.

———. 1946b. *Rehabilitation of Oyster Beds: Hearings before the Committee on Flood
Control.* 79th Cong., 2nd Sess.

———. 1947. *Rehabilitation of Oyster Beds Destroyed by the Opening of the Bonnet
Carre Spillway: Hearing before the Subcommittee on Salt-water Fish and Shellfish
Problems.* 80th Cong., 1st Sess.

US Congress, Committee on Merchant Marine and Fisheries. 1990. *Coastal Wetland Management and Restoration: Hearing.* 101st Cong., 2nd Sess.

US Congress, Select Bipartisan Committee to Investigate the Preparation for and Response to Hurricane Katrina. 2006. *A Failure of Initiative: Final Report of the Select Bipartisan Committee to Investigate the Preparation for and Response to Hurricane Katrina.* Washington, DC: Government Printing Office.

US Congress, Senate. 1989. *Louisiana Coastal Wetlands Conservation and Restoration Act: Hearings.* 101st Cong., 1st Sess.

———. 1999. *Reauthorizing the Coastal Wetlands Planning, Protection and Restoration Act.* Senate Report 106–193. 106th Cong., 1st Sess. www.gpo.gov/fdsys/pkg /CRPT-106srpt193/html/CRPT-106srpt193.htm.

US Department of Agriculture. 1980. "Aerial Photograph, Lafourche Parish, Louisiana, 22057-278-201." Louisiana State University, Cartographic Information Center Collection.

US Department of Agriculture, National Resources Conservation Service. N.d. "Restoring American's Wetlands: A Private Lands Conservation Success Story." www.nrcs.usda.gov/Internet/FSE_DOCUMENTS/stelprdb1045079. pdf (accessed December 16, 2017).

US Department of Commerce, Weather Bureau. 1959. *A Model Hurricane Plan for a Coastal Community.* Washington, DC: US Dept. of Commerce.

US Geological Survey, National Wetlands Research Center. 1994. *Land Loss in Coastal Louisiana 1956–90.* Lafayette: National Wetlands Research Center Open File Report 94–01. www.lacoast.gov/new/Pubs/Report_data/NWRC-OFR 94.aspx (accessed December 2017).

———. 2003. "100+ Years of Land Change for Coastal Louisiana." www.nwrc.usgs .gov/upload/landloss11X17.pdf (accessed December 2017).

———. 2017. "Caring for Coastal Wetlands." www.lacoast.gov/new/Pubs/Report _data/Caring.aspx#act (accessed December 2017).

US Government Accountability Office. 1995. *Restoring the Everglades: Public Participation in Federal Efforts.* Washington, DC: US Government Accountability Office. www.gao.gov/products/RCED-96-5.

———. 2020. *A Climate Migration Pilot Program Could Enhance the Nation's Resilience and Reduce Federal Fiscal Exposure.* Washington, DC: US Government Accountability Office. www.gao.gov/products/GAO-20-488.

Usner, D. H. 2003. *American Indians in the Lower Mississippi Valley: Social and Economic Histories.* Lincoln: University of Nebraska Press.

Vanclay, F. 2012. "The Potential Application of Social Impact Assessment in Integrated Coastal Zone Management." *Ocean and Coastal Management* 68: 149–56.

Van Heerden, I. 1994. *A Long-term, Comprehensive Management Plan for Coastal Louisiana to Ensure Sustainable Biological Productivity, Economic Growth, and the*

Continued Existence of its Unique Culture and Heritage. Baton Rouge: Louisiana State University, Center for Coastal, Energy, and Environmental Resources.

Vaughan, E. 2003. "Louisiana Sugar: A Geohistorical Perspective." PhD diss., Louisiana State University.

Vicente, G., and M. Partidario. 2006. "SEA—Enhancing Communications for Better Environmental Decisions." *Environmental Impact Assessment Review* 26: 696–706.

Vilesis, Ann. 1997. *Discovering the Unknown Landscape: A History of America's Wetlands.* Washington, DC: Island Press.

Viosca, Percy, Jr. 1927. "Flood Control in the Mississippi Valley in Its Relation to Louisiana Fisheries." *Transactions of the American Fisheries Society* 57: 49–64.

———. 1928. "Louisiana Wetlands and the Value of their Wild Life and Fishery Resources." *Ecology* 9, no. 2: 216–29.

Vujnovich, Peter (Louisiana Oyster Dealers and Growers Association) to Hale Boggs. Correspondence, January 20. Hale and Lindy Boggs Papers, MS. Collection 1000, box 1769, folder 8, Tulane University Special Collections.

Waggoner and Ball. 2013. "Greater New Orleans Water Plan: Vision." New Orleans: Waggoner and Ball. www.dropbox.com/s/0v3t7r8i4vwx2sk/UWP%20 Vision.pdf?dl=0 (accessed October 2019).

Wall, D. 2014. *The Commons in History: Culture, Conflict, Ecology.* Cambridge, MA: MIT Press.

Water Institute of the Gulf. 2014. *Diversion Expert Panel Report* no. 2. Baton Rouge: Water Institute of the Gulf.

———. 2015. *Diversion Expert Panel Report* no. 3. Baton Rouge: Water Institute of the Gulf.

Wicker, K. M. 1979. "The Development of the Louisiana Oyster Industry in the 19th Century." PhD diss., Louisiana State University.

Wiek, Arnim, Francesca Farioli, Kensuke Fukushi, and Masaru Yarime. 2012. "Sustainability Science: Bridging the Gap between Science and Society." *Sustainability Science* 7, no. 1: 1–4.

White, Gilbert F. 1945. *Human Adjustment to Floods.* Research Paper 29. Chicago: University of Chicago, Dept. of Geography.

Wilbanks, T. J. 2008. "Enhancing the Resilience of Communities to Natural and Other Hazards: What We Know and What We Can Do." *Natural Hazards Observer* (May): 10–11.

Williams, Michael. 1989. *Americans and Their Forests: A Historical Geography.* New York: Cambridge University Press.

Wilson, A. 2006. *Shadow and Shelter: The Swamp in Southern Culture.* Jackson: University Press of Mississippi.

Wilson, Geoff A. 2013. "Community Resilience, Social Memory and the Post-2010 Christchurch (New Zealand) Earthquakes." *Area* 45, no. 2: 207–15.

Wilson, R. K. 2014. *America's Public Lands: From Yellowstone to Smokey Bear and Beyond.* Lanham, MD: Rowman and Littlefield.

Wood, Joseph S. 1996. "The Idea of a National Road." In *The National Road,* ed. Karl Raitz, 93–122. Baltimore: Johns Hopkins University Press.

Wood, Peter H. 1984. "La Salle: Discovery of a Lost Explorer." *American Historical Review* 89, no. 3: 294–323.

Yang, Kaifeng, and Kathe Callahan. 2007. "Citizen Involvement Efforts and Bureaucratic Responsiveness: Participatory Values, Stakeholder Pressures, and Administrative Practicality." *Public Administration Review* 67, no. 2: 249–64.

Zaninetti, Jean-Marc, and Craig E. Colten. 2012. "Shrinking New Orleans: Post-Katrina Population Adjustments." *Urban Geography* 33, no. 5: 679–99.

INDEX

Note: Page numbers in *italics* refer to illustrations or maps.

Abbot, Frederic, 100–101
Acadians, 27, 53–54
Adamson, George C., 7
adaptation: adaptive capacity, 9–10; adaptive transitions, 9–13, 143; Butzer model, 11; environmental management regimes and, 71–72; human agency and, 6; human contingencies and, 12–13; hurricanes and, 28–34; overlapping disaster recoveries and, 144–48; overview, 16–18; post-Katrina recovery, 34–41; river flood adaptations, 23–28; shortcomings, 42–43; social memory and, 19, 22; sustainability transition, 11–12; transformational vs. incremental, 10
Adger, W. N., 6–7, 9, 22
African Americans: displacement of, 108, 110; emancipation and migration of, 37–38; petrochemical industries and, 27–28; rice cultivation and, 27; "wastes" and, 48
alligator conservation, 58, 60
American Society of Civil Engineers, 54

America's Wetland Foundation, 129–30
"America's Wetlands" campaign, 86
anticipatory planning, 21
Arkansas reservoirs plan, 107–8
Army Corps of Engineers: Atchafalaya outlet and, 100–101, 109; Bonnet Carré Spillway openings, 147; ecological restoration and, 62; environmental impact statements and, 118–19, 139–40; levee construction, 26, 31–32; post-Katrina, 38. *See also* flood-protection systems
Atchafalaya Basin Levee District, 104
Atchafalaya Basin Protective Association, 103
Atchafalaya River basin: Atchafalaya River as outlet, 96–98, *97, 99*–107, 109; as floodway, 51; public concern over, 82
Audubon Society, 76
Avenal v. State of Louisiana, 115
Avoyelles Parish, 100, 108

Bahr, Len, 66
Barras, John, 85
"barrier plan," 119
batture, 49–50

Bayou Goula, 110

Boggs, Hale, 113

Bonnet Carré Spillway: 1937 test of, 111–12; construction of, 108; flood-protection regime and, 51–52; impacts on marginalized populations, 28, 111–15; Jadwin Plan and, 105–6; openings, 52, 147

Booher, David E., 7

BP oil spill, Gulf of Mexico (2010), 146

Breaux, John, 64, 83, 125

Breaux Act (Coastal Wetlands Planning, Protection and Restoration Act, CWPPRA), 63–67, 83–84, 125

Breton Sound, 114–15

budget, state, 69

Butzer, Karl, 11

Caernarvon Crevasse, 102–3

Caernarvon Spillway (proposed), 106

canals, 39–40, 61, 64, 65, 124, 128

cartography: accomplishments of, 89–91; "America's Wetlands" campaign, 86; Breaux Act and, 83–84; *Coast 2050* report, 84–85, *85*; conservation efforts and, 76–77; CPRA plans, 86–87, *87*; CRCL, 82–83; digital and online tools, 88–89; football-field metric, 85–86; Gagliano projects, 79–81, *80*, 84; historical vs. projected land loss, 87; human population, underrepresentation of, 87–88; marsh shoreline as vague or invisible, 73–76; mid-20th century land-loss mapping, 77–78; *Newsweek*, 82; power of, 73; shift from specialists to public attention, 81–88; Tidelands controversy and, 77–78, 79; USGS, 83, 85–86

—maps: coastal population (1752 to 2012), *4*; coastal population distribution, *17*; deltaic and chenier plains, *46*; floodways and levees (mid-1950s), *109*; historical diversions and spillways, *52*; land loss, *80, 81, 85, 87*; Louisiana waterways (2020), *97*; marshes (1752), *75*; New Or-

leans protective levee system, *33*; outlets proposed after 1927 flood, *107*

Castonguay, Stéphane, 95

Center for Planning Excellence (CPEX), 135–36

charitable organizations, 26, 32, 57, 138

Chenier Caminada, 29

Christmas tree fences, 67

Citizen Participation Group, 126

Civil Defense, 26–27, 32

Clean Water Act (1972), 62

Climate Central, 89

climate change: CPRA on, 87; humanities, social sciences, and, 12; Tauzin on, 65. *See also* sea-level rise

Coalition to Restore Coastal Louisiana (CRCL): creation of, 122; ecological restoration and, 63–64; public input and, 122–25; reports, 66, 82–83, 123–24

Coast 2050 report, 66, 84–85, *85*, 127–29

Coastal Protection and Restoration Agency (CPRA): Barataria Bay diversion plan, 139; creation of, 132; flood risk viewer, 88–89; plans and land-loss mapping, 86–87, *87*; public engagement and, 132–37

Coastal Resilience mapper, 89

Coastal Wetlands, Conservation, Restoration, and Management Act (1989), 124

Coastal Wetlands Conservation and Restoration Task Force, 124–27

Coastal Wetlands Planning, Protection and Restoration Act (CWPPRA) (Breaux Act), 63–67, 83–84, 125

Coastal Zone Management Working Group, 128

co-design process, 136–37

Commission for the Protection of Birds, Game and Fish, 56–57

Committee for the Future of Coastal Louisiana, 129

commons, 48–50

conservation policies: alligator conservation, 58, 60; cartography and, 76–77; as environmental management regime, 56–61; oil and gas industry and, 60–61; oyster industry and, 57–58, 60

COVID-19 pandemic, 147–48

Cutter, Susan, 19n, 22

Darby, William, 76

Deepwater Horizon, 146

Delacruz, C. A., 112

Delahoussaye, Jim, 110

Derickson, Kate Driscoll, 21–22

Desbiens, Caroline, 47

digital mapping, 88–89

Disaster Relief Act (1950), 32

diversion structures, 79–80. *See also* outlets

Dufor, General, 103

ecological restoration. *See* restoration, ecological

economic development and safety vs. growth, 40–41

ecosystem services, 69, 90

environmental impact statements (EISs), 118–21, 139–40

environmental management policy regimes: adaptions and negative effects, 71–72; collaboration and, 47; commons, society, and, 48–49; conservation, 56–61; ecological restoration, 61–67; flood protection, 49–53; indigenous strategies, 44; overview, 45–48; public input, 94–95; sustainability, 67–71; wetland reclamation, 53–56. *See also* flood-protection systems

Evenden, Matthew, 95

Federal Emergency Management Agency (FEMA), 34, 148

Fish and Wildlife Service (F&WS), 83

fishing, commercial: Atchafalaya flood-protection systems and, 116; con-

servation policies and, 57, 59; decline of, 60; sedimentation and, 28, 51–52; sport fishing vs., 111. *See also* oyster industry; shrimping

fishing seasons, 59

flooding: 1916, 101; 1927, 26, 28, 51, 93–94, 101–3, *107*; 1973, 113; 2011, 115–16; Morgan City (1912), *105*; rainfall flooding in New Orleans (2017 and 2019), 41

flood insurance, 38

flood-protection systems: acclimation of coastal residents to past changes, 98–99; adaptations, 23–28; after Katrina and Rita, 133; Arkansas proposal, 107–8; Atchafalaya River as outlet, 96–98, 99–107; Caernarvon Crevasse, 102–3; Caernarvon Spillway, 106; diversion into Breton Sound, 114–15; as environmental management regime, 49–53; floodways and levees, mid-1950s (map), *109*; impacts on marginalized citizens, 109–16; impacts on marginalized communities, 28; Jadwin Plan, 104–8; "levees and outlets" approach, 26, 105–6; "levees only" approach, 26, 96, 103, 106; Morganza Spillway/Floodway, 52, 106, 108, 109, 112–15; MRC hearings and redirected risk, 99–104; New Orleans as river city, 92–93; Overton Act (1936) and, 108–9; river cities and waterway management, 95–99. *See also* Bonnet Carré Spillway; environmental management policy regimes; levees; public input and engagement

flood risk viewer (CPRA), 88–89

Foster, Mike, 129

fur trapping, decline of, 60

Gagliano, Sherwood "Woody," 79–81, 82, 84

Garsaud, Marcel, 103

Gay, Andrew, 104

geographic information system (GIS) technologies, 88, 135

Mandelman, Adam, 27

mapping. *See* cartography

marshes, as vague or invisible in mapping, 73–76, *75*

Martin, Laura, 61, 62

master plan, Louisiana: on causes of land loss, 133; cultural heritage in, 69–70; human dimension, need for, 4–9, 16–17; "long-term" 50-year planning horizon, 70; modeling approach, 134; multiple-lines-of defense strategy, 137; nonstructural elements and, 138; public voices and, 138–40; sustainability and, 19, 68–71

Matyas, David, 10

McGuire, T. R., 57

McIlhenny, Edward, 59, 76–77

McNutt, Marcia K., 144–45

memory, social, 19, 22

Meyer-Arendt, K. J., 81

migration and relocation, 29–30, 44, 143

migratory waterfowl refuges, 76–77

Mississippi River: changing hydrology and social role of, 95; early settlement along, 23–24, 73–74; historical diversions and spillways (map), *52*; New Orleans, relationship with, 92–93, 95–96. *See also* flooding; flood-protection systems; levees

Mississippi River Commission (MRC): creation of, 50, 96; flood protection vs. navigation and commerce, 96; hearings, 99–104

Mississippi Sound, 51, 112, 115

Mississippi Sound fisheries, 28, 52, 112, 114, 147

mitigation, compensatory, 62

mobility as adaptation, 29–30

Morgan, James, 77–78

Morgan City, 104, *105*, 108, *111*

Morganza Spillway/Floodway, 52, 106, 108, 109, 112–15

Morris, Christopher, 98

mound building, 2, 23, 44

MR-GO (Mississippi River–Gulf Outlet), 38, 40

multiple-lines-of defense strategy, 131, 137

National Environmental Protection Act (NEPA) (1970), 117–21

National Oceanographic and Atmospheric Administration (NOAA), 89

National Research Council (NRC), 11–12, 21, 67–68

National Wetland Research Center, Lafayette (USGS), 83–84

Native Americans: commons and, 48; mapping of threatened locations, 88; shell mounds, 2, 23, 44

"natural disasters" and humanities perspective, 5–6

navigation: Atchafalaya River and, 97; CRCL on, 123–24; levee construction and focus on, 50–51; MR-GO and, 38; New Orleans and, 92; policies focusing on, 49–51, 63–67, 96, 99, 125; public participation and, 126, 128, 134

New Orleans: hurricane adaptations, 31; levees as iconic in, 93; Mississippi River, relationship with, 92–93, 95–96; protective levee system (map), *33*; rainfall flooding, 41; as river city, 92–93; on Rockefeller list of resilience cities, 40; seawall project, 31; St. Joseph Street Landing, *100*

Newsweek, 82

nutria, 60

O'Brien, Karen, 10

oil and gas industry: canals, 39–40, 61, 64, 65, 124, 128; conservation policies and, 60–61; lawsuits against, 39–40; Tidelands controversy, 77–78, 79. *See also* petrochemical industries

O'Neill, Karen, 51, 125

outfall canals, 38

outlets: Atchafalaya debate, 96–98,
99–107; Caernarvon Crevasse (1927),
102–3; Caernarvon Spillway (proposed),
106; compensation question, 113;
flood-protection regime and, 51–53; impacts on marginalized citizens, 109–16;
Morganza Spillway/Floodway, 52, 106,
108, 109, 112–15; proposed after 1927
flood (map), *107. See also* Bonnet Carré
Spillway
Overton Act (1936), 108–9
oyster commission, 57
oyster industry, *58;* conservation policies
and, 57–58, 60; impact of outlets on,
112–15; outlets and, 52

Pelling, Mark, 10
petrochemical industries, 28. *See also* oil
and gas industry
pine-forest reforestation, 56
planning process. *See* master plan, Louisiana; public input and engagement
plantations, abandoned, 107
Plaquemines Parish, 23, 29, 76
Pointe Coupee Parish, 108
policy regimes. *See* environmental management policy regimes
population maps, *4, 17*
public input and engagement: America's
Wetland Foundation, 129–30; Barataria
Bay diversion and, 139; Citizen Participation Group, 126; *Coast 2050* and,
127–29; Coastal Wetlands Conservation
and Restoration Task Force and, 124–27;
Committee for the Future of Coastal
Louisiana, 129; CPEX and, 135–36;
CPRA and, 132–37; CRCL and, 122–25;
environmental impact statements and,
118–19, 139–40; flood protection and,
94–95; Hurricanes Katrina and Rita
and, 130–32; involvement vs. participation, 134; LOCD and, 136–37; Louisiana
Speaks, 132, 133; master plan and, 133,

137–38; MRC hearings on Atchafalaya
outlet, 99–104; nonstructural elements
and, 138; outsourcing of, 134–37; public
comment method, 121; public participatory methods, 7–8, 120–21, 139; sci-tek
project, 135–36; "stakeholder engagement," 120, 126; Water Institute of the
Gulf and, 136
public lands, 48–50, 55

recovery: CPRA and, 132; disaster aftermath vs. long-term, 21; informal, locally based hurricane recovery, 29–31;
post-Katrina, 34–38; resilience and overlapping disaster recoveries, 144–48
reforestation, 56
Regional Planning Teams, 128
resettlement and relocation, 29–30, 44, 143
resilience: Coastal Resilience mapper, 89;
definitions of, 17, 19; erosion of, 34–41;
hurricanes and, 30–33; impermanence
of, 42; inherent vs. formal, 19–21, 42;
as process, 17–18; resilience curve, 144,
145; Rockefeller list of resilience cities,
40; social, 9; social collapse/resilience
model, 11; start-up businesses and, 40
restoration, ecological, 61–67, 70, 121
restoration ecology, 78, 80
restoration planning, 43, 130, 133, 136
rice cultivation, 27

Scarpino, Philip, 95
science and need for human dimension,
4–9
sci-tek (scientific/traditional ecological
knowledge) project, 135–36
sea-level rise: as cause, perspectives on,
125, 127–28; digital tools, 88–89; levees
and, 39; Louisiana master plan and, 71
sedimentation: as cause, perspectives on,
125; fisheries and, 28, 51–52, 99, 112;
Gagliano project and, 79–80; Grand
Lake and, 110–11

sediment deprivation/starvation: CRCL
report and, 123–24; ecological restoration and, 66–67; levees and, 26, 53;
subsidence and, 26, 98
sediment diversions, 35, 66, 69–71,
138–40
shell mounds, 2, 23, 44
shrimping, 59–60
social collapse/resilience model, 11
social memory, 19, 22
social resilience, 9
Society for Ecological Restoration, 61
Southeast Louisiana Flood Protection
Authority–East, 39–40
spillways. *See* Bonnet Carré Spillway;
flood-protection systems; outlets
start-up businesses and resilience, 40
St. Bernard Parish, 23, 28–29, 38–39,
76
St. John Parish, 39
St. Landry Parish, 108
St. Martin Parish, 107
Strategic Working Group, US Dept. of the
Interior, 128
subsidence: Breaux Act and, 66; as cause,
perspectives on, 123, 127–28; ecological
restoration and, 63; Katrina and, 35;
levees and, 38; "life expectancy" and,
80–81; reclamation projects and, 55;
sea-level rise and, 1, 88; sediment starvation and, 26, 98
sugar plantations, 27
sustainability: adaptive capacity and, 10;
in *Coast 2020*, 128; as environmental
management regime, 67–71; human dimensions in, 6–7; in Louisiana master
plan, 68–71
Swamp Lands Acts (1849 and 1850),
54

Target Areas Plan, 37
Tauzin, Billy, 64–65, 125
Terrebonne Parish, 76, 82, 83, 113
Tidelands controversy, 77–78, 79
tragedy of the commons, 49, 56
transitions: adaptive, 9–13; defined, 11;
sustainability, 11–12
Travis, William R., 10

Unified New Orleans Plan, 37
Urban Land Institute, 36
US Department of Agriculture (USDA),
54–55
US Geological Survey (USGS), 79, 83–86

Viosca, Percy, 110, 112

"wastes" and "wastelands," 48, 50
Water Institute of the Gulf (TWIG), 136
weather forecasting, 30, 32
Wetland Conservation and Restoration
Authority, 132
wetlands: "America's Wetlands," 86, 129–
30; conservation regime and, 57; deltaic
and chenier plains (map), 46; ecological
restoration policies and, 62; loss, falling
pace of, 78; reclamation regime, 53–56;
shift in view from wastelands to valued
ecosystems, 78. *See also specific topics,
such as* adaptation
wetlands loss, mapping of. *See* cartography
White, Gilbert, 6
Wicker, K. M., 81
Wilbanks, Thomas J., 10, 19, 21
wildlife preserves, 57, 59
Winiwarter, Verena, 7
wise use. *See* conservation policies
Wisner, Edward, 55
Wooten, Colonel, 106

www.ingramcontent.com/pod-product-compliance
Lightning Source LLC
Chambersburg PA
CBHW031542260326
41914CB00002B/232